NCIS History

VIET NAM

(A NAVAL INTELLIGENCE MEMOIR)

Marine observation post, "The Rockpile", looms behind the author at Landing Zone Elliot

NCIS, today's Naval Criminal Investigative Service was known simply as NIS during the Viet Nam War. These highly dedicated men of the Naval Investigative Service were comprised of officers, enlisted men and civilian *Special Agents*.

Special Agent Vietnam is the only firsthand account of its kind that takes the reader into the clandestine dangerous world of counterespionage and crime, set amidst the sights, sounds and smells of the war in Viet Nam.

SPECIAL AGENT CONTENTS

FOREWORD

More than forty years have passed, and even for those of us who served in Vietnam, the war has sunk into the recesses of our memories. For some it is because recollections of combat are simply too unpleasant; for others it is because of painful memories of the dreadful internal divisions the war generated between the peoples of the United States. Still others regard as shameful our abandoning an ally whom we had persuaded to make common cause with us.

After decades of books and movies focused on what was wrong with our efforts in Vietnam, the past several years have seen several good books that simply examine how dedicated Americans answered the call of their country and served with honor and pride with some remarkable successes.

This is one of those books. A well-written story…*Special Agent Vietnam,* comes to life with a collection of previously unpublished material and photographs illustrative of those difficult days. It is an important new contribution to the history of the conflict written by a man who served three consecutive Vietnam tours as a special agent.

Here is the story of a highly dedicated and thoroughly professional group of men who served as officers, enlisted, and civilian special agents of the Office of Naval Intelligence in Vietnam, and of some of the equally dedicated Vietnamese with whom they operated. The civilian special agent contingent never numbered more than two dozen; yet they provided counterintelligence and investigative support to the entire force of U.S. Navy and Marine Corps deployed to Vietnam.

Despite their rather uncertain status as civilians, special agents wore uniforms, carried rifles--and worked and lived in the field with sailors and marines, sharing the same dangers and discomforts. I was privileged to be associated with them and found them to be the most dedicated, professional, and capable people I had the privilege of serving with in my thirty-five years of naval service.

Virtually nothing has been written about the Office of Naval Intelligence in Vietnam. This is in part because it was a very small part of a very large war and partially because it has only recently become acceptable to write about things pertaining to intelligence. This is an important story because it captures an interesting and significant history.

What is more, it tells a tale of a unit that served with dedication, honor, and dignity and whose members...myself included, look back with great pride on the part we played.

Thomas A. Brooks Rear Admiral, U.S. Navy (Ret.) Fairfax Station, Virginia Former Director of Naval Intelligence

Commander Donn T. Burrows, right, replaces Lt. Commander Tom Brooks as CO NISOV, 1970

PREFACE

The story of the Naval Intelligence special agents who volunteered for service in the Republic of Vietnam during our nation's most prolonged and controversial war has been waiting to be told for more than five decades. This is a chronicle of events that began in 1962 and continued through to the ignoble fall of Saigon thirteen years later; in many ways, the tales of these men are also a reflection of the political and military events of the Vietnam conflict.

At the peak of American involvement in Vietnam, with more than 550,000 military personnel assigned, the special agent task force was also at its zenith, with only about twenty professionals available to provide support to all U.S. Navy and Marine Corps elements in the republic. These chosen few accomplished much with very little.

Special Agent Larry Coleman, the father of four small boys, comforts a young Vietnamese child at a crime scene in Tu Cau village, south of Da Nang.

Agent volunteers transferred from duty stations around the world, but most moved from the relative safety of a Stateside posting to the most remote, dangerous site the service could provide. Wives and families were left behind for a minimum of one year.

Most agents found upon their arrival that they were expected to conduct complex and demanding investigations of a nature they could only have *imagined* in the United States--and in many instances the expectation was that they would do so alone and without supervision in dangerous circumstances.

More often than not, resources that an agent might take for granted elsewhere -- like transportation -- were difficult to arrange in Vietnam and dangerous when they were available. The challenges tempered these men, and the younger ones matured very quickly.

Vietnam service changed and affected every man who did the twelve month tour of duty, and it has certainly drawn alumni together into the tightest imaginable group -- as close as brothers can be in many instances. These ties endured the passing years, despite the passage of decades between meetings or even communication.

But as the years advanced, agents retired from Naval Intelligence. More alarmingly, they began to die before their stories had been told, and with each death, something of the story of Naval Intelligence was lost. I was both the youngest special agent to deploy to the Republic of Vietnam and the longest serving--from March 1969 to March 1972. Thus it fell to me, more than five decades after the first agent deployment, to tell as much of that story as possible.

This work is a compendium of the recollections of the men who served in Vietnam. My intention had always been to underpin our aging memories through a process of reviewing and researching the original reports that were dispatched for case review at the Naval Investigative Service (NIS) headquarters in Washington, D.C. That unfortunately proved impossible.

Lawyers at NCIS (the new name for NIS) twice refused my requests for assistance under Freedom of Information Act provisions, and less formal requests to headquarters personnel were no more successful. The Navy refused to confirm or deny the existence of all the documents and photographs that we had written and submitted, even though the contents of one important report had previously been published in a U.S. government history.

Special Agent, Vietnam would not have been possible without modern communication and the patient encouragement of my former colleagues and their families. With the exception of a single group reunion in 2000 and various interviews on the fly, it was researched and composed remotely and written in a variety of disparate locales, including Australia and Africa.

The support of agents was a powerful stimulus for me to write of the dedicated and brave brethren who were "Naval Counterintelligence Support Activity, Saigon", and would later be known as "Naval Investigative Service Office, Vietnam".

I had the advantage of familiarity with the people, venues, sights, sounds, and the smells as my predecessors told of the earlier days in Vietnam. I have done my best to capture the experiences and thoughts of my colleagues in ways that communicate the experience and history of each man, including those not individually interviewed or named. It was simply not possible to interview everyone who served, nor has it been possible to name them all.

Many parts of the story that occurred during the period 1969 to 1972 have been written in the first person. I sought to portray fairly what those involved saw and felt, as well as my own experiences…many of which are today nearly as intense as they were more than forty years ago.

Special thanks go to Rear Admiral T. A. Brooks, USN (Ret.), who never lost faith in the importance of this work, and to my parents Doug and Fran Hubbard, both authors in their own right, whose support for the project was unfailing. Judith Anderson Sager, who shared the Vietnam experience with me from afar, returned to help with final editing steps, encouragement, and support. Her critical eye and unerring sense of story context were catalytic in the last days of preparation, when years of work finally coalesced into a complete manuscript. Vietnam marked every person who served there.

For me it was a milestone of such significance that scarcely a day has passed since 1972 that the events and impressions of those days are not somehow considered.

For the men I served with, many profited from the incredible intensity of the year's tour. Those who were scarred from it tipped the scale in the other direction. We all continue to decide in our own way, all these years later, what the experience meant to each of us.

*****

DMZ ???? JEEP ????? SURE I WILL !!!!!!!!!

Agent humor of the day is depicted in this staged photo of the
author receiving questionable "orders" from Senior Resident Agent
Ed Fitzpatrick in Da Nang, 1970

[x]

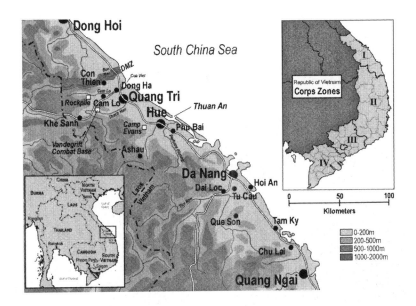

I Corps Tactical Zone was the northernmost area of operations in the Republic of Vietnam. Da Nang, with its substantial natural harbor, was the largest base area and home to the NIS Resident Agency.

Single agent satellite units were located in Chu Lai and at Quang Tri Combat Base, supporting units defending the DMZ.

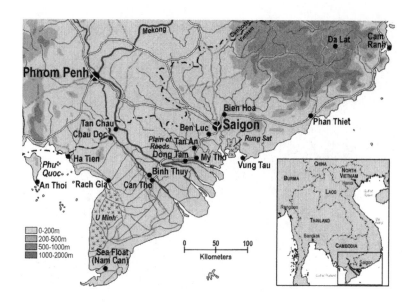

The largely flat Mekong Delta region of South Vietnam (IV Corps Tactical Zone) featured the highest population concentrations in the country and represented a prime target for Communist forces.

The U.S. Navy focused forces on the riverine systems that were dominated by the Mekong and Ba Sac River. The wilderness hideouts of the U Minh Forest and Rung Sat Special Zone adjacent to the national capitol of Saigon were also areas of concentrated operations. NIS Special Agents were active throughout these regions.

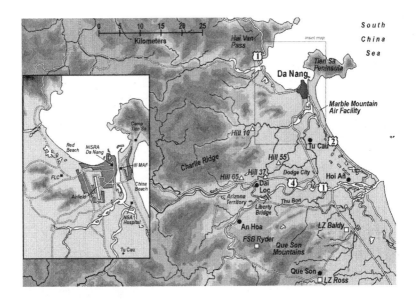

The critical northern port of Da Nang was home to an airbase that for several years was the most active in the world, supporting air strikes along the Ho Chi Minh Trail and the Demilitarized Zone.

Enemy forces did their best to disrupt the airbase, often by rocket attacks that were launched from the hinterland west and south of the city. U.S. Marines regularly engaged North Vietnamese Army and Viet Cong units in protracted, bitter clashes throughout this region.

1   EARLY DAYS, 1962 TO 1964

Saigon slumbered on a Sunday morning in the spring of 1964. The so-called Paris of the Orient was quiet after the preceding night's weekend revelry. Broad boulevards stood still, rows of tamarind trees reflecting morning dew as the tropical sun began its rise over the tiled roofs of villas, business establishments, and squatter camps that characterized the capitol of the Republic of Vietnam…known throughout the Western world simply as South Vietnam.

Split from the communist North by a border called the demilitarized zone (DMZ), South Vietnam's fragile pro--Western regime led by President Ngo Dinh Diem was struggling against both a communist insurgency and shrinking support from its' citizenry. The United States under President John F. Kennedy, while denying that U.S. forces were actually engaged in military operations in the republic, had moved much closer to initiating such operations. By the end of 1962 there were more than three thousand advisers present, including Special Forces, Air Force personnel, and both Army and Marine Corps helicopter units. Fourteen Americans had been killed in operations supporting South Vietnamese forces, and in February the first of hundreds of U.S. helicopters was shot down while ferrying Vietnamese troops into battle.

Nevertheless, life in Saigon for expatriates and the wealthy remained pleasant during 1962 and 1963. The expected amenities were present, the security situation was manageable, and the residue of France's former colonial lifestyle was largely intact. The U.S. military advisory staff had their families with them, often billeted in splendid former--French villas with tall walls and manicured gardens. Behind the growing tension of an expanding counterinsurgency war in South Vietnam, life generally remained quite civilized.

Virtually from the outset, the U.S. Navy provided all of the logistical support for the U.S. military effort in Vietnam. Every ration, round of ammunition, and aircraft part required passed through the Navy's logistical support system.

Responding to the need for the protection of the forces' assets and

[1]

personnel, the Office of Naval Intelligence (ONI) directed that agents be assigned to Saigon to provide counterintelligence and investigative support for Navy commands. Special Agent Robert Kain was assigned as the first full-time special agent in the Republic of Vietnam.

Awakened from a deep sleep at dawn one Sunday morning in May by a banging on his door, Bob Kain, staggered to his bachelor officers' quarters (BOQ) room door and hurriedly opened it. Standing in the doorway was a young Army military policeman who had been dispatched from the Saigon Provost Marshals Office and sent over to Kain's room at the Five Oceans BOQ in Cholon.

"Mr. Kain," he said, "There's a carrier been sunk down at the docks." Stunned, Kain replied, "You've got to be shitting me." Then, recovering his senses, he thanked the soldier and said he would be at the scene as soon as possible. He returned to his adjoining bedroom, quickly dressed, and walked downstairs to where his jeep was parked.

That morning, May 2, 1964, there was little traffic on the normally crowded thoroughfares of Saigon. Kain made good time driving down the boulevards to central Saigon and the dock area where ships were berthed on the Saigon River. Approaching the river, he could see the looming superstructure of USS *Card,* a carrier converted for use as an aircraft transport.

Kain was no stranger to Vietnam. In the days after France's final ignoble defeat at Dien Bien Phu in 1954, the then Navy Lieutenant Kain, while aboard the U.S. Navy landing ship tank *Hampden County* (LST803), participated in the evacuation of Catholic Vietnamese refugees from the northern seaport of Haiphong to Saigon. The evacuation allowed many thousands of Vietnamese to escape control of communist Viet Minh under the leadership of Ho Chi Minh, who was rapidly taking control of the North as the French pulled out. As many as three thousand refugees were packed into the bowels of the vessel, designed to transport tanks and land them through opening bow doors.

After leaving the Navy, Kain was an insurance adjustor for a while. Then in 1958 he joined the Office of Naval Intelligence as an agent and was assigned to the Los Angeles field office. Volunteering in 1961 for duty with the Office of Naval Intelligence at Subic Bay in the Philippines, put him in line for periodic working trips to Vietnam as the U.S. presence grew there. A permanent ONI was set up in Saigon in late 1962, and Kain became its first senior agent.

That Sunday morning Special Agent Kain arrived at the gates of the Port of Saigon to an air of urgency and tension. Identifying himself to a jumpy sentry, he was passed through and drove his jeep toward the towering superstructure of the carrier berthed at dockside.

Kain's experience at sea told him *Card* had been badly wounded. The vessel was settling in the water, and he could hear a clatter of hammers and air compressors from within the bowels of the ship. Crewmembers and shore-based damage control personnel rushed to a multitude of tasks, all designed to save the damaged vessel. Kain boarded, explained his presence to the master, and went below to see the damage firsthand. There he found damage-control parties fabricating temporary patches and reinforcements over a gaping hole. They had placed beams, scaffolding, and patching materials over and around the hole, but water continued to flood the interior of the ship. Pumps hummed in the bilges as sailors began to stabilize the ship's buoyancy.

The rather obvious evidence, both inside and on the ship's exterior, suggested that a number of explosive charges had been placed against the exterior of the hull in tandem below the waterline. These were simultaneously detonated to cause maximum damage, tearing a twenty-five-foot rift in the metal plates of the hull. The damage showed all the indications of an especially audacious attack by Viet Cong swimmer--sappers.

Later, Kain was joined by agent Mord Tucker, who set about photographing the engine room while workers struggled to stop any further flooding. When interviewed by Kain, crewmembers were unable to provide useful information about the events before the explosion, which had come as a complete surprise. Kain focused his attention on the area of the dockside, from where he believed the explosive charge had been fired.

Vietnamese Navy divers conducted a careful search around and under the hull and then began examining the dock itself. A large storm-water sewer was found to open into the river at this point, and closer scrutiny of the drain indicated that the attackers might have entered the sewer labyrinth under Saigon... leaving the scene the same way.

Kain's secret report carefully documented all evidence available at the time, but he could not say with certainty who actually carried out the daring attack. The enemy had clearly been concerned about the arrival of more allied helicopters and their potential effect on the ongoing fight in the field against communist Viet Cong forces. During this period in the Vietnam conflict, VC increasingly used explosives in urban terrorism. The enemy began specifically targeting Americans and places frequented by them. ONI agents responded to a number of blasts at bars frequented by service personnel.

Agents, at the rear of the picture, question witnesses after a Viet Cong bicycle bomb attack breached the wall of this popular Saigon bar

Kain recalls, "One particularly clever means of getting bombs close to their targets was to pack the hollow tubing of a bicycle frame with plastic explosive, then place it against an outer wall or window where the explosion would have maximum effect." With their countrymen being killed and injured on the streets by these attacks, Americans were quickly learning the necessity of vigilance in Saigon. Agents assigned to U.S. Naval Counterintelligence Support Unit, Saigon, had very little leisure time. After his arrival in late 1963, Kain shouldered a majority of the investigative workload, assisted by officer in charge Lt. Bud Siler, USN, and enlisted agents Jake Jacobson, Mord Tucker, and William G. "Sam" Houston. The office in Cholon was shared with the US. Army Provost Marshal, the only U.S. law enforcement agency then in Vietnam.

Kain soon tired of the menu at the nearby BOQ and began exploring the many restaurants of Saigon. For recreation, handball courts were available both at Tan Son Nhut Air Base and at the Cercle Sportif Saigonnais providing another diversion from the daily "grind". Kain's regular handball partner was Marine Capt. Don Koelper. Koelper and Kain went way back, having met in the after math of the Korean War and shortly after *Hampden County's* final evacuation voyage from North Vietnam to Saigon. Kain's ship had been ordered to Korean waters to return elements of the battle weary First Marine Division to Hawaii.

One of the officers who clambered aboard the LST at a small port on the east coast of Korea that day had been 1st Lt. Don Koelper, USMC. Koelper and Kain were roommates and became fast friends in the exceptionally long voyage that followed. (One of the LSTs in the squadron was disabled and had to be taken under tow). The voyage from Korea to Hawaii with speeds seldom exceeding three knots, took thirty-seven days.

Don Koelper had been assigned as an adviser to the Vietnamese Marine Corps...this meant most of his time was spent away from Saigon in the field. During Koelper's periods of leisure in Saigon, the two friends always tried to get together. One Sunday night in February 1964 following a handball game, they agreed to meet at the Capital Kinh Do Theater, a recreational facility operated by the Navy for military personnel in the area, to see *The Diary of Anne Frank.* That afternoon, Kain received an official call out, which forced him to cancel his plans.

[5]

Later that evening he was told by Army military police (MPs) that Viet Cong had bombed the movie theater and that there had been a fatality.

Kain went directly to the theater blast scene to join in the investigation. There he learned that the enemy had shot a military policeman outside the theater and then rushed into the lobby to plant the bomb. A Marine officer, seeing the bomb planted just after purchasing his ticket, had rushed down the aisle calling for people to take cover. That officer was Don Koelper and he was the only fatality in the bombing. Later, at the dispensary, doctors told Kain that the blast had removed most of the rear of his friend's skull. His selfless action had undoubtedly saved many others that day.

*****

The Vietnamese language uses tonal inflection to give meaning to different words. Thus, a word might have many different meanings, depending on how it is spoken. This makes Vietnamese a difficult language for most Westerners to master. Interpreters, therefore, were particularly important for agents needing to interact with Vietnamese who spoke no English.

Bob Kain, like virtually every agent who followed him, was transferred to Vietnam without the benefit of any language training. Upon his arrival, the ONI office was relying on the U.S. embassy translator pool for its communication requirements. Among this pool, one translator quickly stood out as superior; his name was Lo Han Thang.

Kain requested authority from headquarters in Sangley Point to hire Thang and it was granted. Thus, the longest-serving individual in ONI's Vietnam era was hired. Interestingly, a young Lo Han Thang had been evacuated with his family from Hai Phong in North Vietnam to Saigon aboard a U.S. Navy LST, the very same rescue mission that first introduced Kain to Vietnam in 1954.

Thang could not recall the name of the vessel that carried him and his family to the South, but both Kain and Thang have speculated that it may have been the *Hampden County*. Thang remained an integral, important part of the office until its final closure and assisted Naval Intelligence up until the fall of Saigon in 1975.

*****

Bob Kain learned early in his tour that Saigon could be an unpredictable and dangerous place. Though South Vietnam had initially enjoyed relative peace, enemy North Vietnamese activities, Viet Cong insurgents, and internal political strife all contributed to unrest and violence as communists turned up the heat in their attempts to undermine the South. Despite numerous attempts to destabilize and remove him, South Vietnam's Catholic president, Ngo Dinh Diem, remained a titular leader--as he had been since Vietnam's last king, Emperor Bao Dai, appointed him prime minister in 1954.

As many as 80 percent of the people living in South Vietnam were of the Buddhist faith. But ten percent were Catholic. Groups of Catholics led by their priests migrated from the North, assisted by the U.S. Navy under the government's refugee resettlement programs.

They formed a loyal, devoutly anticommunist political base for President Diem, and the president wasted little time appointing Catholics to key positions of leadership. Indeed, it seemed Diem considered Catholics the only Vietnamese he could trust in his bid to stay in power.

During the Eisenhower presidency, Diem was well received in the United States when he toured as a visiting chief of state. U.S. leadership threw their support behind him and his vocally anticommunist government. But eventually cracks appeared in the foundations of his Catholic led regime. Vietnamese students demanded long-delayed democratic reforms.

Even more vocal was the leadership of the republic's Buddhist majority. In the old imperial city of Hue, the Catholic deputy province chief ordered troops to fire on Buddhists celebrating a religious holiday in May 1963.

Controversial monk Thich Tri Quang, himself born in North

[7]

Vietnam and previously jailed on suspicion of supporting the communist Viet Minh in their war against France, began speaking out against Diem. Advising U.S. officials that he considered them responsible for Diem's abuses, the cleric insisted they urge the president to reform or resign. Then, U.S. ambassador to South Vietnam Henry Nolting personally pressed Diem to moderate his position but was rebuffed.

The man behind the scenes in the Diem regime was the president's brother, Ngo Dinh Nhu. Nhu was a shady character well known for his machinations with the secret police, and pulled the strings that kept his brother in power. Madam Ngo Dinh Nhu, the self-appointed and flamboyant first lady of South Vietnam, had the ear of certain members of the press contingent. Defending her own power base, Madam Nhu attacked Buddhist leaders by alleging they were being manipulated by Americans against Diem.

Demonstrations in Saigon

The first lady achieved global notoriety in June 1963 after Buddhist monks, demanding "peace and charity" to all religions, began burning themselves to death on public street corners.

Characterizing the self-immolations as barbecues, she was quoted offering to supply matches to other similarly inclined Buddhist clerics. American leadership became increasingly uncomfortable

[8]

with Diem's leadership. The Vietnamese president had rejected all pleas to moderate policies and find real internal peace. Perhaps sensing an opportunity, a group of Vietnamese general officers began plotting Diem's overthrow.

They were careful to let key players in the U.S. embassy know of their intentions. President John F. Kennedy was given a White House briefing as events unfolded and he directed there be no direct U.S. involvement in any potential change of government.

On November 1, 1963, dissident troops laid siege to the presidential palace in central Saigon. Although Kain was privy to rumors about possible coup plans among Vietnamese general officers, he was surprised by a telephone call from a news source with the news. The newsman said simply that some sort of military action was occurring in central Saigon.

Kain hurried to find the office's radio--equipped jeep, and by carefully navigating through the back streets to avoid potential roadblocks and troop movement, found his way to the downtown headquarters building of Military Assistance Command, Vietnam, where he met Agent Sam Houston.

By now there was considerable gunfire in the area near the presidential palace, some of it near MACV. Parking immediately in front of the headquarters building, Kain began transmitting his observations of the fighting by radio.

He was the sole link Navy headquarters in Cholon had, and thus he was integral to Navy command decisions designed to protect personnel and assets.

South Vietnamese Air Force aircraft roared overhead putting air strikes into the palace grounds a mere two blocks away from Kain's position. Indiscriminate firing ranged up and down the boulevard ahead.

Kain continued the radio transmissions for about forty-five minutes, until a South Vietnamese soldier manning his .50-caliber machine gun at the traffic circle ahead of him, swung the weapon around and trained it directly on Kain's jeep.

[9]

Abandoning the jeep, the special agent entered the MACV headquarters building until the firing subsided, he then returned to his
vehicle and began to patrol the downtown area radioing his
observations as he drove.

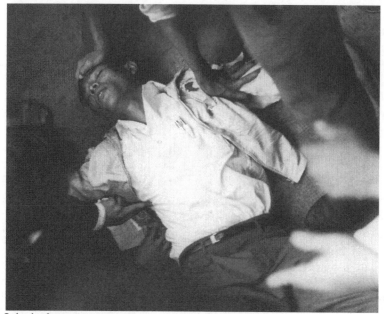

Injuries became common

Diem and Nhu, unable to rally support to expel dissident army and
air force elements, later escaped the presidential palace via a secret
tunnel. Taking refuge at St. Francis Xavier Church in Cholon the
next day, the two brothers negotiated by telephone with coup
leaders who promised to spare their lives.

Diem finally agreed to surrender, and he and his brother were
picked up by rebel troops in an armored personnel carrier. But
instead of being taken to staff headquarters both were shot,
apparently on the orders of South Vietnamese Gen. Duong Van
Minh.

In Washington president Kennedy was shocked by the news of the
bloody end of the Diem dynasty, but in Saigon the generals were
quickly recognized as the new, legitimate power. Embassy officials
were hopeful that General Minh would prosecute the war more

[10]

effectively and without the rancor that had characterized Diem's rule. They were to be disappointed.

Bob Kain and his fellow agents began hearing rumors of Diem's death shortly after the coupe broke out. The next morning the grim details began to surface, together with a rash of rumors as to who was responsible. President Kennedy would be dead days later himself.

*****

2   SAIGON 1964 TO 1967

Something about a three-year tour of duty in the Philippines did not appeal to Special Agent Maynard Anderson. After completing the Agent Basic Course the year previously, Anderson was advised by ONI headquarters in 1964 that he could expect a transfer from Chicago either to Sangley Point or Subic Bay. Concerned by the prospect, he wrote to headquarters and then discussed his options with Special Agent Sherman Bliss. Saigon was, Bliss said, an alternative to the Philippines.

Anderson had heard tales of the Pearl of the Orient, as Saigon had long been known during the halcyon days of French rule. A certain mystique was associated with it and besides, the location augured well for professional travel to other points of interest in Southeast Asia. There also seemed to be a good likelihood of action there…Anderson volunteered. He was to be senior agent in Saigon, but not senior *resident* agent. At that time, the post was not important enough to rate an SRA.

Anderson's trip to Vietnam began on July 14, 1964. Like the many who would follow him, he "overnighted" in San Francisco at the Treasure Island BOQ, leaving nearby Travis Air Force Base on a World Airways midnight flight. This was aboard a chartered Boeing 707 loaded with service personnel and dependents bound for destinations across the Pacific. After Hawaii, they made a fuel stop at Anderson Air Force Base at Guam, in time for a breakfast

[11]

meeting with Supervising Agent Jim Ritchie before flying onward.

A briefing period had been planned at the headquarters element under which the Saigon office functioned. This was known as U.S. Naval Counterintelligence Support Activity, Philippines.

Supervising Agent Harry Doyle met Anderson at Clark Air Force Base, the Philippines, driving him to Sangley Point in the teeth of an impending typhoon. At Sangley Point, Anderson learned a little more about what to expect at his new assignment in Saigon. He was to be met and briefed by the existing senior agent, Robert M. Kain, who he would ultimately be relieving. After an overnight delay due to mechanical problems on the aircraft, the World Airways charter flight once again got underway, Saigon-bound, on August 2.

Also aboard were Lt. Gen. Creighton Abrams, US Army, and his family bound for Abram's new assignment as Gen. William Westmoreland's deputy at Military Assistance Command, Vietnam. Over Saigon at last, a spiral landing approach designed to reduce the likelihood of damage by ground fire, gave passengers their first look at the city that would be home for most of them in the year ahead.

Soon after landing, Anderson was introduced to staff at 0NI: two enlisted agents (the last so-assigned to Vietnam), YNC Mord Tucker and YN1 Sam Houston. The office was situated behind a high wall within the Cholon compound, then home to the U.S. Navy-operated Headquarters Support Activity, Saigon. This was under the command of Capt. Archie Kuntze, USN. (Kuntze was a colorful character who later fell from grace after being charged with "impropriety").

With the Naval Intelligence Detachment assigned as an element of his command, Captain Kuntze was a strong supporter who had supplied agents with transport and office space that would not have been forthcoming from Naval Intelligence resources.

Quartered at the Brink BOQ in central Saigon near the famous Continental and Caravelle Hotels, Anderson shared space with Air Force Capt. Michael Stevens, aide to Brig. Gen. Robert Rowland, chief of the Air Force Advisory Group. General Rowland later provided useful information about the activities and intentions of the Vietnamese Air Force during periods of political upheaval in South Vietnam.

Maynard Anderson set about learning his way around the power circles of Saigon. Special Agent Bob Kain, a skilled criminal investigator, would remain in the office for some months to come, so Maynard saw that the intervening time would be best used in finding out as much as possible about what factors and people made things happen in Saigon--and what effect those forces had on the well--being of the U S. forces he was sent to protect.

He got off to a good, if unexpected start: afflicted with a parasitic disease that baffled U.S. doctors and was only successfully diagnosed by a Vietnamese doctor.

Anderson was hospitalized in Saigon where he met Mrs. William Westmoreland. Kitsie Westmoreland, a long-serving Gray Lady, called regularly at his quarantined private room. It was an auspicious acquaintance that paid dividends later.

Finally out of hospital and back at his Cholon desk, Anderson began the task of establishing relations with agencies, both local and U.S., in earnest. Central to the mission was protection of U.S. assets and personnel.

Information of the right sort could go a long way toward fulfilling this tenet, and a combined effort by the agencies represented in Saigon seemed most likely to succeed.

In 1964 the conflict in Vietnam was not at the stage of a full-blown war. But many activities, both real and potential, affected U.S. personnel: political unrest, theft and corruption, and potential terrorism. The Army Counterintelligence Corps (CIC) had a mandate similar to that of the Naval Intelligence detachment, as did the U.S. Air Force Office of Special Investigations (OSI).

Anderson found agents of the CIC with whom he had associated in Chicago, among them Special Agent Jim Bryant. With Embassy Security Officer Tom Gaffney, CIC, OSI, and ONI formed the Saigon Security Committee to ensure that information developed by one agency could quickly be shared with all with a minimum of bureaucracy. The Central Intelligence Agency (CIA) station chief was also represented.

Though ONI retained its responsibility for investigation of serious criminal matters, the counterintelligence mission became more important as unrest and terrorism became more prevalent. The Saigon atmosphere began changing from one of colonial comfort-- with all the attendant social life to one of a culture touched by unexpected violence. The people of Saigon were a long way from the soldiers struggling for their lives in nearby rice paddies and fields, but they were often reminded of reality by surreal--seeming evening views of firefights in the distance and air strikes visible from building rooftops.

As time went on, these sites were punctuated by the occasional boom of a terrorist bomb detonated somewhere in the city. Naval Counterintelligence Support Unit, Saigon, joined with other allied agencies to ferret out information to provide indicators and warning of activities that might imperil their people and their interests. The focus was on VC activities and intentions, North Vietnamese initiatives and activities, and possible enemy infiltrators and potential enemy agents in their midst.

Reports that may have seemed innocuous to analysts upstream in Hawaii and Washington had real meaning in the Saigon counterintelligence community, where speed had to be balanced against surety of fact. This was especially so when for instance, a potential bomb attack was uncovered. Navy agents then distributed information directly to their affected commands and members of the Saigon Security Committee.

Navy agents developed information sources in many, quite different environments. Mord Tucker and Sam Houston lived in the community with their families. Both were conduits for information, (sometimes gossip), that when combined with other information could produce valuable intelligence. At the time, Buddhist clerics were creating angst with acts of self-immolation in protest over fundamental political issues, including endemic corruption in South Vietnam's high-profile leadership. The Buddhist protests and the news surrounding them were the topic of much discussion in the

[14]

global press and among the Vietnamese. Tucker and Houston both employed domestic staff who visited the market and gossiped with their friends every day. These sources provided accurate information predicting coup attempts on two occasions during 1964-65. Office employees, the translator, and the driver could also report their feelings and predictions. When they stayed away from work, it was always taken as a worrisome indicator of the possibility of unknown events to come.

In September 1964 Maynard Anderson was asked by General Westmoreland to attend a meeting at which he asked Navy agents to investigate allegations that U.S. military supplies were finding their way from Vietnam to Singapore's black market. The information indicated that the trade was of a significant volume: for example, helicopters had reportedly been a part of the inventory stolen.

Anderson subsequently flew to Singapore for meetings with the American consulate, the U.S. naval liaison office, and the Singapore CIA station chief. He asked them for assistance in developing information about theft and the Singapore black market. Although the investigation did not produce results sufficient for criminal prosecution, intelligence was developed that helped plug some holes in the leaky Vietnam supply train.

Counterterrorism initiatives grew in importance when on Christmas Eve 1964, the Brinks BOQ was bombed. A car bomb exploded in the building's underground garage in the early evening. Maynard Anderson was in his room at the time, seated at a desk, writing a letter.

His first recollection was of a muffled explosion, hurling him to the floor and causing the frame and glass of the window above the desk to implode and strike the wall behind him. The room was showered with glass and the window frame fell on him. Dazed, Anderson finally wrenched the jammed door open, hearing other muffled blasts.

At the time, he believed the building was under sustained artillery attack. In the kitchen, he found his Vietnamese maid bleeding profusely from the glass shards that had struck her as she stood in front of a window, curious at the activity occurring outside on the

[15]

street. He assisted her to the stairs, where medical staff met them and took charge…he rushed back to his room to dress.

After a search for his credentials, Anderson started down the stairs to the first floor, where the damage proved to be much more severe. Here he found large blocks of concrete blocking the hall. The air was choked with smoke and dust. A Navy employee had been killed in his room on this floor.

Clean up following the terrorist bombing of a Saigon BEQ

Finally at ground level, Anderson found Special Agent Bob Kain on the scene. Kain had responded to messages on his vehicle radio and had been guided by a growing pillar of smoke on the Saigon horizon. He remembers seeing Anderson standing outside as he arrived and being utterly amazed that so many had survived the blast. The entire central portion of the building directly above the blast had collapsed into the underground garage.

Both agents began assisting in the removal of cars from the burning underground parking area. It proved to be exploding gas tanks in the garage that had prompted Anderson's impression of an enemy follow-up attack after the initial detonation. Anderson was later taken in for treatment of cuts received in the blast. He was relieved to hear that Bob Kain after a careful search of his demolished room had located his missing ONI credentials on top of his armoire.

[16]

Kain spent the next several days sifting through the jumble of rubble at the blast scene, with the help of Army investigators. Their investigation substantiated the theory that a car containing explosives had been driven into the parking area. Collusion of Vietnamese National Police who were guarding the underground area was suspected but never proven. There was considerable speculation that specific individuals were the targets of this bomb attack.

Bob Hope and his entourage, (in Vietnam to entertain troops during the holiday season), were billeted across the street from the Brinks BOQ at the Caravelle Hotel. Bob Kain recalls, "I remember Bob Hope made a special trip to the dispensary to visit and comfort the injured from the attack. Those people really appreciated that." Hope's opening line at the Christmas show was less welcome, "A funny thing happened on the way to the show; a hotel flew by."

*****

The agent force was boosted in January 1965 with the arrival of Special Agent Paul Carr. The product of an Indiana farming community, Carr had served as an Army artilleryman during the Korean War, returning to his native Indiana to attend Indiana University on the GI Bill. He graduated with a degree in business management with police administration as a minor.

With encouragement from his retired FBI agent professor, Carr submitted an application to join Naval Intelligence and was appointed in October 1963.

Carr caught the notice of his trainers during Agent Basic School at headquarters in Washington, D.C. the following year, and was asked if he would consider a tour in Vietnam.

At the time he had been working almost constantly travelling on prolonged road trips out of the Denver office. He was a bachelor with no family obligations and was attracted to the idea of a new challenge and the increased pay and allowances the post offered, and he accepted.

Maynard Anderson wrote to Carr from Saigon, passing on useful

[17]

information regarding his new duty station and suggesting that he bring his own sidearm, as issue handguns were scarce in Saigon. Carr, then on leave in Indiana, bought a Smith and Wesson Chief's Special, which served him well through two tours in Vietnam.

Carr at work on riverine operations

With orders instructing him to report to headquarters in the Philippines, Carr stepped off his charter flight at Clark Air Force Base and boarded a Navy commuter flight to Sangley Point, on the other side of the bay from Manila. Here he received further briefings as to what to expect in Vietnam. Paul Carr was not impressed with the Philippines, and this indoctrination convinced him to stay in Vietnam for his full two--year commitment.

His January 1965 arrival in Saigon was uneventful, and Carr settled into a top –floor room at the Hong Kong BOQ in Cholon, about six blocks away from the office. Since the facility had no operating elevator, he was able to obtain a private room that would normally have been reserved for senior field-grade officers. Soon, he learned that a ladder way provided access to the rooftop. He spent many Saturday nights up there with a cold drink and his portable radio, listening to *The Grand Old Opry* on Armed Forces Radio. In the distance, tracers and flares from skirmishes with the VC would often add to the entertainment.

Shortly after his arrival in Saigon, Paul Carr found his energies being channeled more toward the counterintelligence mission. Because of his origins as a Chicago police officer Special Agent Milt Steffen preferred criminal investigation.

Mord Tucker was nearing the end of his stint, and had carried much of the counterintelligence load. Mord told Carr he thought he might be good at counterintelligence...and he was right.

In the weeks before his transfer, Tucker began to introduce Carr to his contacts and informants...his sources for information about impending unrest and possible enemy targets. One of his first introductions was to the family of civil engineer Frank Hessler. Hessler's Vietnamese wife, Jeanette, was well connected in Vietnamese political circles. She was also sympathetic to the Navy's need for accurate information about local situations. In appreciation, Paul helped the Hessler family with commissary shopping during Frank's absence. At a time when dissident Buddhist elements had been infiltrated by communist agents, Jeanette Hessler utilized her extensive contacts to collect useful information about the monks, their intentions and objectives.

She would also introduce Carr to Lt. Cdr. Nguyen Anh, who held an important staff position at VNN headquarters in Saigon. A northerner who had escaped the communist rule, Anh was the personification of the self-discipline that was characteristic of many North Vietnamese. He had also received training in the United States.

During the time that Paul Carr was learning his way around Saigon, ONI received a lead from agents in Japan about illegal firearms entering their country, most likely from Vietnam. Authorities were alarmed to discover that both semi and automatic military weapons had found their way into the Japanese underworld.

They suspected that personnel from the CIA's proprietary airline, (Air America), were responsible for bringing the arms into Japan; a lucrative business venture.

Given the case, Carr found his way to a nearby Special Forces compound and interviewed a noncommissioned officer at the armory. He learned that the unit had been established years previously, early in the U.S. counterinsurgency assistance program. It was their job to arm groups of sympathetic Vietnamese wanting to fight the Viet Cong. The weapons were mostly of World War II vintage, of both U.S. and European manufacture including German Schmeissers, Swedish K submachine guns, and full-automatic M2 Carbines.

No system for documenting weapons issuance was in place, nor was one planned. Carr learned that Air America had hired some rough characters who didn't mind dabbling in the gun-running business, but little could be done about any of it. Paul Carr wrote up and submitted his findings but he heard nothing more about the matter.

Carr's contacts in the community expanded. He was introduced to a Navy lieutenant whose Vietnamese wife's family was well connected in the transport industry. Her father owned a fleet of trucks that regularly transited the major thoroughfares of South Vietnam, particularly the national highway, Route 1.

Through this contact, he learned Viet Cong "tax collectors" on remote stretches of the highway routinely stopped truckers, removing some of the truck cargo as a levy to "the cause."

Realizing this information had potential value as a means of identifying enemy units, their operating areas and objectives, Carr requested the truck drivers take note of road mile markers when stopped and report details about guerrilla armament and what had been taken.

Large quantities of rice, for instance, might indicate an enemy training facility was nearby, while a desire for concrete and reinforcing rod might be a sign that fortifications were being constructed. As the information began to flow, Carr took it to intelligence analysts at MACV J-2. A number of successful military operations were formulated and effectively launched against the VC as a result of Carr's initiatives.

A man from Oklahoma owes his life to the effectiveness of Carr's trucker network. Realizing that opportunities existed in Vietnam for those with construction skills, he had applied for a position as a dozer operator with a U.S. construction conglomerate with contracts in Viet Nam, and his application was accepted.

S/A Carr catches his flight

After his stint, he completed out-processing from the U.S. Army in Japan and returned to Saigon, where he learned he had been hired.

Though told to wait a few days in Saigon for the next flight north to Cam Ranh, he opted against the advice of many, to ride his motorcycle through "Indian country" to his new job. He never arrived.

Tipped off about the missing man by the American embassy, Carr began checking his trucker contacts that same afternoon, and received a report that a driver on Route 1 had seen a blond man being led by Vietnamese down a riverbank. One of the Vietnamese men had been pushing a motorcycle. Later that afternoon, this information made it into the hands of J-2, and a sweep of the area by U.S. Army infantry was set up for the following morning.

Early the next day, soldiers sweeping riverbanks in the area where the abduction had been reported were surprised when the young American literally ran into their line. It was the Oklahoman, and he

[21]

had successfully slipped his bindings and made his escape. He was very lucky man, in more ways than one.

*****

The Viet Cong continued with their Saigon bombing campaign, next selecting the U.S. embassy as their target. Situated near the riverfront, the embassy had been constructed by the French colonizers years earlier. It had not been built for comfort but with the realities of guerilla warfare in mind.

At about 10:45 AM on March 31 of 1965, a Renault sedan pulled up and parked on the street immediately in front of the U.S. embassy, carrying about 250 pounds of plastic explosives. At about the same time a second man pulled up on his Lambretta scooter on the opposite side of the street. Vietnamese National Police sentries at the embassy challenged the car driver, who responded by jumping out of the car and opening fire.

His accomplice on the Lambretta quickly joined in. The driver of the car was killed, but the motorcyclist escaped into the backstreets. Moments later the huge car bomb detonated causing massive damage to the embassy and a nearby Chinese restaurant. Twenty-two were killed in this latest attack including two U.S. citizens. Another 190 were injured.

In response to the bombing, a meeting of the Saigon Security Committee was convened by the U.S. embassies security officer. Maynard Anderson was there representing Naval Intelligence. The various members rallied to assist the embassy mission and there were assurances that a joint effort would be made to identify those responsible for the bombing, and the CIA began a concerted effort to locate knowledgeable sources. Vietnamese Military Security Service personnel were able to identify the driver of the car as a Viet Cong agent. The identity of his accomplice remained a mystery.

Special Agent Carr revisited the site of the bombing the next day. He was immediately drawn to the blast hole in the street where old train tracks covered years before by pavement, had been re-exposed. Above him in the shell of the damaged embassy were hollow windows reminding him of the embassy staff who had been drawn to them moments before the bomb blast by the sound of gunfire from the street.

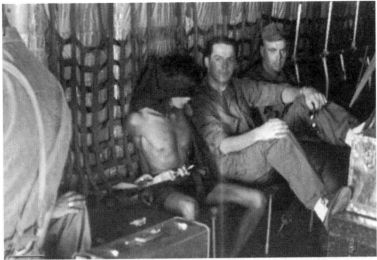

Transporting VC Prisoners was part of the job

Carr would later observe that… "It was this bombing which really added impetus to construction of the new United States embassy in Saigon. This building was in service by the time of the Tet Offensive of 1968, when VC sappers overran part of the compound. It gained global recognition when embassy staffs were evacuated from its roof by helicopters when the South fell in 1975."

*****

The Vietnamese were not the only astute readers of the environment. Members of the Australian Army Training Teams in Vietnam were actively deployed within the South Vietnamese Army field units. A high proportion of these Australians were battle-tested infantry senior NCOs who shared their foxholes with the Vietnamese soldiers in the field. Like good noncommissioned officers in every service, they were well positioned to pick up signs of unrest in the troops. Given that Vietnamese officers were dabbling in politics and plotting coups, the information gathered in this way proved to be very valuable.

[23]

The British MIS officer and the political officer at the British embassy in Saigon were also very generous about sharing important information that came their way. They both continued to be valuable sources even after being reposted to Hong Kong.

One of the strange legacies stemming from the 1954 Geneva Treaty that divided North and South Vietnam was the International Control Commission. With their mission of monitoring treaty compliance, officers assigned to the ICC were in the unique position of being able to travel to both sides of the demilitarized zone.

Staffed by Poles, Indians, and Canadians, the intent of the ICC was to maintain a political balance. The three nationalities were odd bedfellows to be sure. Poland was then a Soviet satellite and was openly hostile to the West. India was a mixed bag…nonaligned but with ties to both the West and the Soviets. Canada was perceived by the others as a staunch member of the North American bloc, overseen by the United States.

Maynard Anderson was a regular at the Cercle Sportif Saigonnais, a Saigon "country club" described as French colonial splendor epitomized.

Situated in the heart of the city on about thirty acres of fenced gardens and trees, the club had tennis courts and a swimming pool known to attract lovely Eurasian women for an afternoon dip. In the days before the war became a fulltime matter in Saigon, the club served as a gathering place for members of diplomatic legations and their support staff, as well as the families of wealthy French rubber and tea plantation owners. These club members maintained Saigon homes and needed a social center for their wives and children. Many families spent most of their time at the club playing tennis, swimming, and socializing.

American ambassadors regularly played tennis, members of the ICC were often in attendance, and MACV staff regularly used the veranda as a quiet meeting place where information could be shared.

Ambassador Henry Cabot Lodge made a habit of visiting the pool at noon to swim and observe the other swimmers. Ambassador

Maxwell Taylor played tennis at least twice weekly at 4:00 PM on court one. Court one was situated just inside the fence that adjoined a busy street, making him an attractive target of opportunity, but he refused requests to change to another court. Bill Bludworth, a CIA agent, often joined Maynard Anderson for a game on a court adjacent to Taylor at those times, just in case there was trouble.

Despite their access to North Vietnam, ICC officers were not considered the best sources of information. Anderson occasionally met Canadian representatives for a social drink and found them to be friendly but guarded. His interests really lay more in the realm of information about potential infiltrators or persons who may have been co-opted to work for the North. Information about what the ICC team was seeing on their trips North was not of as much interest to him. The CIA may have taken a more vigorous interest in this information, but at the time, the Navy did not.

French planters from the tea and rubber plantations northwest of Saigon were not particularly reliable sources of information either. Though many were socially friendly, they were disinclined to show support for the United States because it was not in their best interests to do so.

They had what they felt were valid concerns about maintaining the status quo even if that included paying off resident Viet Cong or groups of marauding robbers.

Navy agents did successfully cultivate members of the U.S. press corps. Agent Anderson found several to be particularly helpful...Garrick Utley of NBC News, Malcolm Brown of the Associated Press, and renowned combat photographer Horst Faas were amongst these.

The press had access to information that was very difficult for others to obtain, particularly about Buddhist unrest and the political situation in general. Much of the impetus for Buddhist unrest originated in the ancient imperial city of Hue. Hue was a center of intellectualism and the home to a university. It was also home to the militant monk Thrich Tri Quang, whose followers had immolated themselves on Saigon streets as acts of protest.

Vietnamese agencies, most notably the MSS, were well developed information sources. Their contacts in the community were widespread, but the reliability of their information often varied widely. Navy agents had their own sources of information in the Saigon community. As sources, restaurateurs heard much of what happened on the streets but were known to be unreliable. One of Anderson's better sources was a Chinese tailor whose side business was exchanging local currency for U.S. dollars at highly beneficial rates. Having established the means to easily export his wealth to a no-questions-asked Hong Kong bank provided the man with a strong incentive to keep American agents on his side.

Understandably the motivation of those who proffered information was not altruism or ideology. It was greed. The units intelligence collection program was enhanced in early 1965 after a shipment of post exchange (PX) liquor and cigarettes was hijacked somewhere between the Port of Saigon and the Navy Exchange.

Agents launched an investigation and began searching for the missing contraband. MPs from the Army Provost Marshal helped.

At about 10:00 PM that first night, the trailer was located with about half the contents missing. The recovered merchandise which included Johnnie Walker scotch and Courvoisier brandy was reloaded into a shipping container and returned to the office compound in Cholon for eventual return to the exchange. But the exchange officer did not want it back.

It was more costly to him to bring it back into the inventory than to simply write the lot off to theft. Agents were suddenly in possession of large quantities of the best "liaison" material available anywhere.

*****

It would seem that a Naval Counterintelligence Support Unit trying to come to grips with worsening enemy infiltration and increasing numbers of attacks against allied personnel would look to the water for the enemy. Saigon had always been dependant on its rivers and tributaries for supply. Now, with growing evidence that North Vietnamese supply vessels loaded with arms and explosives were finding their way into the South, the unit's attention became focused on the river. Vietnamese naval units in February 1965 had engaged and sunk a freighter loaded with arms and medicine destined for Viet Cong forces in the Saigon area.

In those early days, there were no squadrons of U.S. Navy fast patrol craft yet established although they would soon come. The only resource available at the time to counterintelligence agents was Vietnamese Navy junks and patrol boats inherited from the French. Agents would have to improvise to get necessary surveillance photographs of the river and the vessels using it. Light aircraft proved to be a perfect choice for such a mission.

The agents knew that the Vietnamese Air Force had L19 light observation aircraft. But what was required was an inducement to provide their allies with aircraft time, and the solution was quite unexpected.

The Vietnamese liked American combat rations. An enterprising Navy chief petty officer acquired several cases of C rations for the agents who then "bought" the air time.

The flights resulted in sheaves of useful aerial photographs that successfully cast a new light on riverine activities in and around the Port of Saigon. As a result, in April of 1965 the U.S. Navy launched "Operation Market Time", a huge blockading operation designed to deny the communist insurgents resupply by sea. Up until this time, the South Vietnamese coastline had only been patrolled by a VNN motorized junk force. U.S. experts estimated that as many as one thousand junks a day moved in offshore waters.

Operation Market Time put surveillance aircraft into the air, assigned a score of destroyers and escorts to radar picket duty, and began supplementing tired Vietnamese junks with divisions of fast patrol boats. At the peak of the operation, thousands of U.S. sailors were successfully involved in the implementation of the new program.

*****

In the early stages of the Vietnam conflict, the imaginary line between overt criminal action and enemy activity was particularly unclear. The material abundance that arrived with the Americans and their various assistance programs was a tempting target for enemy insurgents and their supporters.

After all, why would anyone run the inherent risks associated with resupply from North Vietnam if products like medical supplies and ammunition could be obtained from U.S. stores? Complicating the situation even further was the temptation that the supply system posed for our South Vietnamese allies.

Vietnamese allied involvement ranged from small-time pilferage from targets of opportunity to major thievery, often planned at very senior levels. It was common knowledge in Saigon that the assassinated South Vietnamese President Ngo Dinh Diem had $1 million cash in his briefcase when he was killed.

That money would find its way into the hands of strongman Gen. Duong Van "Big" Minh. It was rumored that in addition to the million dollars, Minh had also discovered forty kilos of gold before having Diem shot.

Opportunities for theft increased as the U.S. supply system ballooned to support the growing number of troops. From 180,000 in 1965, the number had grown to 540,000 by 1968.

Maynard Anderson characterized the American attitude to property this way: "If it's ours, we put it somewhere and expect it to be there when we return. The Vietnamese felt that if somebody turned his back on property, he didn't care about it and it was thus fair game to steal. The American would simply get another of whatever it was from the infinite supply house."

Anderson believed that it was this attitude that ensured that much of the pilfered allied stores of materials would find their way to both the Viet Cong sympathizers as well as the North Vietnamese regulars along the trails of Cambodia and Laos.

*****

Senior Agent Maynard Anderson was relieved at the end of his one-year tour in July 1965 by Special Agent John Nester. Nester would inherit a staff of three special agents and four military support staff.

Though the primary focus of Naval Intelligence would remain largely in and around Saigon, increasing activity in the I Corps tactical zone, (the northernmost part of South Vietnam bordering North Vietnam), necessitated that agents travel to assist those commands.

Marines had landed in Da Nang and with them had come naval construction and logistic forces. With fewer than a half-dozen agents in Vietnam, it was a strain to send people north but it had to be done. John Nester, Paul Carr, and Milt Steffen were all called to the northern port of Da Nang at one time or another after the initial 1965 landings. Nester and Steffen provided support to Marine units during the highly successful Operation Starlight, when amphibious elements landed near Chu Lai and routed previously secure VC sanctuaries. Lt. Roger Stauback, U.S.N., who later became a legendary football player with the Dallas Cowboys, was there and kindly provided the two agents with their field uniforms.

Steffen and Carr were dispatched together to Da Nang after receiving reports that a Navy LST had been sabotaged in the harbor. Getting there was no easy matter, and when they finally arrived they discovered an all Japanese contract crew manning the ship. None of them spoke English. But reports of the sabotage were accurate…the LST was beached and three decks on the stern had been penetrated. Both agents assumed from the outset that enemy sappers with waterborne demolition charges had been responsible, but they began a thorough investigation none the less. They were assisted by an Air Force master sergeant from Da Nang Air Base who was fluent in Japanese.

The crewmembers were distracted and obviously frightened, and none were keen to wait for the agents to complete inquiries, but they had little choice. Temporary hull repairs were eventually completed and the agents left the scene with explosive residue samples. The crew of much-relieved Japanese civilian mariners immediately set sail for more peaceful waters. The laboratory analysis would later confirm the agent's suspicions about the attack. Shortly after wrapping up the sabotage case, Carr would return to Da Nang. A counterintelligence lead from Naval Intelligence agents in Japan reported that a young marine had been photographed entering the Soviet embassy in Tokyo. What was he doing there?

Embassies of countries hostile to Western democracies were carefully monitored during the Cold War…as were the people who visited them. The unauthorized appearance of a member of the U.S. armed forces at the diplomatic mission of the West's main adversary was therefore viewed with great alarm! The young marine had tough questions to answer. Was he spying for the Russians?

Carr shoved the lead sheet and report from Japan into his briefcase. These papers were accompanied by high quality photographic prints showing the subject with another young American and a male Japanese national at the entrance of the Russian embassy.

At Da Nang Air Base, he changed from his civilian clothes into Marine utilities. He briefed the command, and then set out to locate his subject. He quickly found him standing perimeter guard duty in a large fighting hole. Carr introduced himself and jumped down into the hole with him. The young marine was happy to talk about his recent leave in Japan…he and a Marine buddy had seen all the sites together and had had a fine time.

When Carr produced the photographs taken in Japan at the embassy, the marine said "Yep, that's us". Carr then demanded "This was taken at the Russian embassy. What the hell were you guys doing at the Russian embassy?" With complete sincerity he replied, "Well, it looked like an interesting building, and our Japanese buddy asked if we wanted to see it, so we said sure."

They had been received at the door and allowed to look around the large reception area. In it there had been a large framed picture on the wall, a Russian flag, and a large table, but they hadn't stayed long. Carr questioned him carefully as to whether they had talked to anybody else. "No. They were sure nice folks," he replied.

The marine had no security clearance and access to nothing that might have been of interest to America's enemies. Carr saw nothing that added to his suspicions during the interview. He wished the young marine well and began thinking about how he was going to get back to Saigon.

A report that a Navy corpsman attached to a Marine rifle company was using morphine was the reason for Carr's next trip north. In I Corps, he was met by a young naval officer and learned that the subject and his company were still at sea. They would soon be landing in an amphibious exercise at a nearby beach location. They both climbed into a jeep and traveled to the beach and waited for the landing. They didn't have long to wait for the marines to come ashore.

The suspect was located and questioned. Though he first claimed that the missing morphine Syrettes had been lost, he eventually admitted to his personal use. Their interview was soon interrupted by nearby gunfire coming from a small promontory just down the beach, and this soon led to much more. When the Marines returned from the area, they recounted how they had been ambushed and several VC in a bunker were killed. The experience underscored for Paul Carr the many seemingly innocuous dangers of service in Vietnam.

Carr's last trip to I Corps proved the catalyst for major changes in the Naval Intelligence presence in Vietnam. Dispatched to investigate a reported murder involving marines at Da Nang, he arrived after a difficult trip aggravated by the absence of available aircraft. By the time he arrived, there was no longer a crime scene, the body had been shipped out, and both the suspect and witness had been flown to Okinawa. While Carr was interviewing the division chief of staff about the incident, the colonel jumped to his feet, and Carr followed suit.

Lt. Gen. Lewis Walt, USMC, III Marine Amphibious Force commanding general entered, and Carr were introduced. "Please see me when you're through with the chief of staff," Walt said before leaving.

Shortly thereafter, Carr and the chief of staff were in the general's office. Carr was asked where he was stationed, what area he covered, and how many agents were in Vietnam. Carr answered that their detachment included one senior agent and three others, that their area of jurisdiction incorporated a large tract of Southeast Asia, and that they worked from Saigon. "How the hell can three men cover all that territory?" the general demanded.

Carr explained that with the available resources that they had, they could only work the major events. Turning to his chief of staff, General Walt directed the colonel to message Naval Intelligence in Washington requesting more agents as a matter of urgency. Big changes would be coming, by October of 1965 Special Agent Tom Brannon had established a full-time Naval Intelligence presence in Da Nang, and plans were afoot to further increase agent strength and supporting staff in the north.

*****

The activities of dissident Vietnamese elements often had a direct bearing on the security of U.S. personnel and the prosecution of the war. In one incident, Nester and several other agents drove into Saigon only to be unexpectedly overrun by a crowd of Buddhist monks and students. A bus was burning and more Molotov cocktails were being thrown.

Major General Lew Walt, USMC, with Vietnamese children

The Navy vehicles were seriously damaged, but everyone escaped injury. Because of this unrest, by late 1965 Navy agents were actively collecting information in Saigon about these types of dissident activities. By focusing the attention of his counter-intelligence program on the Port of Saigon John Nester soon

[32]

developed a useful working relationship with Vietnamese Navy staff intelligence officers.

During Nester's supervision of Navy counterintelligence activities, a scheme hatched by an unscrupulous civilian employee at a major construction contractor was uncovered. In this scheme military personnel had been asked to purchase postal money orders in exchange for a small reward.

The money orders were legal tender in U.S. dollars and eventually found their way to a loan company in Hong Kong, with the assistance of the American's Indian business partner.

The majority of the funds had then been dispatched to communist China and the American's share was deposited in various California bank accounts. Agent Nester led the investigation having had a history of covering cases involving U.S. currency. U.S. dollars were highly sought after by the enemy as a means of financing their war effort, and more than $1 million was known to have been transferred in the scheme. The case gained a certain amount of notoriety, and Nester was interviewed by two visiting U.S. congressmen. A strong case was built and the American mastermind was sent to prison for tax evasion.

*****

On the streets of Saigon, Paul Carr's duties remained focused on the counterintelligence mission. American troop numbers continued to grow in accordance with military planners' desire to use U.S. troops to take the fight to the enemy. This, it was hoped, would allow the Vietnamese allies the time needed to build a fighting force that would be effective against the communist onslaught.

Carr continued to expand his growing network of useful contacts and sources, which included retired U.S. Navy Capt. John Pollard, Standard Oil's security officer in Vietnam. Well schooled in the ways of intelligence, Pollard had excellent connections who could quickly supply accurate information about VC activities, particularly as they affected shipping.

Pollard was married to a French woman born in Morocco, and his

Saigon penthouse was a picture of continental charm and chic. It was a gathering point for some important personages of the Saigon intelligence community.

Memories of the British experience in the Malayan Emergency were still very fresh in April 1966, and Carr was receiving disturbing reports that communist agents had appeared in Vietnam as crewmembers of ships originating in Singapore. Britain had just spent nearly ten years and vast chunks of cash in the Malay Peninsula to subdue that insurgency, which was predominantly made up of Chinese guerrillas.

Carr, accompanied by Pollard, traveled to Singapore to investigate and initiate changes that they hoped would remove a serious security risk. South Vietnamese Navy sources had reported periodically that Soviet submarines were seen off-loading military supplies for Viet Cong forces along the coast of South Vietnam.

It was well known that the USSR was supporting North Vietnam with military supplies that were being delivered both to North Viet-namese ports and with the help of the Chinese, who maintained road rail and sea links with its neighbor to the south.

Carr had only heard the stories about Russian submarines, but would stumble across evidence of Soviet support one day in Saigon first hand, and quite by accident. One morning at a civilian motor pool facility, he met an American communications expert who was manning sophisticated radio monitoring equipment there, it turned out, for the CIA. In the corner of the facility were a number of rifles well greased and wrapped in protective paper. These he learned were World War II-vintage German 8mm Mausers. The radioman explained that the rifles were some of the war booty captured by Russians invading Germany in the final days of the war, and the weapons and ammunition had been intended for the Viet Cong and had been delivered via a submarine supply drop. He gave Carr one of the rifles that had been seized as a trophy. He treasures it to this day.

The Soi Rap River was the main tributary and supply line for the Port of Saigon, and was always an area of concern for the Navy. Enemy forces recognized the river's strategic value and skirmishes over it were common. In one of the more unusual incidents, a report was received by Carr that the hull of a Portuguese coastal trading vessel had somehow been ruptured while on the way to Saigon and was sinking in the Soi Rap.

Enlisting the assistance of interpreter Lieutenant Commander Anh, Carr traveled downstream to the scene in a Vietnamese Navy boat until the listing vessel came into view. Carr was surprised to see that very little was being done to save the ship, and his suspicions were heightened by the presence of a Vietnamese Naval underwater demolition team in the water. While never admitting complicity, the "VNN" soon admitted that it had information that implicated the ship's crew in illegal commerce with the Viet Congo. There was nothing more that Carr could do, and he stood and watched as the ship was vandalized and looted. In a final act of disdain, the Vietnamese sailors dumped large cans of peas from the galley onto the deck and the ship was ultimately sunk.

Nha Be was situated on the Soi Rap River, and was far enough away from Saigon to be a safe area in which to off-load dangerous cargo such as ammunition and fuel. This was where the major oil companies had established fuel storage depots, and at the time it was an important venue for unloading supply ships.

Vietnamese villagers and fishermen shared the river with the larger Navy ships and one day a Navy Underwater Demolitions Team discovered a strange object attached to the anchor chain of a fully laden ammo ship waiting to be unloaded. Alerted to the incident, Carr arrived to find the divers scrutinizing a diabolically clever explosive device capable of sending the ship and others nearby it up in a chain reaction.

The Viet Cong sappers had packed high explosives into a five - gallon metal container and had attached two partially inflated rubber bladders. One bladder was attached to each end of the container, and had been filled with only enough air to float the bomb just beneath the surface of the water. There were two clocks within the bladders configured as the primary and its secondary "failsafe" firing devices.

In their plan, the sappers had taken into consideration the tidal extremes that would cause the moored ships to swing on their anchors as the water came up the river at high tide and receded at low tide. The bomb was tied onto a long line from the ship anchor chain…the tide would finish the job. As the water receded at low tide the negative-buoyancy device was designed to be sucked under the ship's hull, where it would cause maximum damage upon detonation.

It was a close call…the timers had only minutes remaining when the divers finally disabled them. There is no way to know the extent of the damage that would have been caused had the bomb not been discovered in time.

A comprehensive report of the incident with sketches, diagrams, and photographs was prepared and dispatched to Naval Intelligence and other interested organizations throughout Vietnam. Immediately after this, Vietnamese fishermen were no longer allowed near ammunition and fuel ships, and soon armed sailors were guarding the anchored ships, further discouraging underwater swimmers by periodically hurling concussion grenades into the water.

*****

Saigon had been considered a Navy town during the early years of the Vietnam conflict. The U.S. Navy, through the command known as Headquarters Support Activity, Saigon (HSAS), provided Americans with facilities ranging from movie theaters and post exchanges to hospitals.

Capt. Archie Kuntze had taken command of HSAS in June 1964, and earned himself a reputation as an approachable leader who got things done. Naval Counterintelligence Support Activity Detachment, Saigon, owed a great deal to Captain Kuntze and his support of their mission. Most notably this included logistical support in the form agent residences, office spaces, and transportation.

The close working relationship between Kuntze and the Counterintelligence Support Agency was of particular value during the unsettled periods early in his tenure. It was during this time that

[36]

Naval Intelligence agents regularly provided situation reports regarding enemy activity that was likely to affect the safety and well-being of naval personnel.

Special Agent Paul Carr held Captain Kuntze in highest regard; however his lifestyle created highly placed enemies for him, and he became known to some as the "Mayor of Saigon." An article in an international news weekly focused further unwanted attention on claims that Kuntze reigned "as a king" over the city of Saigon.

The negative publicity inevitably led to an investigation of a range of allegations against Captain Kuntze. Because of the sensitivity of the investigation, in April of 1966 Special Agent Ken Nickel, the assistant supervising agent of Naval Investigative Service Office (NISO) in San Francisco was flown in to direct the investigation.

As the investigation proceeded, Nickel reported his findings not only directly to the NISO Pacific headquarters in Hawaii but also kept his home office fully informed. In San Francisco, his executive officer, Lt. Cdr. Bill Manthorpe, kept abreast of the investigation while carrying out his own responsibilities in support of the investigation authorizing travel,(and other expenses), and coordinating with stateside naval authorities the delivery of written records and interviews.

Captain Kuntze had been accused of a wide variety of offenses, including misusing the official aircraft to transport a Vietnamese female friend, importing expensive fabric and other items for her, and keeping government money stored in a locked refrigerator. But, it seems that what irritated the increasing number of Army generals in town the most was the sight of a mere Navy captain driving around town in a car resplendent with white-walled tires, air-conditioning and displaying other flashy signs of "high living." (It was rumored amongst the Navy personnel that the real reason for the accusations against the captain was Army interests in a takeover of the administration and support role in Saigon).

When Ken Nickel had concluded the investigation he wrote his report with sensitivity to the situation, emphasizing that Captain Kuntze was more guilty of poor judgment than criminal intent. The captain was punished with a reprimand and the loss of one hundred numbers on the seniority list, virtually ending his once-promising naval career.

In addition to his official reports, personal letters from Ken Nickel to Bill Manthorpe kept him abreast of the changes of military command, administration, and support structures in Saigon along with the changing situation with personnel in the Naval Investigative Service offices there.

In early June of 1966, it was decided to establish Naval Investigative Service offices in Vietnam to serve as the in-country headquarters. This provided more direct guidance and support to the activities of the existing resident agency (RA), putting the organization on an equal footing to NISO Philippines. When Nickel went home to San Francisco he packed his household goods and returned to Vietnam as the new supervising agent upon the establishment of the new NISOV. At the same time, Manthorpe received a telephone call from Capt. Ted Rifenburg the commander of NIS, asking him if he would like to be the commanding officer of NISOV. Manthorpe accepted immediately.

Manthorpe would later recall that although he did not know it at the time, it seems that he had been preparing for his tour with NISOV for several years. While serving as the staff intelligence officer for the Commander of the Second Fleet in 1965, he had preceded the Marines ashore into Santo Domingo to work with the naval attaché, a Marine lieutenant colonel. While the attaché was fully occupied conducting liaisons with U.S. and Dominican Republic government officials and trying to calm the actions of the various private militias, Manthorpe's job was to collect intelligence on the location and strength of the alleged communist revolutionaries. His experience working in this semi-hostile environment constantly alert to surrounding people and activities, was an excellent experience in preparation for Saigon in the 1960s.

Upon completing his sea-duty tour serving on the staff of Commander Second Fleet, Manthorpe took the obligatory tour that all young intelligence specialist were required to have with NIS. As a lieutenant commander, he was offered the position of executive officer with choices of either NISO Norfolk or NISO San Francisco. It was to be San Francisco.

[38]

After receiving his orders to report, Manthorpe was informed that the director of NIS wanted to meet with him. In Washington, Manthorpe met with Captain Rifenburg, who told him how delighted he was that the lieutenant commander had accepted the offer. Without specific details, Rifenburg said that it was going to be a tremendous challenge and that Manthorpe was welcome to communicate directly with him. Strangely, the Captain told him not worry about fitness reports. He would see that they turned out all right.

Bill Manthorpe left the meeting wondering what he had gotten himself into! Upon arrival back in San Francisco, Manthorpe soon found out. The commanding officer of NISO San Francisco and the entire NISO staff were at loggerheads. Morale was low, and the case backlog continued to grow. The two groups were looking to him to bridge the gap and fix the problems.

Lieutenant Commander Manthorpe was in need of help with suggestions and support that would improve morale and efficiency. That help would come from Ken Nickel, the assistant supervising agent with whom he quickly built a good rapport and would work most closely.

From this experience in San Francisco, Manthorpe learned what a dedicated group of professional and highly qualified people NIS agents and their support staff were. He understood how they liked to work and what they needed, (and expected from the NIS military seniors). His relationship with Nickel and his understanding of the agent force would serve him well in Vietnam. He did not fully understand until later that at NISO San Francisco he had also learned the first lesson of leadership, that management is about the processes of an organization and should be left to those responsible, in this case the professional civilian managers. Leadership was about properly caring for and inspiring the people of the organization and must be the role of the commander.

When given the NISOV command in Saigon, Manthorpe moved his family back across the country from the west coast to Springfield, Virginia. He spent several days at NIS headquarters followed by a week in Coronado, California, undergoing the Navy's standard pre-Vietnam indoctrination.

[39]

He was flown out of California on a Military Air Command C141 aircraft direct to Saigon and arrived on July 15, 1966.

The plane touched down at Tan Son Nhut Air Base outside of Saigon in the late evening, where Manthorpe was met by Ken Nickel, Lt. Bob Dothard, and Special Agents Charlie Baldwin and Milt Steffen.

The five went immediately from there to Caruso's, a nice French restaurant not far from the villa that served as the quarters for the senior military and civilian members of the office. After a "steak dinner" which Manthorpe recognized from his previous tour in France as being horse meat, he and Nickel retired to the villa that would serve as their residence for the coming year. The villa served multiple purposes including meetings with counterintelligence personnel from other agencies.

It was sometimes lent to certain MACV counterintelligence officers for meeting with their contacts, and also served as an overnight billet for NISO and other out-of-town visitors.

Their villa was in what had once been the finest section of Saigon, and the neighbors were often senior Vietnamese bureaucrats and CIA operatives of various types. Vietnamese and Army MP protection was supposedly pretty good. The villa was situated in the center of a walled lot with high metal gates and was essentially a square one-floor building of stucco-over-cinderblocks.

The floor plan included a large screened room with tile floors that served as living and dining areas, a kitchen, and one bedroom that had been fortified with a heavy door and equipped with air conditioning.

The staff included a Vietnamese maid, Hai, and her young son, who lived together in separate quarters by the back alley. Because of the neighborhood and its high profile occupants Manthorpe considered the villa a conspicuous target and a disaster just waiting to happen. But it was luxury living compared to the Saigon hotels that served as living quarters for almost everyone else in the city and was worth the risk. The hotels themselves seemed to be regular targets anyway. Fortunately, disaster never came to the villa. The geckos were the only ones to infiltrate the compound and they were welcome, hanging by their suction cupped toes on the walls and ceiling and keeping the bugs under control.

The next morning, Manthorpe got to see the office for the first time. Located at 95 Nguyen Duy Duong Street in the Cholon area of Saigon, it had a separate entrance but lay just inside the wall of what was the former HSAS compound. He was pleased with the organizations "housing" and by how well provided it was with Navy transportation.

The rest of the compound was crowded with facilities that the Army had established upon taking over from the Navy including a commissary, post-exchange, gas station and post office. It had been said that the Army had brought in several battalions of people to do what the Navy had done with fewer than one hundred. The compound was crowded.

So in July 1966 NISOV was formed as a headquarters, manned by Lieutenant Commander Manthorpe and Supervising Agent Ken Nickel, two Navy petty officers, a Vietnamese civilian translator, and a Vietnamese civilian handyman/janitor. John Nester continued in the role of senior resident agent, and assisted in the north as the numbers of NISO staff increased in Da Nang in response to the buildup.

Soon two Resident Agent posts, one each for Saigon and Da Nang were created, were created. Each RA had a lieutenant USNR and an SRA, plus a growing number of special agents as time went on. By early 1967 an agent was also assigned to Cam Ranh Bay.

Manthorpe immediately set about the task of molding the NISO headquarters operations. He and Nickel rapidly reestablished their relationship and procedures for operating the organization, which were essentially the same as in San Francisco…Nickel worried about the management of the investigations and Manthorpe concentrated on leadership of the people.

Nickel was known as the quintessential lead investigator, his guidance to the SRA upon the opening of a case was always clear and concise. He kept himself informed of the details of every case

[41]

and its progress by phone, without interfering or micromanaging. He made a special effort to ensure that all possible leads had been pursued; and he reviewed the interim and final reports meticulously with a phenomenal memory for the details.

He was like Agatha Christie's Miss Marple in that every case recalled to his mind a similar one from the past, which then suggested additional leads and avenues to pursue and potential results for the latest case. The high standards of investigating and reporting that Nickel expected from the agents ensured continued outstanding performance as the caseload continued to grow. To a man, everyone was glad that NISOV was exempt from the tedious conduct of standard background investigations. As the Navy and Marine Corps commitment to Vietnam grew, the agents had their hands full with increasing numbers of cases of serious crimes.

In his leadership role, Manthorpe had no problem keeping in close contact with the agents and staff of the Saigon Resident Agency, since they "officed" in the same building. To further this, he initiated a Sunday brunch at the villa each week featuring Texas chili cooked by Special Agent Fred Givens. But to keep in touch with the increasing number of people in Da Nang, Lieutenant Commander Manthorpe would fly up on a regular basis staying for as long as was necessary.

This close contact soon allowed him to identify festering problems between the assigned officer and the agents in Da Nang; resolving that problem before it worsened by having the officer reassigned.

In addition to being assigned as commanding officer (CO) of NISOV, Manthorpe served as the counterintelligence officer (N22) on the staff of the Commander Naval Forces, Vietnam (COMNAVFORV). His responsibilities as N22 consisted of ensuring the collection of counterintelligence information that was of concern to the Navy, and then analyzing and reporting it to the commander and his subordinate commands.

Manthorpe interpreted this duty to mean that he was to ensure that the NISO conducted regular counterintelligence activities and investigations in support of the Navy facilities in Saigon and Da Nang and, as possible, in support of other Navy locations.

[42]

Unfortunately, given the increasing criminal investigation caseload as the number of in-country Navy and Marine Corps personnel grew, very few assets could be devoted to the counterintelligence effort. Furthermore, as agents departed and were replaced by new faces, many of the previous counterintelligence contacts were lost.

Thus, most of NISO counterintelligence activities declined to a state of liaison with the massive Army counterintelligence activities in Vietnam. Contacts that had already been established with the Vietnamese Navy and with the growing Saigon-Cholon-Giadinh Security Committee were maintained. The latter was led by CIA operative Robert Gambino, in concert with William Colby at the U.S. Embassy, Vietnam.

In Da Nang, liaison was through Earl Sigg, a Navy lieutenant commander who was assigned to the U.S. Naval Activities, Saigon staff. Agents maintained the liaison at the working level, gathering information of interest to the Navy from their counterparts and writing up intelligence information reports (IIRs) for distribution to Navy commands in Vietnam and for dissemination back to headquarters in Hawaii and on to Washington. Manthorpe was responsible for maintaining liaison at the official level, keeping relationships smooth and ensuring the continued flow of their information.

Each week Manthorpe attended the conference led by Bob Gambino that included representatives of all counterintelligence and security organizations in the southern region.

This exchange helped provide a feel for the intelligence threat throughout the southern part of Vietnam. Similarly, he had weekly meetings with Lt. Cdr. Nguyen Do Hai of Vietnamese Naval Intelligence at Vietnamese Navy headquarters.

A less formal liaison was maintained with several officers in the Intelligence Directorate of MACV, most importantly Capt. Larry Tracy, USA, and Lt. Cdr. Frank Killilea who was a fellow naval intelligence specialist. These officers shared much of the information that MACV had, and in exchange Manthorpe let them use NISO's villa as a safe house to debrief their contacts. The resultant information from NISO activities and from the extensive liaison was reported to COMNAVFORV and local commanders by Manthorpe and put into message Intelligence Information Reports for the appropriate Navy commands and headquarters.

In an illustration of how close-knit the intelligence community can be, Bob Gambino and Maynard Anderson would later serve together on the Director of Central Intelligence Security Committee in Washington, D.C. Gambino later became the CIA director of security under Director of Central Intelligence George H. W Bush.

The NISOV organization worked 24/7/365, but life was not all work. Manthorpe, Nickel, and several of the agents belonged to the Cercle Sportif Saigonnais, the formerly elegant, but sadly disintegrating, French social and swim club. Nickel was a dedicated swimmer and fitness fanatic. He and Manthorpe tried to get in an hour of swimming and workout each day, either at noon or on the way home at the end of the day.

In the evening during the early part of his tour, Manthorpe took Vietnamese lessons at the Alliance Francaise, but the language soon defeated him and he would find that any Vietnamese to whom he really needed to speak understood French, in which he was still fluent after a four year tour in Paris.

The year flew by, and before Manthorpe knew it, Ken Nickel had left Vietnam and been replaced by Bert Truxell as supervising agent. Manthorpe quickly became comfortable with Truxell as his roommate in the villa and with his work style as well. Shortly thereafter it was time for his own reassignment, and Bill Manthorpe turned over the reins of NISOV to Lt. Cdr. W F. Brubaker at the end of his tour in 1967.

Upon reflecting on his tour in Vietnam, Manthorpe concluded that: "What I learned in terms of dealing with people would serve me well throughout the rest of my Navy career and into my civilian positions with the Navy. I was fortunate that my time in Vietnam was one of optimism and relative safety. I take my hat off to those who came later and had to deal with the disintegration of confidence and security."

[44]

3   DA NANG, 1965 TO 1967: MARINES AND NIS

Da Nang--the attractive seaport the French designed and christened Tourane-grew along the banks of the Han River, which meanders northward from flat paddy country and terminates in the bay. Da Nang City has been an important trade center to central Vietnam for more than two hundred years.

Da Nang is possessed of one of those natural harbors for which mariners have searched since Phoenicians ventured into the Mediterranean. The bay is shaped like a northward-facing cul-de-sac. To the east, an isthmus called Tien Sa Peninsula protects it, while to the northwest the Annamite Mountains rise abruptly from the waters, forming a gateway--Hai Van Pass--to points north.

During the Vietnam conflict, Da Nang was the northernmost deepwater port in the Republic of Vietnam; its strategic value was immense. Naval construction battalions (the SeaBees) ultimately built deepwater piers on the Tien Sa Peninsula to supply the massive amounts of war materiel.

Also facing northward on the sandy flats behind the beach was Da Nang Air Base, at one time easily the busiest air facility in the world. From sleepy beginnings, Da Nang ultimately supported a U.S. Marine Corps wing, Air Force tactical and fighter aircraft, Navy Fleet Air Support aircraft, a myriad of helicopters from all services, and the VNAF. The commanders knew that this air facility would be critical to the effective prosecution of allied war plans, especially in the interdiction of men war materiel and supplies which were filtering down from North Vietnam via the labyrinthine system of trails and crude roads known as the Ho Chi Minh Trail.

In 1965, facing unprecedented attacks by communist insurgents, South Vietnamese forces were reeling, prompting genuine concerns they might lose control of critical assets to the enemy. In response, President Lyndon Johnson dispatched U.S. marines to protect the Da Nang Air Base.

Landing at "Red Beach" on the western side of the harbor and near the future site of the Force Logistic Command, marines brought most of what they would need ashore with them, while other elements were flown in from Okinawa. In a very short time, the marines sent to protect the airfield and other key installations were doing so by active, aggressive patrolling against the Viet Congo.

*****

As Special Agent Paul Carr recalls it, Naval Intelligence had not planned an agent presence in I Corps in the early days of the war. As happened in later years and in other areas, agent support was requested by affected commands and a permanent presence followed.

Preferring work with the U.S. Marines, Special Agent Tom Brannon became the point man for Naval Intelligence soon after the Marines deployed to the northern sector of the Republic of Vietnam during April 1965.

Brannon had reported to the U.S. Naval Counterintelligence Support Unit, Saigon, on March 7. Transferred from Long Beach, California, he had volunteered to serve a year in Vietnam. At that time three agents were assigned to Vietnam: Brannon, former Chicago police officer Milt Steffen, and Special Agent Paul Carr. All served under the direction of Special Agent Maynard Anderson. Ultimately, they answered to the officer in charge of the Naval Counterintelligence Support Activity, Phillipines at Sangley Point, Lt. Cdr. Glenn Fugate.

Two Saigon agents were living at the 98 Phan Dinh Phoung villa. The others lived in BOQs that were converted hotels and under military administration. The Five Oceans BOQ, an old Chinese hotel, was situated near the Cholon office, perhaps three hundred yards away from it. The Five Os, as it was known, abutted an especially fragrant Vietnamese market and featured prominently with agents who served in later years.

Immediately after Marine elements landed at Da Nang, and then again at Chu Lai, requests were forwarded to Saigon asking for their assistance. Brannon and Carr used scheduled military transport to fly north to carry out their investigations. The process was cumbersome with the agents carrying orders assigning them on temporary duty (TDY) to the requesting element.

In September 1965 the commanding officer of Third Battalion Fourth Marines, Lieutenant Colonel Taylor, requested assistance when he learned that one of his young riflemen had been using issued morphine Syrettes from medical supplies. Brannon joined a heavily armed Marine convoy enroute and drove over Hai Van Pass from Da Nang to the 3/4 rear area at Phu Bai, just south of Hue. At Phu Bai, Third Marine Counterintelligence Team personnel provided support and a tent for interrogation purposes.

Brannon interrogated the marine, who readily admitted he had been frightened during recent combat operations and had taken the syrettes. He also admitted giving several to other members of the command.

This case was of special significance since drug abuse was a rarity at the time and also because the drugs had been stolen, not purchased on the black market. As the case load in the area of operation increased, a full-time agent was requested.

*****

In October 1965, following a request from provost marshal Major Les Barrett, USMC, Tom Brannon agreed to remain in Da Nang. The Director of Naval Intelligence (DNI) orders dated November 16, 1965, would officially establish the U.S. Naval Counterintelligence Support Unit, Da Nang Detachment.

As happened to other agents in later years, Tom Brannon was left to his own devices when the time came to requisition whatever was needed...even uniforms.

Marines pointed out that an individual in civilian clothes stood out, might draw fire, and issued the agents dungarees.

The Naval Support Activity (NSA) was established in the riverside building known as the White Elephant, where it would remain for six years. Marine command elements were set up opposite NSA at

[47]

Camp Horn, and it was from there that the active war in northern South Vietnam was directed. Brannon was given a small office cubicle near the commodore's office at the White Elephant from which to work. Not too many days would pass before the workload reached horrendous levels...men awaiting their interviews lined up outside the tiny office.

Brannon had little time for anything besides work, but the Navy provided him a small room in a dingy waterfront building that served as a BOQ. The mess was several blocks away. Fortunately a Navy jeep was requisitioned for his use.

No extra agents were available locally in Da Nang though Special Agent Carl Sundstrom came on special assignment from Naval Air Station Atsugi, Japan, to assist. Provost Marshal Barrett, upon seeing Brannon's case load predicament, assigned him infantry first lieutenant Mike Anderson, and later Criminal Investigation Division (CID) agent S.Sgt. Dan Buckle to help.

While neither was empowered to act independently, both participated actively in investigations. Anderson, as a junior officer, was especially good at finding his way through the inevitable difficulties in the Marine command maze. Buckle acted as Brannon's partner in both interviews and interrogations. Buckle, a marine with broken service, had initially enlisted in 1947. He was a mature, seasoned marine who was later commissioned and rose to the rank of lieutenant colonel. With no clerical assistance available to him, Brannon typed his reports in the rough and mailed them to Saigon, where the final product was produced and dispatched to commands.

*****

Goaded on by what seemed like a permanent line of shuffling witnesses and suspects with no place to stand but outside the commodore's office, the Navy rented a house for its Da Nang office in October of 1965. The house at 20 Duy Tan Street would serve for more than five years in this role. Brannon left the details to Lieutenant Anderson, and soon everything was moved in.

No security arrangements were made for the house, though it was located in a central Da Nang neighborhood, but a field phone was soon installed and linked to the Navy switchboard at the White Elephant, where Brannon retained his BOQ room.

By then two Marine divisions were in I Corps. The headquarters element that would control the war effort in northern I Corps, III MAF, was newly established on the east bank of the Han River, opposite the White Elephant. Telephone communication was undependable.

I Corps Navy and Marine Corps commands were learning about the NIS presence in the region. As Command representatives and Marine military police learned to find NISRA Da Nang at their backstreet address, demand began to increase.

*****

In 1965 agents were dealing with a military that was an almost entirely volunteer force. Dissent against the war was minimal, and there were few signs of narcotics usage.

In January 1966 however, Brannon began receiving reports that things were changing in Da Nang and began using informants to learn more. He suspected correctly that there was a Vietnamese drug trade operating through the totally unregulated pharmacies that were prevalent in most settlements.

He also suspected that the drugs were being offered to service personnel while frequenting unauthorized bars and brothels in the ramshackle settlements just outside the military facilities.

As an initial step, Brannon visited the Army Provost Marshal in Da Nang, but was told that they had seen no evidence of any illicit narcotics trade in the area. They also informed him that they did not believe any such problem existed.

Special Agent Tom Brannon pictured at the left, buys narcotics in Dogpatch

Recognizing the potential impact of narcotics on the battle efficiency of troops, Brannon decided to conduct an undercover investigation at a notorious shantytown outside the gates of Hill 327. The location was just west of the Da Nang Air Base and was home to the Marine headquarters elements. Known as Dogpatch to the marines, it was both insecure and dangerous, but sexual favors and illicit goods attracted visitors nonetheless.

Drawing $100 from the supply officer at Naval Support Activity, Brannon approached the Marine Provost Marshal to request the assistance of a young Puerto Rican marine whose upbringing in a tough area of New York gave him the skills to act as a streetwise narcotics buyer.

With Lance Corporal Rivera in tow, Brannon went into Dogpatch dressed as a Marine sergeant. They bought narcotics, and took photographs of the transactions as they occurred. Both cannabis and opium were plentiful

Still undercover, prescription drugs were then purchased without prescription at the Vietnamese pharmacy across the street from the Army Provost Marshal. Other purchases around Da Nang confirmed their suspicion that a ready source of narcotics existed for anybody with a desire to purchase them. Intelligence reports were prepared and forwarded to senior command elements. These were very likely the first early reports of what in later years would grow into an uncontrollable problem in Vietnam.

As Christmas of 1965 approached, two things occurred that were pleasant changes in the "Da Nang routine". The first was that Brannon was ordered to the Philippines for a special assignment. Better yet Bob Hope, Raquel Welch and the Rockettes, visited Vietnam.

Tom Brannon reported to the Naval Intelligence headquarters element at Sangley Point, Philippines. After the on-going grind of Da Nang, a trip out-of-country was something he really looked forward to. Upon his arrival, Supervising Agent Jack Donnelly briefed him.

A U.S. Navy sailor named Edwin Ross Armstrong had defected to the Chinese Communists while in Hong Kong, and had now been returned. Armstrong was the first defector to the Chinese since the Korean War. He had been a determined man, jumping ship from his U.S. destroyer and travelling from Hong Kong to rural Kowloon. He then apparently swam to awaiting Chinese sentries. The Chinese had exploited his antiwar sentiments for propaganda purposes and then returned him when his usefulness was over. Brannon was ordered to "maintain a low profile and get him back to U.S. control." His contact would be the U.S. defense attaché, who was a Marine lieutenant colonel.

Flying to Hong Kong via Navy transport, Brannon checked into his hotel, and then made his way to the consulate to contact the attaché. He would learn that unspecified U.S. embassy personnel had played key roles in recovering Armstrong. They had been assisted by their British counterparts who enjoyed excellent contacts in mainland China at the time. Nothing more was said to him about the operation.

Armstrong was closely watched at the embassy but was not in restraints. The Navy hoped to spirit him to the airport and out of the British colony without anyone realizing that he had been in Hong Kong.

Hidden from public view, Armstrong was escorted aboard a waiting US. Air Force cargo aircraft already loaded with military passengers. He and Brannon were soon en route to the Philippines.

Armstrong was perhaps eighteen, a gangly adolescent standing about six feet three, and weighing no more than 150 pounds. He looked like the high school student he could have been. Passengers had been told that a defector was aboard but not which of the oncoming passengers he was. Brannon to this day believes that most thought he was the traitor simply because of Armstrong's youthful appearance.

The marines at the brig took Armstrong into custody as soon as he reached Sangley Point. From all reports, the baby-faced sailor did not have an easy time with his Marine jailers, some of whom were Vietnam vets. He was tried by general court-martial and was awarded a sentence of twenty years confinement and a dishonorable discharge.

Finished with his assignment, Brannon began his return trip to Vietnam. He flew from the Philippines back to Hong Kong first, where he surprised his wife in California with a phone call. Soon after Brannon's return to Da Nang, Bob Hope and his entourage visited I Corps, entertaining several thousand marines gathered appreciatively for what was always an unforgettable show. Brannon recalls, "Raquel couldn't have looked better to the men, many of whom had not cast an eye on a round-eye for months." Brannon and Staff Sergeant Buckle were part of the security detail for the group, and enjoyed an up-close view of the show. True to form, Bob Hope returned to I Corps for the next five Christmas seasons, carrying on a tradition of sharing Christmas that he had begun during World War II.

He has a special place in the hearts of the thousands that he entertained on their first Christmas away from home.

*****

The Da Nang operation remained a single special agent post until March of 1966, when SRA Charlie Baldwin reported. Soon after, several other special agents arrived to work for him. Tom Brannon

[52]

only had two days to brief new agents, before he flew to Sangley Point to report to his new duty station.

Special Agent Dave Roberts was awakened on his first morning in Vietnam with a face-to-face greeting by the "house gecko", arising in fright to the delight of the housekeeping staff at the ONI villa in Saigon. This was his first-ever trip outside of the United States, and Roberts had left his home in the Virginia suburbs of Washington, D.C., two days earlier, in the midst of a record snowfall. It was December 1965 and his final destination was Da Nang.

He first flew cross-country to the San Francisco Bay Area, where he found himself in a crowded waiting room at Travis Air Force Base. He sat waiting with scores of others destined to fly in chartered air-liners to Saigon and points between. Following a seemingly endless flight, he was picked up by agents at Tan Son Nhut and driven to the Cholon office. On day two, and after all the formalities of his check-in at Saigon headquarters, he was on a military flight on his way north to Da Nang.

Dave Roberts was one of several agents hurriedly recruited to staff the new office in support of a rapidly expanding Navy and Marine Corps presence in northern I Corps. He had been attracted by the opportunities for accelerated promotion and a preference in future assignments. The surety of training in an environment guaranteed to expose an agent to every variety of investigative challenge was also a factor; this was a major career move for him. As with every agent who followed, an element of uncertainty accompanied the final arrival at the place that would be home for the next year.

Roberts was met upon his arrival at Da Nang Air Base by Special Agent Milt Steffen and 1st Lt. Mike Anderson, USMC, and was driven to their office-quarters at 20 Duy Tan Street. Steffen had extended his tour in Vietnam to work in Da Nang after his year in Saigon. More agents transferring in from other duty stations in various parts of the world were expected at any time. SRA Charlie Baldwin arrived soon after and took command. He would be followed by Special Agents Jim Levett and Carl Merritt.

Dave Roberts did not have to wait long for his first major investigation, an apparent suicide involving the officer in charge of the classified control center. The Navy lieutenant had shot himself in the head, and a full crime scene examination was required in addition to in depth investigations into any apparent motive.

In the world of counterintelligence, suicide is often symptomatic of pressures borne by those who have compromised national secrets. The fact that the victim was in charge of scores of highly sensitive documents caused alarm bells to ring and detailed inventories were carried out in haste.

For Roberts, the tasks were much more mundane with detailed measurements and photographs of the victim in his small hot room. This was conducted in soaring humidity amidst the blood and brain tissue spatter and was followed by a trip with the body to the Navy hospital known as Charlie Med for an autopsy.

Roberts felt distinctly unwell by this point, and his discomfort was recognized by a sympathetic pathologist who suggested he wait outside until the post mortem procedures were completed. Having returned to the office at dusk after the long and unforgettable day, Roberts looked forward to extra drinks that night at the officers' club.

*****

Special Agent Carl Merritt was also destined for the new office in Da Nang, and had been the last agent offered a split tour with one year in the Philippines followed by twelve months in the Republic of Vietnam. Merritt, with orders in-hand and his bag of personal effects, boarded a C130 Hercules flight at Naval Air Station Cubi Point, Philippines. He and several dozen other travelers crowded into the bowels of the four-engine transport, made themselves as comfortable as possible in their sling seats, and began the flight across the South China Sea. They made a late-night landing at Tan Son Nhut Airport in Saigon.

A former marine, Merritt had well developed skills for making the best out of challenging new situations. Confronted on arrival with the frustration of an unreliable Vietnamese phone system, he found himself unable to contact the Navy enlisted man who was to pick him up at the airport. The plan had been for him to be driven to the

[54]

supervising agent's Saigon villa for an overnight sleep before beginning the final leg of his journey.

But on the flight from the Phillipines, he'd befriended a Navy chief petty officer who had guaranteed him a seat on the next day's Navy flight to Da Nang. He couldn't contact anybody, why not just stay put and have a few beers at the airport bar?

Bier 33 was a product of Saigon, and was not a great example of the brewer's art. The standing joke was that lawn trimmings were used in the fermentation process instead of the traditional hops and barley. Nevertheless, it was wet if not cold.

Merritt and the chief drank through what remained of the night. Awakening to a painfully brilliant tropical morning, Merritt learned to his growing discomfort that the Da Nang aircraft was an old World War II vintage C47 and that the pilot was his drinking buddy. The Navy still had a few pilot NCOs back in 1966.

Thankfully that morning's flight north to the Da Nang Air Base was uneventful. Arriving at the 20 Duy Tan address, Carl Merritt began a memorable year, and SRA Charlie Baldwin and the other agents welcomed him to the fold. Hungry and thirsty, the group decided to properly introduce Carl to Da Nang's very limited nightlife with an evening visit to the NCO club at the air base. It was known as the Take Ten Club. Special Agent Dave Roberts remembered it as an especially warm night. A comedian was scheduled to perform and Merritt had changed into an embroidered white shirt like was worn in the Philippines. Finding a table the group sat down, ordered drinks, and waited for the show to begin. Unaware of what was happening in the street, they visited as Viet Cong terrorists shot the sentry and rolled grenades in through the open door of the club. Though the explosions injured many, somehow the agents were spared.

Bolting for the backdoor, they took shelter behind an air-conditioning condenser, anticipating a follow-up attack. Fortunately, none came. They returned to the club and did what they could to assist the wounded and injured, and then drove back to the office in silence.

Charlie Baldwin remembered that the agents returned to the Duy Tan quarters in an atmosphere of both tension and excitement.

Special Agent Carl Merritt

"Some of the tension dissipated, when I noticed right in the middle of Carl Merritt's back the perfect imprint of a tennis shoe.
In the melee which followed the blast, someone had run over him and his white shirt, and the combination of the grime and beer from the floor had stenciled a permanent imprint."

*****

Carl Merritt recalled that agents in Da Nang settled easily into their new neighborhood. Vietnamese families, most of whom had no electricity, surrounded the location. An array of extension cords running from different points of origin within the office soon allowed the agents to share with their grateful neighbors up and down the block. One neighborhood family in particular, who were the survivors of an ARVN soldier, received regular help from the agents. The men adopted the family and regularly shared their food and other necessities.

Despite the arrival of thousands of American service personnel, vestiges of an earlier and more refined era still remained. Several small

[56]

restaurants in the neighborhood continued to offer high-quality French cuisine. A favorite of the agents, the Golden Dragon, was operated by a black French Algerian whose restaurant featured an impressive wine cellar.

The role of a traveling agent at NISRA Da Nang was created when Carl Merritt volunteered to manage the growing demand for NIS support in the field.

This was a role that other agents continued to support until 1969, when satellite offices reporting to Da Nang were finally established at Quang Tri Combat Base and at Chu Lai.

1965 brought another year of change and transition in northern I Corps as two Marine divisions deployed and then redeployed to meet changing tactical conditions. Uncomfortable to a man with the task they were assigned, (static defense of the air base), senior marines soon began to extend their control by traditional Marine techniques utilizing patrol and pacification. Communication with deployed field marines was sketchy and transportation was largely a matter of the agent's capacity for innovation.

Merritt soon learned that he could guarantee himself a seat on any service aircraft by carrying a colorful mailbag. If asked, his answer was obvious... that the bag contained mail "for the troops". In reality, the bag was used to carry case files and a supply of trade goods for bartering with those willing to provide transport, a shower, or a dry place to sleep. Liquor was especially effective since marines were limited to beer rations. A bottle of Crown Royal would buy just about anything that might be needed.

The mailbag ploy worked with other branches of the service too. In Phu Bai, home of the Army Security Agency's secret Eighth Radio Research Station, Merritt assured himself a shower and clean bunk by leaving 9mm Swedish K submachine guns with friendly Army contacts.

At that point in the war, the army station had established facilities that were far better than most other organizations that were just getting settled in under canvas. The K was a favored weapon in Special Forces units but the then uncommon 9mm caliber sounded different enough that there was a real risk that "friendlies" would interpret its chatter as "nonfriendly" and react accordingly. Merritt elected to stay with the 7.62 caliber M14 rifle that was then standard issue to all marines.

The task of finding a marine or the scene of an incident always began with the parent unit, either regimental headquarters or the battalion command post (CP). At that location, the situation could be assessed and a plan drawn up to allow for travel forward to the final destination. This might well involve helicopter travel, or a jeep or truck ride. Sometimes the going was on foot, accompanying a sweep. Merritt effectively established the model for travelling agent rounds men who would follow.

*****

In NISRA Da Nang's operational area of I Corps, 1966 brought with it a new military threat from the buildup of regular North Vietnamese Army (NVA) forces in the border regions. Along with it came growing signs of political instability within the fragile Saigon regime of the colorful Premier, Nguyen Cao Ky. Buddhists remained unappeased by Ky's attempt at a piecemeal approach to democratic reform, and tensions remained between the underrepresented Buddhists and Catholics in power.

Premier Ky recognized I Corp commander Lt. Gen. Nguyen Chanh Thi as a serious rival. Thi was a respected military leader as well as an astute politician, and he was not above capitalizing on traditional distrusts that the regional people held for the Saigon government and its policies.

The city of Hue had long been the epicenter of Buddhist unrest, and it was also Thi's home. In March of 1966, Premier Ky flew to Hue to personally investigate allegations that Thi had been agitating against his Saigon government. Immediately after the trip, Thi was forced to resign. Although he did so gracefully, the people of I Corps were in shock. Unrest, demonstrations, and strikes in the cities of Da Nang and Hue would erupt following his dismissal, and the "Struggle Forces" opposing the Ky government in Saigon was formed.

[58]

Despite this civil unrest, III MAF commander Lt. Gen. Lewis Walt, USMC, pressed ahead with combat operations in the region south of Da Nang in concert with his Vietnamese allies.

After Thi resigned, he returned to his home in Hue, where many rallied to him, furthering the political foment. Perceiving the threat posed from the support of the "Struggle Forces" by key military, police, and political leaders in Da Nang, Premier Ky dispatched the Vietnamese Marines. Suddenly General Walt was in a very difficult position. While wishing to avoid any U.S. involvement in Vietnamese politics, he nevertheless had a responsibility to prosecute the war against the communist forces.

Moreover, his professional relationship with Thi had been cordial and effective. The Marines did all they could to stay clear of the Vietnamese turmoil, hoping matters might resolve themselves with efforts quickly returning to the effective prosecution of the war.

In early April however, an ARVN group from Hoi An responded to news about the arrival of the Vietnamese marines from Saigon. They left their barracks south of Da Nang towing artillery, intending to bring their guns to bear on the air base where the Saigon marines were located. General Walt ordered elements of his Ninth Marines to block the force. With the aid of Marine fighters overhead and the threat of distant artillery zeroed in on their positions, the rebel Vietnamese were halted at a bridge on Route 1 and ultimately returned to Hoi An.

On April 15 Premier Ky, covertly reinforced forces loyal to his regime in Saigon and critical areas within Da Nang were seized. The widespread arrests of Struggle Forces leaders soon followed. During the operation, Vietnamese Air Force A1 Skyraiders fired rockets and machine guns at positions near the III MAF headquarters, wounding nearby marines. Somehow a full blown confrontation was avoided.

Three days later General Walt played a firsthand role in regaining control of the strategically critical bridge connecting Tien Sa Peninsula with Da Nang.

With opposing South Vietnamese forces facing one another on

opposite sides of the span, Walt confronted the Vietnamese warrant officer that was in command and urged him to remove the demolition charges that had been placed. The warrant officer refused and with a flourish announced to Walt that they would die together. Though he proceeded to give the command to detonate the charges, the explosives didn't fire and the bridge was saved.

Demolition charges were quickly cleared by the awaiting U.S. marines, and the critical war materiel movements from Deepwater Pier to the storage areas resumed.

The NISRA Da Nang office and billet in downtown Da Nang City was a place of unrest throughout the troubles. Though U.S. civilians and others had been evacuated, the Naval Intelligence agents remained at their home and office on Duy Tan Street. All other agencies left.

Driving to the U.S. Army Military Intelligence Compound to visit detachment commander Maj. Neil Hock, SRA Charlie Baldwin was surprised to find their compound vacant. The Army had burned their files and taken refuge on Tien Sa Peninsula. There was a growing and palpable tension in the streets of Da Nang as Vietnamese political events continued to unfold. Factions technically allied to the same cause aligned against each other, and it became difficult for outsiders to know if a former ally posed a danger to them. Agents went about their jobs but with a heightened sense of awareness.

One day while in the home of their Vietnamese language teacher, two agents overheard a heated conversation between Vietnamese that not only indicated an imminent uprising in I Corps but identified key players. SRA Charlie Baldwin immediately reported their information to Da Nang's CIA station chief, who arranged for them to brief the deputy ambassador in Saigon.

During the meeting, the deputy ambassador announced to Baldwin that his report confirmed information developed in Saigon, presumably by the CIA. The Navy report added further credence and detail to intelligence the embassy had been using to formulate contingency plans for Vietnam.

[60]

Agents remained in the small office compound during the periods of high alert when Da Nang City was evacuated. They carefully observed events around 20 Duy Tan for firsthand indicators of developments in the Vietnamese political crisis.

One morning, the unmistakable sounds of an ARVN tank maneuvering down the street drew the attention of the agents. The tank was seen slowly driving down the block adjacent to theirs. As it approached the nearby Buddhist temple, the turret turned to the side, training its main gun at the building.

Taking a safe position on a nearby curb, the agents waited to see what the response from the temple would be. They didn't have to wait for long, as a Buddhist monk rushed toward the tank climbed up onto it, and doused himself in gasoline, but did not set himself ablaze.

His ruse proved ineffective though, as later the boom of the gun could be heard. Several rounds were fired into the uppermost part of the structure and there was little damage, but a clear message had been sent.

One morning in early May 1966, Dave Roberts awoke to find Duy Tan Street strangely quiet. Barbed wire and sand-bagged positions blocking both ends of the street had been erected and were being manned by armed Vietnamese. The agents weren't going anywhere, but fortunately they had a substantial supply of C rations stored in the office. Any movement outside on the street would be unnecessarily hazardous. A Navy supply truck was allowed through to deliver drinking water, and the agents stayed at home for more than a week listening to the sounds of gunfire in surrounding Da Nang.

When tensions reached their height in Da Nang on May 15, agents were occupying themselves on the front porch of the house in an endless game of pinochle. There had been more firing than usual that day, and the arrival of VNA FA1 Skyraiders over the eastern edge of the city quickly drew the agents' attention. They watched with growing concern as the planes fired rockets and strafed positions that appeared to be in the vicinity of General Walt's headquarters.

[61]

Isolated and without any means of communication, Charlie Baldwin decided that an effort needed be made to reach the Da Nang Combat Information Bureau (CIB) to assess the situation. Reporters could be expected to be found at the CIB, and they would have news. Furthermore, they might be offered something other than the C rations that they had subsisted on throughout the emergency. Accompanied by Special Agent Milt Steffen, they set off by jeep. Rounding a corner in downtown Da Nang, they were confronted by a fire fight between Vietnamese National Police and ARVN troops. With rounds cracking around them, Steffen swung the jeep back around and returned them safely to the office in record time.

*****

Bob Powers transferred to Da Nang to join Charlie Baldwin's team in November of 1966. A single agent, Powers had volunteered for the new duty assignment after serving a stint in Iceland. He enjoyed overseas work a lot, and in Vietnam he would be joining his two brothers, one a career Army intelligence officer, the other a young marine.

That December, Bob Powers and Carl Merritt were called out late one night to investigate a reported shooting at a Marine engineer unit on the far side of Da Nang. As always, the city was locked down tight since "the country belonged to Charlie."

Armed to the teeth, they set off in a Navy Ford Bronco, with Merritt in the back, where he could better defend them in the event of an attack. As usual, there were roadblocks everywhere.

Powers was new in-country and knew none of the passwords that the nervous sentries were expecting to hear, but with the help of their credentials they managed to talk their way through. Still set up in the back, Merritt frantically banged on the roof of the truck every time it appeared that Powers was taking a wrong turn into Indian country. At last they arrived, safely and without incident.

[62]

Senior Resident Agent Charlie Baldwin with two National Police colleagues in Da Nang

The Marine victim's body had already been removed, which complicated the crime scene search for forensic evidence, but there were nine eye witnesses. According to them, the suspect had entered the darkened hooch full of sleeping marines and began shooting. The dead marine had been a bunk mate of the intended victim and had been shot dead as he tried to escape.

On the surface the case was not a difficult one, but before the case had come to trial all but three of the nine marine witnesses had been killed in combat! The shooter was ultimately found guilty and received a lengthy sentence.

*****

Like Special Agents Merritt and Powers, New Englander Peter Segersten volunteered for Vietnam service while serving at NISRA in Newport, Rhode Island. The young special agent arrived in Da

Nang aboard a Navy C54 on New Year's Day 1966 and reported to Charlie Baldwin's team. Like most of the other agents, his work would be almost exclusively with the Marines.

Segersten began by assisting with his support of forward deployed USMC units; in particular the Third Marine Division. The Third Marines were just beginning a rigorous series of operations to rid the areas between Da Nang and the DMZ of North Vietnamese Army units and the VC cadre that supported them.

The process of getting out to the marines location normally began with an aircraft ride, either into Phu Bai or Dong Ha. Aircraft could belong to any of the services, but Marine CH46 and C130 aircraft were the most common.

NIS special agents working in the north of South Vietnam went to great pains to be sure that Marine commands knew that they were in-country and available to assist. Segersten and Merritt regularly visited Marine units deployed along the outer edges of South Vietnam, in the dangerous areas most commonly considered Indian country. The agents also visited Khe Sanh before the big NVA buildup and siege when it was a forward artillery base, and once again when it was surrounded by enemy forces and under intense artillery and rocket attacks.

Agents working the north soon learned that in an environment of primitive under-canvas living, it was wise to seek out a billet with either a SeaBee battalion or a Marine engineer group. Both organizations were accomplished at minimizing the hardships of living in the field.

Peter Segersten inherited an interesting investigation in October 1966 that was to have far-reaching ramifications in military legal circles. The question would prove to be how the Uniform Code of Military Justice (UCMJ) applied to civilian employees of the Navy serving in a war zone.

Segersten, backed up by Special Agent Howie Dilkes, was called out late one afternoon to begin the investigation of a fatal stabbing that had occurred at a small Vietnamese bar on the Tien Sa Peninsula, just opposite Da Nang City.

Segersten found the scene with some difficulty. It was a nondescript shack made of scavenged material, and was located near the north end of China Beach. It had been erected where it was to take advantage of nearby ship berthing. Inside the structure were a few chairs and tables, a bar, and a number of entrepreneurial females.

Marine MPs at the scene informed the agents that the victim's remains had been removed to the morgue. An able seaman civilian employee of the Navy named James Henry Latney had been arrested in connection with the killing. Latney was assigned to the Military Sea Transportation Service (MSTS), and was jailed in their brig. The investigators found little physical evidence, and the Vietnamese employees were uncooperative.

Realizing that they needed a skilled interpreter to successful interrogate the Vietnamese witnesses, the agents drove to the nearby naval advisory detachment that adjoined Camp Tien Sa. For many years the NAD had supported clandestine Vietnamese operations into North Vietnam utilizing fast patrol torpedo boats called nasty boats. At the detachment, the agents found a former ONI special agent, a Marine captain, who offered his Nung interpreter. The Nung were an ethnic group widely involved in the shadowy world of the Special Forces.

At the crime scene, the Vietnamese witnesses were skillfully interrogated by the NAD Nung, who had honed his skills with captured enemy soldiers.

Witnesses said that Beyethe Arthur Trimm, the victim, had come ashore earlier in the day while his ship was off-loading fuel at a berth near Tien Sa Peninsula. He had been drinking quietly until Latney's arrival later in the day, and the men had argued and scuffled. The witnesses saw Latney slash Trimm repeatedly with his pocketknife, and Trimm fall to the ground. They said that Latney folded his knife and put it in his pocket, only to pull it out once again and stab Trimm in the heart.

Segersten set out to learn all he could about the two, who were crewmembers aboard the bulk fuel transport *Antank*. He quickly discovered that Latney, was considered the ship bully by the crew. Trimm had been a marine and had been discharged under other-

[65]

than-honorable circumstances. He had just signed on in Manila. Segersten knew the murder weapon would be critical evidence in the case against Latney. The bar proprietor, known to all as mama-san, reported that Latney had thrown his knife out the door after the stabbing. A careful grid search of the beach and water produced nothing. Mama-san then told the Nung interpreter that a Popular Forces (PF) soldier had picked it up. The Nung began asking Vietnamese in the area about whom the PF might have been and later that night located a young Vietnamese soldier who admitted retrieving the bloodstained knife. He took agents to the nearby sand dunes and dug up the murder weapon. The soldier willingly provided a statement acknowledging what had occurred.

Latney languished in the Marine brig for several months while legal officers and diplomats argued about how the trial was to be conducted. The UCMJ stipulates that civilians assigned to a theater of war are subject to the laws of that code, but under it the lawyers were not confident a prosecution would succeed. Finally, the presiding Marine authority ordered that a general court-martial be convened to try Latney. An incident of such blatant criminal be-havior as this could not go unpunished.

The court-martial found Latney guilty of murder, and he was shipped to a federal penitentiary to serve his sentence. Ultimately however, he was released after a successful appeal of the conviction. The appellate court found that a formal state of war did not exist in Vietnam, and because of this the UCMJ did not apply to the civilian, Latney.

*****

In March 1967 SRA Charlie Baldwin's tour ended and Special Agent Jack Myer, who had just completed a three year tour in Japan, replaced him.

Missing his scheduled flight from Tachikawa because of a wake-up call that never came, Myer was lucky to find a seat on the Air Force C130 that ferried the day's edition of *Stars and Stripes* newspaper to Saigon.

After being briefed by supervising agent Ken Nickel, Myer began his trip up-country that next day aboard the Market Time shuttle, an aging C47 loaded to capacity with Vietnamese Navy personnel and dependents.

It was a long trip, made more tolerable by the fact he was assigned one of the ten seats, while the other passengers squatted on the deck. Myer remembers the flight that morning especially well since the same aircraft crashed on its return leg...killing everyone.

Myer had a pretty good idea of what to expect in Da Nang, the plane crash notwithstanding. As a Japan-based agent, he had carried out many investigations afloat offshore at Yankee Station, where U.S. naval forces were actively carrying out the aerial campaign against North Vietnam

He had experienced the flight into Da Nang on a Navy replenishment aircraft from the fleet on the first leg to Japan. It was a hot and dirty trip. In the few days Myer had before the handover from the departing Charlie Baldwin, he was shown the ropes. As added excitement to a party thrown by the local Army Military Intelligence detachment, a firefight broke out on the street between sentries and infiltrating VC. It was an appropriate baptism for Myer's, welcoming him officially to Da Nang.

*****

Soon after arriving in Da Nang in late 1966, Bob Powers established himself as a particularly capable criminal investigator. His reputation followed him through three decades of service with the organization. Powers holds the dubious distinction of having investigated what is believed to be the first "fragging" in NIS history.

Fragging, the use of fragmentation grenades to commit murder, would most often be carried out against disliked officers and NCOs. The investigation began with a call for assistance from a Marine artillery unit deployed along the corridor south of Da Nang, north of the Marine enclave at Chu Lai. The battery executive officer, who was a captain, had been very seriously injured by the explosion of a booby trap rigged outside the tent he shared with the commanding officer. The victim lost both of his legs in the blast of the US manufactured M26 fragmentation grenade.

Powers was assigned to a month of temporary duty with the Marine enclave at Chu Lai, where he billeted with Marine military police. A Marine senior NCO from CID accompanied him to the artillery encampment on Route 1 and left him there. Powers began by reconstructing what remained of the crime scene and searched for any remaining physical evidence.

He found that a wooden stake used in aiming an artillery piece, had been used in this case to secure one end of a trip wire. The other end was connected to the pin of the grenade. The stake he found was one of what normally would be a set of three, and on it he found residue from adhesive tape.

Powers carefully preserved the post and its tape as evidence, then began asking questions. He soon discovered that one of the unit troublemakers worked in a supply tent that allowed limited-access.

It was thoroughly searched. A set of gun laying stakes like the ones used in the attack was soon discovered, the package had been opened, and one was missing. Forensic laboratory examination later established that the stake used to fashion the booby trap had come from this packet of three. Since access to the supply tent was strictly limited, this was an especially important discovery.

Powers soon realized that this investigation would not be concluded quickly. He would have no choice but to remain in this forward area until it was. He was wearing an unusual composite "uniform" consisting of utility shirt, white tee shirt, and chinos.

His appearance set him apart from everyone else at the position and likely rendered him an attractive target because of it. He had no rifle with which to defend himself, only his .357 magnum handgun.

On the first night, when there was little else that he could do safely, Powers began looking for a place to sleep. A Marine Major named Mimmor, who had originally thought Powers to be an itinerant journalist, was particularly helpful once he discovered that he was carrying out the investigation, and offered Powers a bunk in his tent.

The gun battery and battalion areas were separated by Route 1, and at that time the investigation was being carried out among 155mm gun batteries. The road was an obvious avenue of enemy attack, and Marine defenses reflected that fact. Early the next morning Powers was led in the dark past sentries demanding a password, and then through an antipersonnel minefield before reaching the highway. On the opposite side, the process was repeated. Powers stayed very close to the major.

Interviews that took place during the days that followed were conducted in a two-man tent equipped with nothing but a table and two chairs. In accordance with regulations in forward areas, all marines interviewed were armed with their issue rifle. Attacks on the gun position did occur. Powers' first experienced a mortar attack during the interview of a young marine who immediately bolted from the tent upon hearing the sound of incoming rounds. Powers remained, uncertain of where to go or what to do once he got there, his revolver lying on the table.

Powers interviewed scores of marines including the one from the supply tent. He had been warned of his rights against self incrimination, but waived them and spoke freely. Bob Powers thought the man came across as a particularly cool and streetwise character, deserving of a careful record check back in Da Nang.

The investigation lasted several weeks, and interviews turned up a variety of other offences. Men guarding the perimeter would often throw grenades at friendly defensive positions during the night... something they jokingly referred to as War Call. This invariably resulted in a general stand-to, during which every marine rushed to defend the position against the "enemy attack". Another marine produced over thirty pounds of marijuana and admitted he was the main supplier in the battery. Because of his cooperation, Powers burned it without filing a report.

While the investigation proceeded, physical evidence was forwarded to the U.S. Army forensic laboratory at Camp Zama, Japan, for examination. Their report confirmed the agent's findings. Additional inquiries sent to the United States disclosed that the primary suspect had an extensive criminal record.

Senior Resident Agent Jack Myer, left, in the Demilitarized Zone at Con Thien firebase with Special Agent Carl Merritt

He had in fact been given the choice of military service or jail at his last court appearance. With this in mind, Powers decided to interrogate the suspect again. With Special Agent Pete Segersten accompanying him, he drove from Chu Lai back to the battery site, where they attempted the follow up interview. This time, when confronted by two agents, the suspect chose to remain silent and was ultimately arrested. They handcuffed him and drove him to the Marine brig in Da Nang. The agents were taking no chances with this man.

A break in the investigation came when a fellow marine at the gun battery mailed marijuana to the suspect. It was intercepted and as might be expected, led straight back to the sender. When he was interrogated, he said the suspect had admitted to being out on the perimeter smoking marijuana on the night of the attack. He had been angry about being passed over for promotion, and decided to set the booby trap in retaliation.

Witnesses helped to build a circumstantial case against the suspect, which was not very strong. The suspect eventually accepted a plea bargain and was sentenced to five years in prison.

*****

Another case for NISRA Da Nang involved a teenage Vietnamese girl who had been killed in one of the outlying villages near Da Nang. Marine MPs had somehow neglected to report the incident to Naval Intelligence, and their CID investigators began working the case on their own. Few leads were produced, and even less evidence.

Headquarters Fleet Marine Force Pacific in Hawaii sent a message to Da Nang agents when they were made aware of the Vietnamese girl's death. Why, they asked, was Naval Intelligence not conducting the investigation? SRA Jack Myer gave the case to Bob Powers.

Powers began by interviewing Marine MPs and CID to obtain as much background as possible. There was a lot of joking and "good lucks" from the marines, who had yet to produce a useful

[71]

investigative lead. The physical evidence consisted of one spent .45 caliber cartridge case, which had been inadvertently stepped on by one of the men while conducting the crime scene search.

On the second day, Special Agent Powers was accompanied by a Vietnamese interpreter, and traveled to the victim's village to interview her mother. He found the woman to be a cooperative and competent witness who provided excellent information about the Marine suspect. She had obviously not trusted the Marine investigators, since they wore the same type of uniform that the suspect had worn when he killed her daughter. Inquiries in the village had to be made with care. Powers would learn that the accused Marine had been involved with the victim's family in a black-marketing scheme. He had shifted his allegiance to another family when the victim's father had not allowed him to have sex with his daughter.

Anxious to obtain corroboration, Powers set out to find other witnesses. The victim's mother tried unsuccessfully to get the other family to cooperate, but they would not. Infuriated, she attacked the patriarch of the family, which led to a full blown melee as his family retaliated against her. Powers was caught in the middle as he struggled to extricate his witness. Trying to settle things down, Powers was frustrated to find that his interpreter had disappeared. He didn't locate him again until later in the day. Next, the Vietnamese doctor who first examined the girl and had pronounced her dead was located and interviewed at Da Nang's hospital.

An identification lineup was held to see if the victim's mother could identify the suspect, which she did successfully. Powers arrested the suspect in this so-called "cold case". He later faced a general court-martial, was found him guilty of murder and was sent away for life.

*****

[72]

4   SAIGON, 1967 TO 1968: TERRORISM AND TET

As 1967 began, many signs of the war's escalation were evident. U.S. forces in Vietnam had increased in number during the previous year from 180,000 to 280,000.

In addition, 60,000 Navy and Marine personnel were serving on ships offshore and 35,000 Air Force servicemen were in Thailand, where air bases supported both the bombing campaign against North Vietnam and the covert war in Laos. American forces were also supplemented by allied countries. South Korea, Australia, New Zealand, Thailand, and the Philippines all boosted their troop numbers. South Vietnamese service numbers stood steady at about 750,000.

The Ho Chi Minh Trail continued to be the primary supply route for communist forces operating in the South. Supplies continued to flow despite constant air attacks against both personnel and vehicles as they threaded their way along the trail through the mountains and jungles of North Vietnam, Laos, and Cambodia. The Soviets and Chinese kept a regular supply of military commodities and aid flowing to their North Vietnamese ally.

To keep up with the ever-increasing Navy presence in South Vietnam, NIS assigned a lieutenant commander, W F. Brubaker, as commanding officer in July of 1967. By then NISOV Supervising Agent Bert Truxell had taken over the reins from Ken Nickel, Nickel having been promoted.

Truxell had more agents at his disposal than Nickel had, but he knew right away that they were not enough. With six years' experience in ONI and two years as an Army CIC agent, Bert Truxell nevertheless found himself ill prepared for the chaos that was the Vietnam War. Upon his arrival at Tan Son Nhut Air Base, the new senior agent was subjected to a rapid trip through Saigon in sweltering heat with car windows closed against grenade attack.

He would recall… "The unexpected was always the expected in Vietnam. Where else would one's office feature a courtyard with edible bananas and a heavily armed Vietnamese guard?" The office was set up under an organizational structure typical at the time. "Code 20", the Investigations, was essentially the domain of the supervising agent, whereas "Code 40", Counterintelligence, was largely under the CO's jurisdiction.

This arrangement was not set in stone and left ample opportunity for a cross-over of interests, which did occur. Though the Saigon senior resident agent was managing cases for the bottom half of South Vietnam, oversight of the Da Nang resident agency was more a matter of guidance from afar. Da Nang SRA Jack Myer, a seasoned veteran, was known to sometimes "lose his connection" on uncertain select long-distance telephone calls, depending on the topic. It was a tactic his supervisor understood well and admitted he would have used had roles been reversed.

Agents, who often worked alone, were dispatched to wherever it was that they were needed. Truxell, saddled with the ultimate overall countrywide responsibility was constantly confronted with the practical difficulties of the task. He recalled that "Hopping aboard logistic flights and helicopters was a way of life. Time loss was phenomenal; it could take days to get to a case and just as many to return."

Every agent who served in Vietnam was a volunteer. The organization stipulated that the volunteers have a minimum of one year of experience in ONI/NIS, but many had never worked a criminal investigation until their arrival in Vietnam. Truxell and his two SRAs had further challenges. How does one supervise an agent out in the boondocks of a war zone when reliable communications don't exist? The agents grew up and learned quickly, it was a matter of survival. If they missed a lead, they were sent back to cover it. There was no room for compromise in the quality of the investigations. The organization would not tolerate it, nor would the military justice system.

The NISOV commanding officer's counterintelligence role at Naval Forces, Vietnam, remained focused on counterterrorism and the protection of our forces. At the time, a close working relationship with South Vietnamese National Police authorities provided a regular flow of information about VC activities in the area. These were reports not only of terrorist incidents in Saigon and the Gia Dinh sector of the city but also information gleaned by Police Special Branch in its investigations and interrogations. This information, combined with in-house sources and further intelligence provided by ONI's Vietnamese Navy counterparts, helped intelligence officers form a picture of enemy activity and occasionally their intentions.

Lt. Cdr. Bill Brubaker furnished the commander of U.S. Naval Forces, Vietnam, with a weekly briefing at the COMNAVFORV headquarters in central Saigon. While desk officers briefed on activities in their respective areas of responsibility, Brubaker used a large map of Saigon to illustrate VC activity and its proximity to Navy assets and personnel.

*****

The VNNSB was a valuable conduit of counterintelligence information. A permanent adviser to the VNNSB, normally a junior U.S. Navy intelligence officer, provided the link between the Vietnamese and NISOV.

In June of 1967 Lt. Clint Schneider, U.S.N. reported to Vietnam as a counterintelligence adviser to the Vietnamese Navy. Lieutenant Schneider had been a naval aviator, an Al Skyraider pilot, until flight surgeons discovered he had developed night vision problems.

Uninterested in a career in the back seat, he had opted to leave naval aviation and start a new career as an intelligence officer. After schooling at the Air Intelligence School and a particularly grueling time in escape-and-evasion training, he was dispatched to Vietnam for assignment to VNNSB. It was his first operational intelligence assignment.

Schneider began his assignment as quietly as a conspicuously large man who towered over his counterparts could do. Quickly, he learned that the Vietnamese were very competent counter-intelligence and counter subversion operatives and ascertained that he could learn much from the people that he had originally been sent to advise.

[75]

VNNSB adviser Lt. Ron Lodziewski and Lt. Cdr. Brooks with VNNSB Officers

"I figured out the job on my feet," he said. "The Vietnamese primary mission was protection of the regime, though they were often very good at their security tasking too."

NISOV Commanding Officer Bill Manthorpe provided practical advice for his new arrival, but Schneider was quick to pick up that he would have to use his personal initiative to figure out the operational aspects of the job and to decide how best he could assist the Vietnamese. He realized that the Vietnamese had the potential to provide very good intelligence if he could provide them with the basic support requirements of transportation and logistics.

Schneider installed a bunk in his office at the VNNSB compound and spent an increasing amount of time with his counterpart, Lieutenant Commander Hai. "Hai had forgotten more about intelligence than I would ever know. In the first days of my assignment, he was often unavailable to me, but this changed over time as his confidence in me grew."

An impromptu trip to Da Nang via a VNAF C47 was a stark reminder of the logistic challenges the Vietnamese allies faced in running a countrywide intelligence and security program. Schneider and Hai boarded the aging transport together with Vietnamese military dependents, who were accompanied by their worldly goods, including goats and chickens.

The aircraft lumbered into the air with its noisy and odorous cargo, diverting its course part way through the flight to avoid a known area of enemy activity. Out of curiosity, Schneider asked his counterpart what he thought might happen if they were to survive a plane crash in this part of the jungle. He said, "You, after all, could strip down to your skivvys and nobody would be the wiser," Commander Hai smiled and replied, "No, it's not that simple; they'd get me only a little while after they found you. Unlike the peasantry, I've spent my life wearing boots. My footprints would be a giveaway."

Although one of the engines was running roughly throughout the trip, they landed safely in Da Nang. This same aircraft would crash soon after their flight due to an airframe failure.

Knowing he had a lot to learn about the craft of intelligence, Schneider decided he could make the most immediate impact on VNNSB's effectiveness by providing his counterparts with materiel and logistic support. He established relationships with the Army helicopter units who could fly the Vietnamese to their field elements, U.S. Air Force assets and Air America was used for longer distance flights.

He commandeered NISOV evidence that was scheduled for destruction for use by the Vietnamese, most notably the firearms and ammunition.

The Vietnamese provided support to Naval Intelligence also. The VNNSB detachment at the Port of Saigon gathered information about visiting merchant vessels, including crew lists, and provided these to the Americans. On several occasions, they provided surveillance teams for NISOV, in localities where Americans would have been highly conspicuous. In late 1967 a VNNSB surveillance team assisted in the apprehension of a Chinese gang in possession of counterfeit printing plates.

VNNSB agents at the Port of Saigon discovered two grenades of Russian manufacture concealed in the bottom of a metal cookie container. These were in the possession of a port employee, and they seized this opportunity to recruit an agent for use in their war against the Viet Congo. The Vietnamese man quickly confessed to hiding the grenades, telling authorities that his family lived in an area under the control of the Viet Cong.

The Viet Cong had learned that he was a port employee and had threatened his family. They then offered him a chance to prove his loyalty to their cause by using the grenades to attack Americans. He was instructed to use one grenade to destroy a target at the port and to use the other against American personnel at a popular Saigon bar.

Schneider was asked to assist in an operational plan to mislead the enemy into thinking that the port employee was complying with the VC orders. A spectacular, and nondestructive, blast was staged at the Port. Soon after that, one of the Russian grenades was taped to the leg of a table at the bar. But a patron soon "discovered" it and raised the alarm before it exploded. U.S. Army explosive ordnance disposal (EOD) soldiers disarmed the device, and the incident was widely reported by the Vietnamese press. Despite all the theatrics however, the Vietnamese informed VNNSB that he was unable to operate as their double agent. He simply could not jeopardize the safety of his family.

The capture of terrorist team leader Nguyen Van Sam, was a major success for VNNSB and their parent command, the Military Security Directorate (MSD). Acting on good information, an MSD team snatched Sam in a dingy alleyway off the backstreets of Gia Dinh. Whisked to MSS interrogation facilities, the Viet Cong officer soon identified four other cell members. All were quickly apprehended. These sapper teams were active in carrying out attacks against both the Vietnamese and their American allies, and the apprehension and neutralization of VC sapper cells proved to be a very important victory. Intelligence experts were reasonably confident that Sam had told them everything that he knew.

A Vietnamese newspaper had reported his capture, and that the VC was being subjected to torture. It was decided to have the newspaper report that the captive had cooperated fully with South Vietnamese authorities and had then been released. Sam was never heard from again.

LT Schneider and his VNNSB counterpart

[79]

The communists had their fair share of wins too. A report received by VNNSB in Saigon contained information regarding a crewman on watch aboard a Vietnamese Navy monitor that had killed all of his crewmates as they slept, and had then slipped anchor at Can Tho. The heavily armored vessel was then taken upriver under the cover of darkness toward Cambodia. Schneider obtained help from an Army helicopter squadron, and the search for the hijacked vessel began. It was never found, and the search was abandoned when the chopper started taking heavy ground fire as they approached Cambodia.

Later a Cambodian newspaper article translated from the original Khmer to Vietnamese turned up at VNNSB headquarters. The article extolled the achievements of the South Vietnamese sailor who had murdered his crewmates, describing him as a true patriot. The report was that the sailors had been "overthrown", not that they were murdered in their sleep. A photo of the chief petty officer accompanied the article.

Because the Cambodian press claimed that U.S. advisers were absent from the VNN ship during the takeover, Schneider received orders from the U.S. senior naval adviser to investigate the circumstances of the report. No evidence that the allegations were anything other than propaganda was ever discovered.

*****

Bombings and individual attacks against vulnerable Americans continued. One young Navy lieutenant walking to work from his Saigon billet in his dress whites, fell victim to a notorious VC assassin known as the Dragon Lady.

He was shot and killed by a young Vietnamese woman riding as a passenger on a motorcycle. Intelligence agencies focused their attention on this mystery killer as the list of victims grew. Finally, the Vietnamese National Police apprehended a twenty-four-year-old Vietnamese woman of Chinese descent after she made an unsuccessful attempt on the life of a Nationalist Chinese intelligence officer.

Clad in traditional *ao dai,* Phung Ngoc Anh had used a .45-caliber pistol to shoot her victims at close range.

Some witnesses had described her as having long hair. Others reported that she had short hair and covered it with a red or blue scarf. When police arrested her at her apartment, they discovered wigs and scarves matching both descriptions.

Anh admitted to killing three of her victims, including two Americans. Ballistic tests would tie the weapon seized at the time of her arrest to a total of five.

*****

Acts of terrorism characterized the war in Saigon as 1967 drew to a close. Both the Americans and their South Vietnamese allies continued search-and-destroy missions against Viet Cong forces and the North Vietnamese regulars. The staff officers in the rear areas created charts and diagrams attempting to establish a means of measuring military activity whether by body counts, villages and hamlets repatriated, or rice harvest statistics. The war's progress was certainly not static, but neither could it be said that either side was clearly winning.

In North Vietnam, the architect of France's defeat at Dien Bien Phu in 1954 had hatched a plan to turn the tide in the communists' favor. Gen. Vo Nguyen Giap and his staff formulated a strategy that was dependent on assistance from the general population in South Vietnam to swing communist fortunes toward eventual victory. The "General Uprising Plan" was clever and ambitious, and relied heavily on insurgent Viet Cong elements to spearhead coordinated attacks against South Vietnamese and U.S. installations and personnel.

In 1967 the Viet Cong infrastructure was a viable military and political force. Northerners marching hundreds of miles down the Ho Chi Minh Trail bolstered the ranks of southern communist elements and communicated directions from the Hanoi Politburo. Southern communists sensing opportunities in a defining future military event, readied to join their brethren in attacking the South

[81]

Vietnamese and their American allies.

General Giap's comprehensive strategy called for coordinated attacks against hundreds of targets ranging from small provincial outposts to the American embassy in Saigon. The timing of the operation was set to coincide with annual celebrations of Tet, their lunar new year and the most important religious holiday for Vietnam's overwhelmingly Buddhist majority.

What would become known as the 1968 Tet Offensive was a well kept secret. Commander Brubaker received a general warning from his National Police sources intimating that VC attacks were expected against allied installations in Saigon. He included the warnings in his regular staff briefing at the headquarters of Naval Forces Vietnam, just before the close of January 1968.

For emphasis, during the same briefing, he advised the staff chaplain not to expect his Vietnamese driver to show for work…he had been arrested as a Viet Cong the night before. Nonetheless Brubakers' warnings were not taken as seriously as they might have been. Such warnings had become pretty routine.

He did wonder why VNAF General Nguyen Ngoc Loan had not mentioned intelligence about potential Tet attacks at a recent luncheon with their U.S. Air Force counterparts, OSI. The VNAF general who commanded a police force of over seventy thousand men later gained a degree of notoriety in new films and still photographs of his street corner execution of a captured Viet Cong. The VC had been implicated in the slaughter of National Police dependents. The .38 caliber revolver Loan used to carry out the execution had been a gift to him from OSI.

At VNNSB headquarters in Saigon, Lieutenant Schneider noticed in-creased levels of activity among Vietnamese counterintelligence personnel as the observance of Tet grew closer. He remembers that "Something was in the wind. The Vietnamese were busier than usual in the final days before Tet. The enemy couldn't keep something that big a secret forever." They prepared for festivities but at the same time issued nonspecific reports of ongoing enemy activity. The Vietnamese at naval headquarters near the Saigon River were prepared for an attack.

The information moving through Vietnamese Navy channels and then to NISOV for translation was out of date by the time it made its way through channels. But the reports had a common theme - ongoing enemy buildups.

In Da Nang, CIA agent Foster Fipps provided the marines with clear warning before the attacks broke out. Brubaker characterized Fipps as the exception to the rule…he got his own information. Most others depended heavily on Vietnamese provided intelligence. Fipps and NISRA Da Nang representative Lt. George Wheeler met almost every day; the bases in I Corps were covered at least.

Brubaker himself relied on Vietnamese police information only once before the Tet offensive began, in a warning to AVFORV staff.

"I thought it was important. The defense of Saigon had been turned over to the Vietnamese in the month before the offensive, with the redeployment of the U.S. Army 199th Light Infantry Brigade. I knew the ARVN were planning to give upward of half their troops leave to go home for traditional Tet celebrations; that left only the National Police and a few Army Military Police to defend all the pencil-pushers …"

With Tet celebrations formally beginning on January 29, 1968, a round of celebratory receptions began. The American embassy held a well-attended social function. That same night, Bill Brubaker and Supervising Agent Bert Truxell were invited to the home of Saigon's police chief, Col. Nguyen Van Luan. Brubaker would reflect; "If the police knew something specific about enemy intentions, they hid it well. Luan passed nothing of this nature to me or the others."

The colonel's guests at the party were entertained by his six-year-old son, who rode his miniature motorcycle around the yard, protected by the high concrete walls that separated the chief's quarters from central police headquarters.

Tragically, Luan would be killed days later when Vietnamese Army Rangers guided helicopter gunship strikes on a high school that was serving as his command post during the offensive. Other ranking

[83]

Vietnamese officers were also killed or wounded in the incident. We now know that North Vietnamese planners scheduled the Tet offensive to begin on the night of January 30, but communication problems kept the communist units involved from receiving synchronous information. Because of this, some attacks occurred on January 29 while others came as much as twenty-four hours later. Alerts were posted after the initial attacks, but for some reason NISOV personnel received no warnings.

At 2:00 AM on January 31 a large explosion woke Brubaker and Truxell at their villa near the American embassy. Brubaker would later find that the explosion was caused by a satchel charge placed to breach the embassy security wall. Their villa phone was dead, so the men decided to drive to the NISOV office in Cholon. Truxell drove with Brubaker riding shotgun...the streets were remarkably quiet.

Arriving at the office, an agent standing guard at the entrance greeted them; the Vietnamese guard was nowhere to be found. Truxell took stock of the strategic situation at the office, taking into consideration the information that enemy units were nearby and an attack on the compound seemed imminent.

"The compound may have withstood attack by marauding Indians, but there was little chance it could repulse heavy weapons. I thought we were doomed if faced with a concerted attack in force. It appeared we were facing scattered elements of the VC and their armed sympathizers."

"The office had an ample supply of small arms and ammunition and the compound's surrounding wall would be pivotal to their defense plan. The enemy had to be kept far enough back that grenades could not be thrown over it. A couple of well-placed grenades in the courtyard would likely injure everyone inside. Also, we had to keep the enemy clear of the next door service station, as blowing that up would almost certainly do us in and give them entry into the compound. Had the enemy breached the wall and thrown their grenades through the only firing points available, NISOV would have been overrun."

[84]

Street fighting in Saigon near the American Embassy during the opening hours of the 1968 Tet Offensive

The issue became whether the compound could hold out until allied forces could relieve them. Truxell began drawing up an evacuation plan knowing full well that there were no "friendly" military elements anywhere near Cholon.

Next, a plan for watch duty was drawn up with four men assigned to each watch of two hours. Truxell would not recall whether the office came under fire on the first night. The next day though, a small group of Australians were caught by heavy fire just outside the office and somehow made their way safely inside.

Those Australians provided much needed military experience and gave the defenders a big lift in morale. Truxell remembers, "It became apparent that our watch-standers had little understanding of fields of fire. The enemy was diagonally across the street in the upper floor of an apartment building."

[85]

The aftermath of Tet

"At one point, a .30-calibre machine gun manned by U.S. Army troops in another sector of the compound tore into the building with return fire. Some of the guys would not fire because they couldn't see anyone to shoot. I could hear the AK47s and see puffs of smoke from windows."

"When I pointed this out, they replied that it might be a little old lady making tea. I told them that if they didn't fire soon, that little old lady making tea was going to shoot their ass off."

The ragtag force of agents and sailors was relieved on day three, and things in Vietnam were never the same after that. Agents started wearing greens and carrying military weapons. "So much for noncombatant status," said Truxell. "I found that the thing that generated the most fear was the unknown and we knew almost nothing about the situation surrounding us. Would we have surrendered had we started taking casualties? Not while I was still alive. I thought that solution assured a bullet in the back of the head for all survivors."

There would be casualties of a different sort however. NISOV YN1 John Springer, one of the defenders at the compound, was abruptly ordered from Vietnam before the Tet hostilities were concluded.

[86]

Springer had served three continuous years as an intelligence yeoman, had developed scores of useful contacts, and had fallen in love with a Vietnamese Navy employee in Saigon. They had two daughters together. He was refused permission to extend his tour into year four, and Springer had only enough time to collect his things from the house he shared with his Vietnamese wife and two small daughters before bidding a tearful goodbye. Springer survived several fire fights en route to Tan Son Nhut Air Base to catch his flight out of Vietnam. It is not known whether their family would ever see each other again.

*****

Tet '68, as it became known, was a milestone in the American involvement in Vietnam, but it would not be the only occasion when the enemy chose this important holiday period to stage attacks around South Vietnam. Although the allied forces virtually destroyed the Viet Cong infrastructure during the offensive, media coverage helped change attitudes toward the war both within South Vietnam and in the United States, and support for the war began to erode.

Supervising Agent Bert Truxell was relieved in March 1968 by Bob Morrice, and Texan Royce Logan became the senior resident agent in Saigon. Shortly thereafter, Lt. Cdr. Bill Armbruster would replace Lieutenant Commander Brubaker.

Despite these personnel changes, Tet left an active legacy.
In counter-intelligence operations, NISOV executive officer Lt. Jim Law U.S.N., headed up several important initiatives. His primary focus was to acquire information about the tactics and organization of the enemy sapper units that had spearheaded the attacks against U.S. facilities during Tet.

Working with his counterparts at the VNNSB and COMNAVFORV intelligence staff, Law pursued every opportunity to gather information about enemy sapper tactics. Certainly there was much that could be learned to assist the Navy in devising more sophisticated defensive measures. Law would be rewarded for his perseverance when U.S. Army troops captured a North Vietnamese Navy sapper during operations near the Cambodian border; an area

[87]

known as the Parrot's Beak.

Law and his team would drive for miles through the rubber plantations and more open areas, considered "Indian country", to successfully recover the prisoner from the Army. The drive back to Saigon was every bit as dangerous as the trip out, but was undertaken without any major events. Their prisoner was successfully interrogated over the next several days, and useful new information was shared widely within the U.S. naval commands of South Vietnam.

NISOV ensured other counterintelligence successes by developing information about arms caches buried and left by the enemy when preparing for Tet. With the intent to arm the peasants with these at the onset of some future anticipated mass uprising, the loss of the weapons further slowed the ability of the Viet Cong to recover from the catastrophic offensive.

*****

5   DA NANG, 1967 TO 1968: AGENTS IN THE FIELD

Lt. George Wheeler, USN, did a good job when he sought out a suitable billet for NISRA Da Nang in 1967. The original office at 20 Duy Tan Street and the billet were situated on parallel streets in the center of Da Nang, accessible to commands serviced by NIS but independent of all.

The billet that housed all NIS personnel was on a corner at 23 Doc Lap Street. A former hotel of three stories, it was surrounded by a wire-topped brick wall and metal gate. Front gardens had been concreted over providing an excellent if unforgiving surface for jungle-rules volleyball matches. On the first floor was a foyer with a rather graceful stairway. One room doubled as a library and lounge, where several years' collection of well-worn pocket books graced wall bookshelves, revealing the most common recreation at NISRA Da Nang.

[88]

Decor was worn contemporary Vietnamese. The senior resident agent and the representative (a Navy lieutenant reserve intelligence officer) bunked in a sandbag-protected room off the first deck porch, and a second room was situated off the foyer. The top two decks had similar rooms, each shared by two men. A central arms locker on the first deck housed long arms, but each man had his helmet and body armor and at least a handgun in his room at all times.

The billet at 23 Doc Lap was renowned for its bar, which was carefully constructed by an itinerant SeaBee with superb carpentry skills to resemble a small German *hofbrau.* It had stained rustic benches, false beams, and a gabled bar, which was considered unique in Vietnam.

Christened the Boom Boom Room by the troops (but called the Blue Elephant among more genteel company), the bar enjoyed the status of a military club, offering discounted liquor and soft drinks. Significantly, the billet became an important social gathering place for guests from other agencies and of course Marine compatriots traveling to and from the bush. Navy lawyers, the American consul, and even occasionally German nurses from the hospital ship *Helgoland* were eager visitors.

Da Nang had an after dusk curfew and remained off-limits to military personnel throughout most of the war, meaning those who could not demonstrate a legitimate reason for being there were subject to arrest by Marine MPs.

Da Nang City was dusty, dirty, and noisy, but its accommodations were a vast improvement over billeting elsewhere, especially in the cantonments and the field. Large tamarind trees populated street verges and vestiges of lawn and behind some high fences were hibiscus and even some bougainvillea blossoms.

The office at 20 Duy Tan Street, which had originally served simultaneously as a billet, was a converted Vietnamese residence rented to the Navy. By 1968 a high security barrier with a gate had been erected, in front of which a U.S. Navy sentry was posted at all times. Vehicles were parked next to the sentry, where they could be watched.

[89]

NISRA DaNang billet, 23 Doc Lap Street

A tiled walkway led to the porch, which doubled as a reception waiting area and had a connecting door to the office occupied by the yeoman chief petty officer. Three former bedrooms housed, respectively, the senior resident agent, the representative, and three or four special agents. A converted garage held the balance of special agents, and there were also spaces for interrogation and an office for the Vietnamese interpreter.

Little excess room was to be found anywhere, and was it not for agents traveling away almost constantly; the office would have been as claustrophobic as a warship.

Opposite the office on potholed, muddy Duy Tan Street were houses of the Vietnamese citizenry. Their children and pets played in the street through the day and seldom missed the early arrival of the chief, who passed out apples and oranges from the chow truck on morning breakfast rounds for the sentries. NISRA Da Nang looked like most of the better houses on the street, except for its fence and sentry, and by Da Nang standards it was in one of the better neighborhoods. Around the next corner on a cross street, which ran through to the NIS billet, was the American consulate. Guarded by members of the Marine Security Battalion, it maintained a lawn and gardens and large tropical trees.

Although the walk from office to billet may have been only five hundred yards, few chose to travel on foot because of concerns about personal vulnerability. Smart Americans moved quickly and without regular pattern if they wanted to improve their chances of getting home. There was ample rolling stock for the trip and meals to think about before the drive.

The Navy officers' club in Da Nang was called the Stone Elephant. Conveniently situated at the top of the Da Nang Peninsula just a few blocks from the NIS billet, it was an eating spot and favored watering hole. Agents began their day at the Stone Elephant, where a smorgasbord breakfast was the norm and Vietnamese waitresses in *ao dais* rushed around with pots of steaming black Navy coffee. By evening, the atmosphere at the bar changed with happy hour, with beer and cocktails at give-away prices and often a floorshow presented by visiting bands. Most common were Filipino and Korean bands but the favorites were Australians.

Packed with Navy officers and Marine aviators from Marble Mountain Air Facility, the Stone Elephant crowd showed real enthusiasm for their entertainers, particularly if they were Westerners. Without doubt, the most popular song always guaranteed to have patrons enthusiastically joining in was "We've Gotta Get Out of This Place." The British band The Animals created a Vietnam classic with this song. Unlike Saigon, Da Nang had no authorized town nightlife, meaning men who worked together every day often under high pressure had no place to go on liberty.

Except for the occasional night at a Navy club, playing it safe meant personnel were inside the guarded billet gate by dusk. Surprisingly, there was very little friction between men, but there were some memorable "horror shows" in the hofbrau bar, where patrons were known to pour mixed drinks and popcorn into a roaring twenty-four-inch fan to top off an evening's celebration.

Jungle-rules (meaning "no rules") volleyball was another favored after-work activity, always pursued with aggressive spirit. Body blocks and net pull-downs were favorite winning tactics.

Nearby neighbors were Vietnamese National Police families, who were billeted on the adjacent corner in a two-story former French villa, resplendent with a balustraded tower. Farther along down the block, Vietnamese Lt. Gen. Hoang Xuan Lam, ARVN, had his quarters. Lam commanded all ARVN forces in I Corps, making him a prime target for enemy guerilla attack. Thus, virtually every night an ARVN armored car would position itself opposite 23 Doc Lap. Far from making the billet occupants feel more secure, it instead kept them aware of the potential effects of the .50-caliber machine gun on the flimsy masonry walls of the old building.

Therefore agents had little to do at NISRA Da Nang but work; a seemingly endless caseload occupied everyone's attention. With responsibility for more than one hundred thousand Marine and Navy personnel deployed throughout I Corps, NISRA Da Nang answered regular requests for assistance from commands faced with serious incidents such as murder, rape, fraud, and theft. This caseload was supplemented by lead requests from global NIS components and federal agencies without representation in Vietnam, and the demands of a counterintelligence program. Agents were asked to locate individuals and conduct on-the-spot investigations about things as diverse as an individual's activities in the Black Panthers, a stolen or missing government check, and matters pertaining to the transmission and safe custody of classified material.

NISRA Da Nang shared central Da Nang with Commander Naval Support Activity, Da Nang, where the command remained in the imposing waterfront colonial structure known by all as the White Elephant. The admiral had responsibility for a command that oversaw most of the supply and support function for the northern end of South Vietnam, I Corps.

Camp Tien Sa, sprawling around the base of Monkey Mountain at the head of the peninsula, housed the majority of NSA's personnel who manned the Deepwater Pier, ship repair facilities, and warehousing facilities.

By 1968 NSA detachments had also been established at key points along the coast where resupply was often carried out by lighters and landing craft. Rivers in the northern part of I Corps served as secondary highways carrying supplies, especially large-caliber ammunition, to inland dumps.

Behind the white facade of SA's command headquarters was a court-yard surrounded by a warren of offices and workspaces, none of which ever seemed large enough. The daily mail pickup was made at the White Elephant.

One street back from the waterfront, Da Nang Cathedral stood to re-mind all who passed of the more gentile times of the 1920s, when French settlers erected the church and adjoining convent. Packed in opposite it, a mass of commercial storefronts supplied every imagined need. All this was considered off-limits to U.S military personnel, and it was a temptation to many.

A little farther upstream, the Han was bridged by a critically important structure constantly guarded by roaming sentries who fired at every bit of floating detritus that might shield any underwater swimmer or sapper intent on blowing it up. Barriers, including a cage of concertina wire surrounded pylons, and concussion grenades were frequently thrown in their vicinity as a further safeguard. The bridge was the only viable link to Tien Sa Peninsula, from which all material including ammunition from the port originated.

On the Da Nang side of the bridge, a ship-landing ramp had been constructed especially for use by Navy LSTs and heavy landing craft. Known to all as Bridge Ramp, it was a hive of activity at any time of the day or night. Sweating sailors atop bellowing loaders and industrial forklifts jockeyed huge pallets of ammunition and other supplies into the waiting maws of the berthed ships, under the glare of the floodlights at night.

Intelligence indicated that Bridge Ramp was a favored enemy target for a potential long-range rocket attack. The presence of large volumes of explosive and volatile cargo was attractive because of its potential to damage both ships and men.

These attacks were normally carried out with a barrage of Soviet 122mm rockets, fired from a point far to the southwest and well outside the Marines' perimeter. They did periodically cause serious damage, and always major concerns. The Vietnamese civilians, who were often crowded into makeshift improvised housing, undoubtedly suffered the most casualties.

Peter Reilly flew into this scene to assume the senior resident agent post from Jack Myer in March 1968. Reilly, a linguist who specialized in Chinese and had begun his Navy career in the Naval Security Group (NSG), had just completed a four-year stint in Taipei, Taiwan, before volunteering for the Vietnam post.

To the consternation of the NIS command element in Saigon, he used a regular Marine Corps C130 logistic flight to travel directly from Taipei to his new duty station, without the usual entry formalities and briefings at NISOV in Saigon. Peter Reilly was demonstrating, and not for the first time, the independence and direct action that would characterize his thirty-year career in Naval Intelligence. Jack Myer had already left Vietnam, and Peter Reilly once made aware of his error, boarded a plane and flew to Saigon to meet his new supervising agent Bert Truxell.

Former Tucson police officer Mike Nagle had come to Vietnam in July 1967 after completing his probationary year of service as a street agent based in Pasadena, California. Nagle had completed his degree at the University of Arizona while serving with the Tucson Police Department, and as his graduation date neared in the spring of 1966, he began looking for federal law enforcement career opportunities. He submitted applications to both ONI and the FBI. Mike Nagle had never known his father. Ens. Patrick Nagle, USN, had trained in Pensacola, Florida as a Navy fighter pilot in the dark days just before Pearl Harbor As the war was looming; Nagle had been part of the Navy's accelerated training program. He then participated in the vanguard of America's first attacks against Imperial Japan with the storming of Guadalcanal in the Solomon Islands.

While returning from a mission on August 8, 1942, (the day after Maj. Gen. Alexander Vandegrift's First Marine Division waded ashore into the tropical hell of Guadalcanal), Ensign Nagle's aircraft ran out of fuel.Telling his wingman that he could go no farther, Nagle ditched his F4F Wildcat in the dark waters of the Solomon Sea.

[94]

He was never seen again. Mike Nagle's only link to his lost father was a trunk containing his father's treasured personal effects and photographs of him as a newborn in his arms.

Despite the prestige of an FBI career, Mike Nagle really wanted to serve his country overseas. When in early 1966 the FBI came to him with an offer to become a special agent, Nagle telephoned ONI to determine the status of his application, and ONI responded with their own offer.

Mike Nagle was soon a special agent with ONI, working personnel security investigations on the streets of Los Angeles. By the time he received orders in February 1967 to attend Agent Basic School at headquarters in Washington, D.C., Nagle had volunteered for duty in Vietnam. He was told while at Basic School that he would be assigned to NISRA Da Nang, his transfer scheduled for July 1967.

Mike Nagle was one of the few agents dispatched to Vietnam arriving via a commercial aircraft rather than by the charters most personnel endured. He boarded a Pan American flight to Saigon at Los Angeles International Airport, with Special Agent Dick Ryan, who also held orders to Da Nang. Ryan, a former Los Angeles police officer and veteran of the Watts Riots, had volunteered for Vietnam service with Nagle. Their flight traversed the Pacific with stops at Hawaii, Wake Island, and Guam before crossing the bomb-blasted red soil of coastal Vietnam at high altitude.

Nagle remembers of his arrival, "As we neared Tan Son Nhut, Saigon, the pilot pushed the aircraft nose down into a steep descent; this was not really reassuring for a new guy."

Once safely on the ground, they were enveloped in the hot, muggy blanket of a July day in Saigon. After meeting a few NISOV personnel, Nagle and Ryan were driven to the office to begin in-processing.

[95]

Da Nang Ammo Dump

Nagle recalls saying to himself upon seeing the office for the first time, "My God. What have I got myself into?" Very little could prepare anybody for the initial shock of immersion in Vietnam at war.

The new agents were issued the identification necessary to get along in Vietnam. These included modified credentials that excluded the word "intelligence", Vietnamese identity cards issued by MSS (guaranteed to frighten any sane Vietnamese citizen), a MACV identity card showing the bearer to be an engineer at the Office of Civil Construction, and a PX ration card. Two days after their arrival, Nagle and Ryan both boarded a USAF C130 for their flight to Da Nang.

"I remember very well my first night in Da Nang. The air base was hit hard by VC attacks, and men were killed. Rockets were hitting the base and falling in the city too. One of the agents, who will remain anonymous, was in a skivvy house enjoying the company of some Da Nang ladies of the night when the first incoming rounds hit and he found himself marooned. The supervising agent in Saigon somehow got wind of it and tried to find out who it was, but none of his fellow agents were going to give him up."

Nagle quickly learned that many forms of excitement were available in Vietnam's I Corps. He joined a team of agents under the capable control of SRA Jack Myer. His roommate Peter Segersten was already an old hand. Bob Powers was even then considered one of the organization's most capable investigators, and Howie Dilkes was also well seasoned.

In the fall of 1967 Special Agent Joe Rodriguez, also a former Tucson PD officer would replace Powers. The new agents settled into the routine of six or seven day work weeks.

It didn't take long for Mike Nagle to realize that the residence that housed the American Red Cross girls was a mere three blocks away. "I got into a little trouble. Jack Myer came and got me one night, reminding me about Da Nang's curfew hours."

On the work side of things, the agents were exposed to professional jealousy and obfuscation by some members of Marine Corps CID. Investigations were sometimes given over grudgingly after having been legally compromised by zealous but untrained MP investigators. Mike Nagle would soon begin to share the caseload that required agents to travel alone through northern I Corps.

As 1967 drew to a close, agents working the north along the DMZ began noticing increased enemy activity. The NVA were clearly on the move, particularly pressuring Marine outposts defending the border area between North and South Vietnam. Nagle found himself at Khe Sanh Combat Base near the Laotian border, in the final week of December. The reason for his journey has been lost to time, but he still remembers the fighting at and around the base as communist numbers grew in the hills around the outpost, as they prepared to besiege the marines.

"I had flown into Khe Sanh with Major General Tompkins, USMC, in his helicopter from Phu Bai near Hue. I was hoping to get back out on the same day, but it didn't happen. My work was done, but there just were no seats available on any of the aircraft."

Special Agent Mike Nagle at Khe Sanh, Dec 1967

This was Nagle's first exposure to life at the front. He could hear Russian 122mm rockets being fired from the mountains and hills surrounding them, followed by the distinct double detonation as they struck the ground. "We were taking incoming rounds constantly."

[98]

Men were dying at Khe Sanh, while increasingly the enemy probed the hilltop Marine bases. A constant stream of wounded men came in by helicopter, seeking attention from the Navy medical team. Generous marines found a spot for the special agent in a deep underground bunker festooned with a sign that announced simply, "The Womb". Here Nagle slept in a hammock like the other bunker occupants to keep out of reach of the rats.

"The damned rats were huge. The grunts entertained themselves by shooting them with a pellet gun, and by keeping a Rat KIA tally sheet on the bulkhead."

The worst part for Nagle was having nothing to do. Marine defenders all had tasks; they seemed to be on the run constantly. Nagle stayed out of the way and attended intelligence briefings, at which it was reported that thousands of North Vietnamese were around them. Between briefings, he hung out with Marine aircraft control personnel at the airstrip, ever hopeful of a ride to the rear.

"There was a lot going on at the airstrip. C130s and C123s were touching down, kicking cargo out on the run, then turning and trying to take off before enemy incoming rounds could find them on the ground." After four unforgettable days at the busiest combat base in the north, Special Agent Nagle was finally able to hitch a ride on a Marine helicopter heading to Dong Ha. With considerable relief he flew away from the cauldron that would become known to history as the Seige of Khe Sanh.

Finally arriving back in Da Nang, Nagle learned that his former Tucson Police colleague Joe Rodriguez had arrived and been promptly sent north to Dong Ha to run a case.

"That was a hell of a fast introduction to the life of a special agent in Vietnam for Joe Rodriguez," Nagle recalled.

As January 1968 drew to a close, agents in Da Nang were conscious of the preparations for the celebration of Tet. They failed to realize though that the VC were building up its forces, until the communists actually launched their offensive.

Nagle's home away from home

"As I recall, we first got word that Saigon had been hit, and that the compound where NISOV offices were situated in Cholon had come under attack. Soon after, we heard that Hue was being attacked, and we started making hurried preparations to defend ourselves at the Da Nang billet."

The agents rushed to 23 Doc Lap Street, and began filling sandbags to enhance the billet defenses, and stocked up on drinking water, rations, and ammunition. The nearby offices at 20 Duy Tan Street was closed and left in the care of Navy sentries.

Agents didn't have to wait long for the war to come to downtown Da Nang. The night reverberated with the sound of small arms, mortar, and rocket fire. Allied red and communist green tracers arced through the sky, and the schoolyard on the opposite side of the street became a rallying point for VC attackers. Later it would become the scene of an intense skirmish. South Vietnamese tanks were deployed nearby to defend General Lam's quarters.

[100]

Touch and Go: C-123's on Khe Sanh airstrip

"We all had issued rifles, flak jackets, and helmets at the ready. We were very careful to keep lights down at night; we really wanted to keep a very low profile."

The agents were on their own in Da Nang, as the VC and allied forces fought at night for control of the city. Communications were spotty, and the tactical situation was unknown. The men began to consider what they would do if the billet were attacked and overrun. "The Marines at III MAF were our closest help. Some of the guys actually planned to swim the Han River if the worst happened."

Nagle himself had no such option. Injured in one of NISRA Da Nang's infamous jungle-rules volleyball matches, he was sporting a cast on his broken foot. There would be no evasion by swimming with that cast, and he began to think about sawing it off.

After two or three days behind the walls of 23 Doc Lap, the situation normalized enough that the men were able to leave during the day. All enjoyed hot meals after the steady diet of C rations.

To their north beyond Hai Van Pass, U.S. Marines fought on at Khe Sanh while the media tried to draw parallels between their defense and that of the French at Dien Bien Phu.

"Jungle Rules". Special Agents Sundstrom (left) and Hemphill, NISRA Da Nang billet 1969

Communist forces tried to encircle Khe Sanh just as they had done when the French were finally defeated.

The Marines, however, were never in danger of being starved in any extended siege at Khe Sanh. Massive, extended air strikes by B52 bombers kept the communists at bay, though the base was subject to many days of artillery and rocket attacks, and Marines fought desperately for the mountaintop bases that defended the base approaches.

Ironically, the North Vietnamese Army found itself drawn into a massive meat grinder as allied airpower systematically eliminated troop concentrations. Air strikes and artillery destroyed the enemy by the hundreds.

Hue, symbolically important to most Vietnamese, had been largely overrun in audacious attacks by VC and NVA units. The Citadel was taken by the enemy, who were quick to raise the National Liberation Front (NLF) flag atop the flagstaff overlooking the Perfume River. VC troops captured a number of Americans, including civilian government employees, and they began a program of systematic execution of suspected Southern sympathizers, the magnitude of which became known months later when hundreds of bodies were exhumed from shallow graves.

[102]

Marines, from their Phu Bai enclave south of Hue began a drive northward, fighting house to house to reach the Perfume River.

After days of bitter costly fighting, they joined in an allied offensive that finally pushed communist forces out of the Imperial City. Hue and its inhabitants were bled white by the 1968 Tet Offensive, and many U.S. troops died recapturing it.

*****

Dave Hall's regular exposure to Marine Corps rifle companies made him the logical choice to manage a counterintelligence investigation into reports of U.S. personnel sighted with VC and NVA troops. One such case was codenamed Salt and Pepper. Two men, believed to be marines, were alleged to be cooperating with the enemy. It had even been reported that the men, one black and the other white, had been seen carrying Eastern bloc pattern military weapons. Hall came to the case ably assisted by the ongoing work of a select group of Marine Corps counterintelligence specialists.

Across the river from NISRA Da Nang in the old French military compound that housed Lt. Gen. Robert Cushman and his III Marine Amphibious Force headquarters was a small file filled office. Here Maj. John Guenther, USMC, III MAF staff counterintelligence officer, directed the Marine counterintelligence initiatives in I Corps.

Major Guenther and his counterintelligence marines formed a highly trained group of professionals who served as the eyes and ears of the commanding general, collating and analyzing information from many sources.

Most came from counterintelligence teams deployed with Marine rifle companies in the field, where interrogations of both enemy and friendly Vietnamese produced important information on an almost daily basis.

A strong spirit of professional cooperation existed between the counterintelligence marines and NIS. In this instance, the marines held the majority of the intelligence dealing with alleged defectors, missing in action personnel, and prisoner of war marines.

Capt. Ken Klem, USMC, was assigned to Major Guenther's staff and was assisted by Gy.Sgt. Galayzin and a Sgt. Davis. They maintained extensive files on missing marines made up of sighting reports, interviews, and prisoner interrogations as well as relevant reports from other intelligence agencies. Klem could recite from memory the names and histories of any captured marines and the known circumstances of their loss. Moreover, the Viet Cong often paraded captives through villages for propaganda purposes, thereby providing indicators of the general area of the camps in which they held the prisoner.

Many of those marines captured in Da Nang and points south were marched to a remote area in far west Quang Ngai Province for incarceration in horrifying, primitive prisons.

Those captured farther north in Thua Thien or Quang Tri Province, seemed more likely destined for ultimate internment in North Vietnam. This was after prolonged captivity in the desperate circumstances of a jungle holding camp and a grim trek up the muddy Ho Chi Minh Trail.

Klem recalls: "Two marines were lost in 1964 while sightseeing on a motorcycle outside Da Nang. Garwood was lost in September 1965 outside of Da Nang. Other marines disappeared after being enticed into Vietnamese hooches in the Da Nang area during 1966... One marine escaped from the III MAF Brig in late 1967 and was subsequently captured by the VC. Later, another was scooped up by Viet Cong while in a restricted liberty area and ended up in captivity. The U.S. Army also had a few I Corps personnel grabbed by the VC while engaged in "non-authorized activities.""

Besides the pressing information about captured Americans, Major Guenther's marines had been receiving multiple reports from different sources alluding to sightings of a tall Caucasian operating with Viet Cong in various enclaves within I Corps.

These came both from allied South Vietnamese military sources and from interrogations of captured Viet Cong. Physical descriptions of the defector's garb, hair color, and eye color varied considerably. Moreover, attempts at identifying the missing personnel from photographs were equally ambiguous.

[104]

Special Agent Hall became involved in the uncertain, (and so far secret), investigation because the Salt and Pepper case had apparently been compromised by the appearance of a series of wanted posters. Command was concerned that information leaked about possible defectors and persons known to be held by the enemy could endanger other U.S. prisoners of war.

They were also concerned that it might also provide the enemy with intelligence that would hamper ongoing efforts to free the Americans. A classified program managed by MACV called "Brightlight" used Special Forces personnel to target possible VC prisons to free American and allied prisoners. Hall, with the assistance of another intelligence agency, succeeded in locating and retrieving all remaining wanted posters. The posters carried grainy, distant images of two men: one was black, the other Caucasian.

The press corps, seemingly always hungry for a "bad news" story, never was able to make much of this one. Hall continued following up every lead that came his way, but a satisfactory identification of the two men was never made, nor were they captured.

Major Guenther's counterintelligence marines became convinced that many of the reports they had received of the pair assisting and training the enemy were actually Viet Cong proselytizing and propaganda feeds.

NISOV commanding officer Thomas A. Brooks, a longtime intelligence officer who rose to become the director of Naval Intelligence, remembers that both Salt and Pepper were finally identified as Marine deserters but that most of the allegations about their activities could not be proved.

Many aspects of the reports had been exaggerated. Commander Brooks, who later interviewed the war's most infamous alleged defector, Marine Robert Garwood, had an intimate knowledge of the men believed to have switched sides. He does not know whether either Salt or Pepper survived the war.

The Garwood investigation had been far more definitive than Salt and Pepper. Not only were Vietnam-based counterintelligence marines involved, but so was Headquarters Marine Corps in

Washington, D C. The Counterintelligence Branch worked closely with the Casualty Branch on all matters pertaining to missing and captured marines.

They monitored intelligence and open source reporting for information about American MIAs in an effort to confirm whether they were alive, and if captured, their health and overall condition while in captivity.

Capt. Chuck Bushey, USMC, then assigned to the Counter-intelligence Branch, Headquarters Marine Corps, and recalls, "In the case of Garwood, propaganda leaflets purported to have been written and signed by him were found in South Vietnam and forwarded to HQMC through Marine Corps channels. Thus began the compilation of a substantial file regarding Garwood."

"Perhaps noteworthy, we would hand carry the leaflets to the FBI laboratory for handwriting analysis in an effort to confirm they were written by him. It took several leaflets and several handwriting examinations before the FBI finally confirmed they were his. If I recall correctly, Garwood was listed as a deserter in 1969. Also, around 1969, POW releases in South Vietnam indicated that Garwood was cooperating and working with the VC. His dossier at HQMC continued to grow."

Later reports would indicate that CIA analysts had also independently evaluated propaganda material believed to be written by Garwood for use by his captors. Agency analysts reported that they believed at least six documents had been written by Garwood. They profiled his personality traits based on their document examination.

In part, the Garwood file was growing because more released prisoners of war had observed him at enemy detention camps. They described his activities, conversations they had with him and his relationship with their Vietnamese captors.

Captain Bushey and fellow counterintelligence marine Robert Wingfield interviewed returned marine Lance Cpl. Jose Agosto Santos at Bethesda Naval Hospital after his release from a VC jungle prison camp. "We gleaned a great deal about Garwood's activities at that time, including information about his collaboration with his captors. As I recall, he was living separately from the other prisoners," Bushey recalled.

It was reported that Agosto Santos asserted in his debriefing that not only was Garwood billeted separately from other U.S. prisoners but that he had "crossed over" to the enemy, refusing repatriation to U.S. forces and actually accepting a commission in the North Vietnamese Army.

Other released U.S. Army prisoners said that Garwood had carried arms and ammunition for the enemy, was billeted with enemy guards, and assisted in U.S. POW interrogations by virtue of his understanding of the Vietnamese language. Finally, in late 1969 a repatriated U.S. Army captive related a conversation with Garwood in which Garwood said he would soon be traveling to North Vietnam to meet with leaders of the U.S. Black Panther and Black Muslim parties. The evidence suggests that he made the trip to North Vietnam four years after his capture.

Garwood was not returned to the United States following the formal release of POWs by Hanoi in March 1973. He did not return until 1979, with many unanswered questions as to his intentions and loyalties remaining.

As for the possibility that Garwood was the elusive Salt of the duo, Captain Klem said, "I do not doubt that Garwood did a lot of moving about the countryside, but while remaining under VC control. Many sightings and broadcasts have been attributed to his movements from 1967 to 1970. To my knowledge, there has been no known connection of his movements with another person that could be construed as being Pepper."

Many years after he had returned to the United States from Vietnam, Special Agent Dave Hall, met a former recon marine who had served in I Corps at the same time as he had. Their conversation eventually led to the topic of Marine defectors, and the marine said he had firsthand knowledge of Americans joining enemy units and related a strange story.

He had been part of a four-man reconnaissance patrol operating in contested country outside of Da Nang. The group stopped to eat a short distance away from a stream. Sitting back-to-back, facing outward silently eating their meal, they were surprised by an enemy group that appeared and prepared to cross the stream. Among the lead elements in the group were several Caucasians, and the marines took them under fire. One Caucasian dropped face first into the stream, causing the marines to believe that he had been killed along with several of the Vietnamese.

Seriously outnumbered and aware that they had completely compromised what should have been a clandestine reconnaissance, the patrol moved as fast as they could to their scheduled extraction point where a helicopter picked them up.

*****

In 1968 NISRA Da Nang's caseload was mostly the investigation of criminal activities. Nonetheless, the organization's intelligence mission was never overlooked, and when NISOV was tasked with a particularly sensitive collection mission, it fell to Dave Hall.

A global positive intelligence operation aimed at compromising Soviet intelligence efforts had been initiated in Washington, requiring a suitably qualified agent to carry out tasks in Southeast Asia. Civilian Special Agent Hall met the requirements of the Washington spymasters. He would work alone, independent of even his own immediate superior. The command structure of NIS made this arrangement workable, while perhaps it might not have been with other intelligence organizations active in Vietnam.

Hall received orders which took him to remote areas, to wherever particular persons or information sources were, and there he developed the information that he was assigned to collect. Everything helped to fill in the gaps on a global chessboard designed to compromise the Russian's and their intelligence acquisition apparatus. As is typical of such operations, the men controlling the information requests provided no feedback to the agents on the ground…they had no need to know the master plan, and what they didn't know couldn't hurt them.

*****

[108]

In addition to a seemingly never ending supply of leads and investigations on the criminal side of the house, NISRA Da Nang's agents managed information sources in the city capable of providing intelligence of a more immediate nature. Attacks by enemy sappers, (and by rockets), were a constant concern because of the concentration of U.S. forces in the Da Nang City area.

Rockets were a particularly indiscriminate weapon that killed many more innocent Vietnamese civilians than they did Americans. Enemy abilities to launch attacks from well outside the perimeter was a continuing thorn in the side of U.S. commanders.

Thus, when Special Agents Fred Beatty and Dave Hall received reports from informants about planned Viet Cong attacks on Navy shipping, they reported it as soon as possible.

Agent reports by their very nature were uncertain. Many factors determined the amount of credence they received from intelligence analysts and responsible commanders. These included how reliable the informant had previously been and how credible his information seemed in the context of known factors. In this case Hall and Beatty's informants told them that a team of enemy sappers planned to target the U.S. Navy shallow-draft vessels that used the Da Nang Bridge Ramp. Here ships received and discharged a variety of cargo, much of it ammunition destined for artillery units deployed along the coast and waterways of I Corps.

With their reports filed, Hall and Beatty could do little more. It then became the duty of Naval Support Activity, Da Nang, to decide what countermeasures should be taken…Apparently none.

Agents sleeping at 23 Doc Lap were abruptly awakened in the predawn hours by a massive explosion at nearby Bridge Ramp. The shockwave shattered the panes of glass from their billet windows.

When dawn finally arrived, NISRA Da Nang agents were witness to a scene of utter devastation. A landing craft, utility (LCU) loaded with ammunition had been the target, and the explosion had effectively laid waste to all nearby vessels. Divers were in the water attempting to recover bodies…as many as seventy men were believed dead. Early on, naval authorities speculated that an enemy rocket had scored a direct hit on the vessel. Later, a below water examination of the hull pointed more toward the sapper attack that they had been warned of earlier.

In mid-1969 however, a 122mm rocket did barely clear the third floor of the NISRA Da Nang billet. It slammed instead into Vietnamese National Police housing of mostly dependent wives and children. Penetrating the roof of the old French villa, the explosion killed many of the occupants leaving shrapnel marks on the nearby Navy house. The Americans could do little for the victims, most were beyond help.

*****

Few secrets are more closely guarded by their governments than those regarding communication security. The U.S. government has huge organizations tasked with the protection of its secrets while it collects those of other nations.

Historically the weakness in the system has been that very few sensitive messages were actually passed by safe hands, instead, they were encrypted at various levels and then transmitted as electronic signals.

The continuing struggle to safeguard secrets while attempting to learn as much as possible about others is not new. During World War II cryptographers breaking enemy codes gave their commanders a substantial advantage in determining decisive military engagements. The business of signal intelligence has grown even more important in the years following World War II.

When NISRA Da Nang SRA Pete Reilly received information that a U.S. Marine Corps officer assigned to sensitive communication fa-cilities in Da Nang had been trying to sell classified communication equipment to Russian agents, his reaction was swift. The first lieutenant, an Annapolis graduate, had apparently planned to sell the equipment to a Russian agent while on leave in Bangkok. Instead, other interested U.S. agencies had intercepted him in Thailand and quickly bundled him up for his return aboard a military flight back to Da Nang.

Special Agent Dave Hall was assigned the case. His directions were to learn as much as possible about "Ivan" in Bangkok, the circumstances of the marine's contact with him, and then to build a criminal case.

When the lieutenant arrived in Da Nang, Hall was there to meet him. His plan was to arrest the accused, then launch his investigation by interrogating him. Instead, Dave Hall would learn that military protocol requires that the first steps taken in the arrest of an officer, is the presentation of the accused to his commanding officer.

Understandably, the communication facility commanding officer was quite unimpressed with the young agent's oversight, but SRA Pete Reilly successfully calmed those concerned and the agent began interviewing witnesses. His investigation of the first incident was not complete but about a month later, an informant called Hall. He reported that the same officer had taken another sensitive piece of communication equipment and was on a military aircraft bound for Saigon. His final destination was to take him to Bangkok... and presumably the Russians.

Agents were there to meet the plane when it arrived at Tan Son Nhut Air Base in Saigon and again turned the young man around for Da Nang.

Hall was there when he arrived. Seeing the same agent awaiting him and still carrying the communications equipment, he attempted an escape. Knowing that he would once again face vehement protests from the commanding officer, Hall arrested him and took him into custody anyway.

This time, Senior Resident Agent Reilly was less conciliatory with the upset marine. Two such serious breaches clearly underscored substandard security practices at the communication station, and this time the CO was forced to agree. Authorities would determine that the young accused was mentally unbalanced and returned him to the United States. But procedures at the communication station underwent a major overhaul, and Naval Intelligence learned the identity of one more Soviet agent lurking on the fringes of the Vietnam War.

[111]

In April of 1969 a Soviet 122mm rocket hit this National Police family billet, killing a number of women and children. The NISRA DaNang quarters can be seen in the background

*****

Special Agents Dave Hall and Frank Orrantia, who served at NISRA Da Nang in 1968 and 1969, were among the last established northern rounds men. Introduced to the north by Special Agent Joe Rodriguez, Orrantia soon was joined by Hall, who was assigned by SRA Pete Reilly to help him learn the ropes. Hall and Orrantia would often pair up to travel to a particular area and then split up to run assigned leads. Both were improvisers, especially with transportation. Frank Orrantia developed a useful contact in an Army aviation unit at Da Nang Air Base; a captain who could often fly them directly to a northerly unit in his single-engine DHC Beaver.

Air Force and Marine C130s also flew regularly, but over time the agents grew to prefer a trip by sea. Through their contacts with Navy staff at Operation Market Time headquarters on Tien Sa Peninsula, space would be found for them aboard a northbound Swift boat or Coast Guard cutter. Frank Orrantia had made the trips before, disembarking at Cua Viet, the last stop before the DMZ began.

[112]

Cua Viet had been little more than a remote river estuary until the war effort became focused on its strategic value. The Cam Lo River debouched into the South China Sea next to the dunes and broad sandy beach where Cua Viet was situated. Though subject to attack from NVA units ranging south of the DMZ and also to frequent mining, the river remained a vital logistic link.

Most supplies for Third Marine Division units defending the northern border were boated up the river in LCUs or LCMs, (landing craft, medium). Agents needing to access the marines rode the landing craft upstream to the hardstand ramp on the riverbank at Dong Ha, adjacent to National Highway 1.

Naval Support Activity Detachment (NSAD), Cua Viet, was established at the river mouth to facilitate the movement of war materiel inland to the Marines. Fuel, ammunition, and rations were mainstay items. Within easy rocket and artillery range of the NVA, it was one of the most dangerous Navy duty stations, despite deep protective bunkers surrounded by thousands of sandbags. Sailors worked every day, and they worked hard. Other than a Marine amphibious tractor battalion and other ground security elements, they had the area to themselves.

In late 1968 NISRA Da Nang received a desperate plea for assistance from NSAD Cua Viet, where death threats had been made against an officer. The threats were of such credibility that command believed a homicide might be imminent. Dave Hall and Frank Orrantia were given the case.

The request arrived during the monsoon season, at a time when typhoons were ranging around the South China Sea. The weather was foul, even at protected Da Nang. Winds were up, visibility down, and rainsqualls had grounded all aircraft. Logically, the agents first approached the Navy for transportation north; operations staff at Market Time told them no vessels were sailing except for combat essential missions.

Taken aback, they next approached the Coast Guard, who operated cutters in support of the Navy's Operation Market Time surveillance and interdiction mission. They were a different story.

[113]

Told of the threat at Cua Viet, the duty officer reached for his radio and summoned a cutter for the immediate emergency mission. Soon aboard, the agents and the small crew of the cutter began pushing their way northward through surging seas.

Once they were clear of Da Nang, conditions improved markedly though, seas smoothed, and they made good progress. Dave Hall wondered why the Navy hadn't gotten the word.

As the cutter pushed its way northward with the long sweeping miles of beach to its port side, an alert lookout spotted a motorized Vietnamese junk navigating the shallows between a sandbank and the beach. The junk was ordered to heave to but ignored the order and took evasive action. Local mariners had an intimate knowledge of the rules in these waters. Similar vessels had frequently been used to bring arms and supplies from the North to insurgent groups fighting in South Vietnam.

The Vietnamese were struck by a single high-explosive round from the 81mm mortar mounted on the after deck. The round struck the bow of the vessel, and it began to sink in the shallow water.

The sandbar was more than a mile long, and given the urgency of their mission, the cutter commander elected to continue on course.

A pump on the cutter began to fail, and they slowed. Since they were nearing Thuan An at the mouth of the Perfume River, the commanding officer decided to seek Navy assistance. They sailed over the bar and made their way up the river to Hue.

The navy personnel at Hue were not particularly interested in the Coast Guard mechanical problems, and concerned by their impasse, Frank Orrantia quietly took a Navy chief petty officer aside. He identified himself, and explained the nature of the mission. He patiently explained that it would not reflect well on Navy Hue if a threatened officer was killed while the Coast Guard waited for assistance. The chief saw the wisdom in Orrantia's comments. Parts were quickly found to repair the pump, and Navy mechanics assisted with a record-time installation. The cutter was soon under way once again.

[114]

Several hours later the cutter approached the shifting sandbars at the river mouth at Cua Viet. A combination of runoff from the rains and the huge tidal ranges had transformed the river mouth into a mass of churning white water.

Naturally there was concern on the bridge as the captain and the helmsman decided the best way into the river. Hall and Orrantia were both alarmed by these conditions, which they had never seen before. After several minutes observing the water, the helmsman suddenly gave the cutter full throttle, and after a bumpy ride over the sandbar, they were into the river reducing headway to avoid the anchored vessels. The agents disembarked moments later and the coastguardsmen wasted no time getting back into open waters. There was a palpable tension at NSAD Cua Viet, but an attempt against the commanding officer had not been made, and word quickly spread that the agents had arrived. The CO was the first to be interviewed. He reported that he had been in his quarters the night before, lying awake in bed, when he heard the distinctive sound of the "spoon" flying off a grenade. He dove to the deck of his sandbagged hut when the fragmentation grenade exploded outside. The hooch was damaged, but the he was uninjured. He reported that he had not been threatened in any way before the attack and had no idea who might have thrown the grenade.

No clues still remained other than the spoon from the exploded grenade. With this being all that they had, Hall and Orrantia made a production of having recovered it. Next they began interviews of everyone who had been in the area at the time of the attack. It was their hope to not only determine "movements and whereabouts" but to see if they could sense any undercurrents of dissention. But the interviews failed to produce even one logical lead.

Finally, in desperation, they announced that the grenade spoon would be forwarded to the FBI labs for development of latent fingerprints. The agents announced that they would be returning to Cua Viet to arrest the offender as soon as results of the scientific examination were known.

As every member of the U.S. armed forces is fingerprinted upon induction, this was something more than an idle threat. By this time, both agents were of the opinion that there had not been an intentional threat on the CO's life. The explosion had been due to carelessness in an area of the compound where sentries were routinely heavily armed with access to all manner of weapons and ordnance.

The next day the agents boarded a landing craft loaded down with ammunition and bound for the Marine logistic bridgehead upriver at Dong Ha. This experience was always a slow, anxious voyage as the LCM battled currents and hidden sandbars and the crew watched carefully for mines in the muddy waters.

There was a history of mining's on the Cua Viet, and Hall and Orrantia walked down the sloping ramp and onto the steel matting at Dong Ha feeling relieved. They walked up to the nearby National Highway, and were soon hitchhiking to Dong Ha Airstrip. Seats were secured on a Marine C130 returning to Da Nang, and they were back in their own quarters that night. The origin of the threat against the CO, (if there had been a threat at all), was never identified.

*****

6   DA NANG, 1969: A YOUNG AGENT'S LESSONS

What would induce a young man to volunteer for service in Vietnam, particularly in 1969, the year after America's press had transformed the Tet Offensive from a tactical victory to a strategic defeat? In hindsight, I would have to say it was a cocktail of ambition, spirit of adventure, and a sense that it was time for me to serve, as my father had done before me.

I was born on April 1, 1945, the day U.S. Marines stormed the beaches of Okinawa, one of the deadliest campaigns in the corps' history. Dad was then a junior naval officer in a destroyer escort, the USS *Joseph Conolly* (DE450), in the buildup to the anticipated assault on the Japanese homeland. He returned home from the Pacific in 1946 and took up an appointment to begin a career as a park ranger in the National Park Service.

My early childhood was spent in the idyllic surrounds of Hawaii National Park. Dad, in his uniform, set off each morning for the walk through rainforest to park headquarters while we children spent long hours exploring among towering fern trees and the nearby volcanic crater. We enjoyed occasional trips with Dad into the Kau Desert in his GI jeep. One of my favorite spots was a practice range used by marines during the war. It was strewn with the sort of refuse a young boy finds very interesting, including unexploded ordnance. There I first fired my dad's 1903 Springfield rifle at the tender age of four.

Transferring to Yosemite National Park in 1952 was a shock for my siblings and me. Gone were the gentle tropical climes and the equally gentle Hawaiian folk, the fat mammas who would feed me *poi,* and most particularly my very close friends.

Yosemite was a community of perhaps fifteen hundred souls nestled around the fringes of one of the most beautiful valleys on the planet. Cliffs that started, quite literally, one hundred yards behind our home rose vertically two thousand feet. The base of Yosemite Falls was a ten-minute walk away, and when the spring thaw of high country snow came, it rattled the windows in the National Park Service homes clustered near its final drop.

Here I attended Yosemite Elementary School and later commuted to high school in Mariposa California, some forty-five miles away.

I had completed two years at Fresno State and a four-month trek across the South Pacific, when Dad was transferred to Washington, D.C., where he had an office in the Interior building. It must have been a shock to him after nearly twenty years as a field naturalist and interpreter.

*****

I was a criminology major at Fresno State, working part-time and focusing simply on getting a degree behind me as soon as possible. There were no frills to my existence. The folks helped me when they could, but getting the necessary education was certainly my own responsibility.

[117]

I thought the California Highway Patrol (CHP) might be a good organization in which to begin my career in law enforcement, and I successfully passed both the written and the oral examinations. The CHP Academy accepted me in the summer following my graduation.

When I did finally complete my degree in the summer of 1967, I took up my parent's invitation to visit them in Washington. Soon after my arrival, Dad suggested I might like to talk with people in federal law enforcement to consider what career options they might also offer. This seemed like a good idea. I had a job, I was saving money for a car, and Washington was an exciting place. But what I really hoped for was a job that would allow me to serve overseas.

When I explained this to a Secret Service colleague of my father's, he referred me to people he knew in State Department Security and at the Washington, D.C. field office of the Office of Naval Intelligence. This field component had recently been renamed the Naval Investigative Service.

I applied for special agent billets at both agencies and began the long wait while a detailed background investigation was conducted. In the meantime, I applied and was accepted for Officer Candidate School at the U.S. Army Military Police Command. I was hedging all my bets, I thought.

I also continued my job as a butcher in Springfield, Virginia, while my background investigation slowly went forward--doubtlessly complicated by my 1965 travels through French Oceania, Fiji, New Zealand, Australia, and New Guinea. The State Department had the means to do checks in each of these countries; the Navy did not.

But as the domestic phase of my background neared completion, NIS obtained State's investigation reports. State Department Security in early 1968 was battling with a funding freeze and could not hire until the new fiscal year. The Navy was not so fettered. In the first week of March 1968 the commanding officer of Naval Investigative Service Office, Washington, interviewed me in his office in building 200 of the Navy yard.

[118]

He told me that my background investigation and screening had been successfully completed and that he was prepared to offer me an agent appointment.

He would however expect me to promise not to leave NIS if State made me an offer later in the year. I promised, and we shook hands...I was on board.

In July, State called me and asked me to accept an appointment. Feeling a strong sense of obligation to NIS, I declined.

NISO Washington, my first assignment, was established in one of the massive buildings that had once been part of the Naval Gun Factory, within the confines of Washington Navy Yard. The historic yard constructed on the waters of the Anacostia River, was a hodgepodge of eighteenth century brick buildings and others added during the two world wars.

On my first day and wearing a new suit, I reported to Special Agent Cecil Boggs in his office in the bowels of building 200 and began in-processing. At the Naval Dispensary, I discovered that the documents I presented listed me as a research analyst. Obviously, the medical arm of the Navy had no need to know that I was in fact a fledgling special agent. My temporary credentials did identify me as an agent however and thus cleared to "top secret". I was ready to hit the streets for the Navy.

New agents invariably began their jobs by conducting background investigations. In March 1968 the Naval Investigative Service was charged with the conduct of all of the services' background investigations (BIs), which were used to determine a candidate's suitability for exposure to classified material. In the Washington office, we had a massive workload of BIs. All agents did at least some. A lucky few got the criminal investigations, and a couple of counterintelligence specialists did liaison work and were often seen snipping newspaper articles for their files.

I quickly learned that every background investigation followed a clear matrix of what we called "leads." What these were depended on a variety of factors in particular the level and type of access the candidate required. A Marine officer candidate attending the

[119]

Communication School at Quantico might need only a secret clearance to complete initial training. On the other hand, a cryptographer at the Nebraska Avenue headquarters of the Naval Security Group would require periodic upgrades and a number of coworker and neighborhood interviews to establish suitability for continued exposure to some of the nation's most closely-guarded secrets.

The starting point in a BI was normally a local agency check, literally a check of any agency in the area in which the subject had served or resided in during a particular period. At NISO there was a dedicated staff just for this. Later, I would learn to run checks in the old courthouses of Stafford and Fredericksburg, Virginia.

When I was handed my first background investigation lead sheets, I was patiently told what was required, then paired up with an experienced agent. This was Special Agent Ralph Robillard, a retired U.S. Air Force OSI major with two decades of experience running BIs. I soon assimilated the elements that were required to be covered in any BI interview; how long the subject had been known to the interviewee and in what capacity, whether the subject had any questionable foreign connections, whether the subject was considered to be honest and trustworthy, whether the interviewee was aware of any reason why the subject should not be granted a position of trust and responsibility, and whether he recommend the subject for such a position.

I was soon running leads in the decaying halls of the temporary buildings erected along Constitution Avenue, known to all as Main Navy, and to a lesser extent within the labyrinth of the Pentagon. In the afternoon to beat rush hour traffic, we would do neighborhood checks-interviewing the subject's neighbors, past or present. Neighbor interviews were often a good opportunity to identify what was called a developed informant by asking the interviewee to identify another person who could supply information about the subject.

The results were sometimes startling and could lead an investigation down a derogatory path. A "derog" BI demanded detailed interviews, statements from interviewees, and a detailed report.

[120]

That report would be used by command to decide whether the subject should have continued access to classified material.

In many instances investigative results had a direct bearing on a person's job assignment. Although the Washington military and civil environment was very interesting, I never really enjoyed doing background investigations and could not contemplate a career centered on this type of work.

In May 1968 I was ordered to NIS headquarters, then located in the Hoffman Building in Alexandria to attend the Agent Basic School. This marked a real turning point in my career. Basic School classes were quite small. Several experienced street agents who acted as mentors were assigned to students in each course. My mentor was Special Agent Jack Renwick, a likeable and highly capable man just back from a one-year assignment at NISRA Saigon. Renwick sat at the table through the lectures, answered questions, and provided guidance.

Holding Basic School at headquarters was wisdom at work. We had regular exposure to the men who led and drove the organization. If they were not on the same floor as our classroom, they were a short elevator ride away. Thus, we were exposed to counterintelligence specialists, received briefings on the communist bloc's current activities against the free world, and were taken step by step through major espionage cases. We were frequently reminded that our primary mission was to be spy catchers. At Basic School, I developed a far clearer concept of the NIS mission and some idea of how I might participate in it.

Although the hippy revolution had its liberalizing effects, the United States was a different, more socially conservative country four decades ago. Because a good number of the agents at Basic School had had previous careers in street law enforcement, there were not any prudes in the group.

As we were exposed to more case histories involving espionage and attempted espionage, it became increasingly apparent that sex, perhaps even more so than greed, was an underlying issue in many of the cases. The Western nations had learned to their detriment that homosexuals could be particularly vulnerable to manipulation by foreign agents.

This so-called aberrant sexual behavior could be a weakness our enemies might exploit to learn national secrets...even a healthy libido could spell trouble in certain circumstances. Thus, NIS took sex cases seriously. They were all managed and monitored from a vault known as the Cat 8 shop. Its overseer had dossiers guaranteed to make the most seasoned agent blanch.

As Basic School drew to a close, I began to consider carefully what I had learned from Jack Renwick. He had never tried to sell the concept of Vietnam service to any of us. I soon discerned, however, that duty with NIS in Vietnam could immediately expose me to just about every type of investigative challenge on the books.

Agents who successfully completed their year tour were permitted to take the promotional exam to full journeyman level, were given preferential assignments, and were sought after because of their well-rounded vocational experience. Vietnam service was clearly a short cut to the top. I was twenty-three; the world was my apple. I volunteered and was told I would be eligible after my year of probationary service was up in March 1969. I specified Da Nang as my choice of duty station.

*****

In 1969 the First Marine Division, headquartered at Hill 327 west of Da Nang Air Base, had battalions actively deployed in an arc beginning at the northern boundary of the area of operations which was Hai Van Pass. It extended westward and to the south. This was the An Hoa Basin, beyond which was Que Son Valley. Both areas had been bitterly contested during the entire period of the U.S. involvement in Vietnam.

Not only was there a strong Viet Cong infrastructure present there, but An Hoa Basin was also a natural exit point from the mountains to the west and the extensions of the Ho Chi Minh Trail beyond. Marines often spoke of seeing small units of NVA marching in step out of the mountains on their way to valley battlefields.

[122]

In more peaceful times a coal mine had operated at An Hoa, and the French had constructed a serviceable airstrip there. This made An Hoa one of several important strong points selected by the Marine command from which to embark on operations focused on finding and destroying the enemy. The area was not, unfortunately, in an ideal location for resupply by land. To address this problem, SeaBees and Marine engineers constructed a large bridge which they christened Liberty Bridge, across the Thu Bon River. The northern approaches to the bridge were muddy roads not much better than cart tracks which had been originally built to access the village of Dai Loc.

During the war these roads passed a series of Marine firebases on Hills 55, 37, and 65. Overlapping artillery "fans" allowed the guns on these hills to drop massive fire power virtually anywhere in the area. Tank-escorted convoys preceded by engineers checking for mines, regularly trucked large amounts of materiel into the hostile environment. Supplying ammunition for the scores of artillery pieces in the area was a major logistical headache, and once completed, the Liberty Bridge became the focus of the enemy's interest. It was fortified with mortar pits, concertina wire, and dozens of marines. The marines endured endless monsoon rains observing the rushing waters while watching for enemy sapper-swimmer attacks.

Manning armed strong points is the antithesis of Marine Corps practice, which emphasizes going to the enemy. The hills and bases were considered protected venues for artillery, logistics, and command. Marines patrolled and engaged the enemy on his turf. Marine command also had a strongly developed belief in the value of civic action and pacification, prompted by hard lessons learned in the Banana Wars of Central America earlier in the century. Marine combined action groups (CAGs) were made up of volunteers who lived in villages with Vietnamese to assist them with basic needs such as security, medicine, and hygiene.

All of this could make it difficult for a NIS agent to go directly to a command venue and expect to find a particular individual. Agents who worked an area normally had a good idea which units were operating in what area.

This knowledge was supplemented by good contacts in the Marine postal system that could usually ensure accurate information about where a subject's battalion was receiving its mail. After obtaining information from his sources, an agent could sally forth to the command rear and start asking questions.

Flying to the base areas was always preferable to driving, except perhaps in the case of Hill 55, which was the nearest to Da Nang. This well-fortified hill overlooked surrounding paddy fields and villages with its eight-inch howitzers staring down the throat of the An Hoa Basin to the south.

"Elliot"

[124]

As with the other hill strong points, Hill 55 was an important rear area for battalions and small-unit groups screening the country, putting in ambushes by night, and hurting the local VC. By 1969 the Viet Cong around 55 were finding tax collection and intimidation far more difficult than in earlier years.

Marine patrols were taking their toll. Marine snipers with rifles and night-scope equipped .50-caliber machine guns accounted for mounting casualty rates amongst the nocturnal VC. Life may have been easier for the enemy in the southerly rice fields, known by marines as Arizona territory, but it was not improving for them at Hill 55.

*****

Fragging became more common in the later years of the Vietnam War. After Bob Power's first 1967 investigation, the practice became more and more prevalent. By 1969, commands were looking much more closely at suspicious deaths caused by grenades. Most victims were either NCOs or officers, and when a Marine staff sergeant was blown in half while asleep on his cot on Hill 55, the First Marine Division requested assistance from NIS.

Special Agent Larry Coleman was officially Da Nang SRA Don McCoy's assistant. A solid, mature agent and highly skilled investigator, Coleman was respected by his peers and was a quiet source of advice to those less experienced. He took over investigation of the Hill 55 fragging and got started with a careful examination of the scene. The victim was a cook, and was assigned quarters in what was known as a Southeast Asia (SEA) hut. This was a lightly framed and screened rectangular building with a metal roof and sides of plywood. Early indications were that the attacker had cut the fly screen immediately adjacent to the victim as he lay sleeping.

The grenade was introduced through the opening, and quietly put in place. The blast had disemboweled the victim, but caused surprisingly little damage to the upper torso and face.

A postmortem examination provided little additional information ex-cept to confirm that death had been caused by the blast and unique stainless-steel wire fragments utilized in the manufacture of the M26 fragmentation grenade. The screen panel with its cut was removed for further examination, and the sentries were interviewed to see whether any had seen movements around the victim's hooch that night.

Neither the sentries nor his colleagues were able to provide anything helpful, nor were any footprints discovered around the building's exterior.

Clues discovered during the search of the victim's personal effects pointed more to suicide than homicide. When the scientific examination of the screen confirmed it had been cut from the inside, suspicions became even stronger. It was also hard to imagine anybody creeping unnoticed across a squeaking plywood floor and, after managing to place the grenade, making good his escape.

Agents in the United States followed up in an attempt to learn more about the victim and his state of mind at the time of his death. Ultimately, it was determined that he had in fact killed himself. The only doubt lurking in Larry Coleman's mind was the fact that the pin from the grenade that killed the victim was never found.

Fragging on Hill 55. The victim's shattered cot shows high explosive effects of the grenade.

Hill 55 was later the scene of several intimidation efforts using fragmentation grenades. Disliked COs, ("lifers" to the discontented), became targets for expressions of anonymous defiance. Grenades were placed as warnings, though all could have detonated. In one case, trip wires were attached to a gunnery sergeant's desk chair and then to the pin of a grenade that was affixed to the desk interior.

Another act of intimidation involved an M26 "frag" with its pin removed and electrician's tape wrapped around the striker lever. The tape rendered the grenade safe temporarily until it was placed in a can of gasoline; this was intended to provide a time-delay explosion. The solvent would gradually dissolve the adhesive on the tape and allow the striker lever to be released, striking the detonator. An explosion could be expected three to five seconds later once the fuse had burned.

Unfortunately the perpetrators were never charged or brought to justice due to the lack of evidence and the carefully maintained code of silence within the ranks.

But those responsible were eventually identified, and transfers of the men by command neutralized the problem.

*****

Often, a NIS special agent would go to forward areas to conduct investigations initiated by leads and requests sent from other components within NIS. U.S. postal inspectors were a frequent source of referrals. Mail in Vietnam was always treated as a high-priority item and deliveries occurred daily in most instances. There was a large volume of return mail and parcels destined for home, quite often items purchased from the excellent PX facilities.

Injuries, attrition, and death sometimes produced opportunities for some to mail arms and other stolen property home. Questionable items might be "lost" in the unit weapon accounting system or acquired through barter with a Vietnamese ally. Although they were disassembled in most instances, mailers hoped goods would pass scrutiny at the point of entry and be waiting at home for their arrival back.

[127]

Even more common, particularly from 1969 onward, were cases of narcotics mailed in various guises. Tape cassettes, a favorite communication medium between Vietnam and the home front, were a common receptacle for these.

Forward Marine commands were usually disturbed when a special agent visited them carrying reports alleging narcotics use and exportation by the same men who were riflemen in the field. Most grunts, (who depended on each other to stay alive), had a code of conduct forbidding narcotics…at least while on operations. But a responsible commander could not rely on an informal code of conduct alone when his troops' effectiveness and welfare were concerned.

A trip taken in 1970 illustrates the unreliable nature of this code. Carrying three cases involving members of the Fifth Marines, I embarked on a Marine CH46 resupply mission early one morning. I shared the bird with five or six enlisted men returning to their units, and we flew southwest across rice paddies and the choked, dusty road that led to Dai Loc and the Arizona territory. On that day the road streamed with tanks and trucks carrying marines returning to Da Nang.

Interspersed among them were Vietnamese pedicabs loaded to the bursting point with people, pigs, chickens, and other rural impedimenta. Even more prevalent were small motorcycles and pedestrians balancing huge loads on carrying poles bouncing rhythmically as they shuffled to the next village. Beyond, the mountains rose above verdant rice paddies. It might have been a peaceful picture were it not for artillery bursts on the slopes and the impatient convoy surging along below.

Hill 55 was the first stop on the resupply mission. Several men got off, taking personal gear weapons and cargo with them. Then they moved away from the big chopper shielding their eyes and grasping caps in the rotor wash. Clouds of red dust and loose debris blew from the landing zone (LZ) through wire entanglements. Nothing grew on these firebase hills and the dust was ever present.

Taking off again, the CH46 gained altitude and continued a southwest course skirting the massif on the right known to the

[128]

Marines as Charlie Ridge. It was from here that the artillery fire had earlier been observed.

Ahead, the Vu Gia River curled down from the mountains and across the paddies and plains to the south before joining the Thu Bon. Hill 65.overlooking the river and situated near the base of Charlie Ridge, was our next destination.

Skimming over hooches and the upward-pointing muzzles of momentarily quiet artillery batteries, the CH46 landed slightly down-slope on the metal helipad. I got off and moved away, watching the helo rise again and clatter off over the Vu Gia in the direction of An Hoa Combat Base.

An Hoa could be identified only as a smudge of smoke and circling aircraft far in the distance on the opposite side of the Arizona. Up the hill at the battalion CP I was redirected to the battalion executive officer, who unhappily read official NIS reports indicating that one of his men had attempted to mail a disassembled M16 home.

The XO knew the accused, describing him as a fairly quiet young country boy originating from a town in the Deep South. He sent an NCO to find the marine and to arrange a suitable location for the interview.

Surprised to see an agent, the marine quickly confessed. The weapon had been issued to a man wounded in the most recent operation and had been left unattended at the LZ afterward. The marine saw an opportunity and had taken the rifle field stripped it into the smallest pieces possible, and mailed them home in several packages. "I just really wanted it for next deer season at home," he said.

The interview completed, I briefed the battalion commander in the presence of his sergeant major, promising that I would forward a complete report to assist with any disciplinary procedures. It was late in the day, and in the charge of the sergeant major, I had been escorted to accommodations normally used for transient officers. My host then offered a spare bunk in his hooch asking if that would be suitable.

[129]

I had been around marines long enough to know that battalion sergeants major are a force to be reckoned with. Smart, astute, and all knowing, they are the eyes and ears of their commanders. I gratefully accepted the invitation and settled into his small private hooch with its panoramic views of the position and the villages and fields beyond. The hooch included a private shower, replenished by young marines toting water in five-gallon jerry cans. It was as close to luxury as is possible in a war zone.

As the shadows lengthened, a squad quietly walked down the base access road and through the perimeter fence to set up a listening post and lay ambush for errant enemy patrols. Soon after the squad cleared the perimeter, three batteries of 105mm howitzers fired in unison at a distant tree line where contact had been reported.

The fire from the 105's was supplemented by an eight-inch howitzer battery on Hill 55, which dropped a string of rounds with uncanny accuracy across the tree line where it faced the paddy fields. Massive explosions tossed full-sized trees into the air like toothpicks. It proved that it was not a wise thing for "Charles" to take pot shots at marines with this sort of firepower on call.

The Marines had several tall sandbagged observation towers that were used to monitor the surroundings and to provide fire support. A 106mm recoilless rifle's business end pointed northward from one tower, its breach open to the elements. Commands were shouted and the 106's spotting rifle was fired, sending a red tracer reaching out into the growing darkness.

It was quickly followed by the blast of the main gun firing in support of patrols skirmishing on the steep slopes above. It was, the sergeant major said, a fairly routine evening on Hill 65.

The war had gone on as it had for several years, but there was little doubt that friendly forces were gradually gaining advantage in a traditionally hostile region. The batteries fired through the night as rains fell over the Arizona.

I could not help but wonder what sort of a miserable night the grunts were having outside the wire. But the answer was "another just like the last one." Marines had it hard in the bush.

[130]

Needing to travel on to An Hoa Combat Base to conduct my next investigation the next morning, I walked to the CP to learn what air movements were planned for the day. The hills had regular helicopter visits, but they were certainly not events one could set his watch to. A low cloud ceiling and continuing drizzle caused delays for all except the most urgent air missions. "Maybe this afternoon," I was told.

Having learned by then the unpredictable vagaries of Vietnamese monsoon weather, I opted instead to join a Marine Roughrider convoy to An Hoa. They were expected within the hour at the nearby village of Dai Loc. A jeep from Hill 65 was scheduled to join the supply trucks and I joined the driver and his shotgun escort, winding down the road to Route 4 and the rendezvous.

The convoy was waiting for us perhaps twenty heavily loaded five-ton trucks and several tractor-trailers, each with a gunner manning a coaxial .50-caliber machine gun. Drivers were out kicking muddy tires, doing a last-minute check before the upcoming journey into the Arizona territory.

Gunners wearing radio-linked headsets wiped weapons and checked ammunition levels. Slotting into position within the procession, our jeep moved off in convoy, navigating water-filled ruts and seemingly bottomless holes, seldom shifting out of second gear.

Once outside the village and paddy fields, the terrain adjacent to the road became increasingly barren and inhospitable. Here was the "Arizona territory", a scene of virtually continuous conflict between marines and the enemy since NVA/ VC control here had been challenged.

Flashes from artillery impacts and columns of smoke rose in the distance. Approaching the northern banks of the Thu Bon River, the convoy passed a squad of marines preparing to march from their overnight defensive positions.

Tanks led the convoy into An Hoa

Amongst the water filled holes, hooches made from ponchos and shelter halves had provided some cover from the rains and a place to sleep. The marines had that skinny, hard-staring look of those who spent their lives in the field. They ignored the convoy completely, either intentionally or because of their preoccupation with the march ahead.

Marines at their fighting holes in the Arizona Territory pause for a C ration breakfast

Slowly, the trucks began to cross the Liberty Bridge, recently completed by SeaBees and Marine engineers and built from U.S.

[132]

timber imported for the job. The Song Thu Bon is a wide river, even when there has been no rain. Monsoon rains caused rapid rises, and the brown waters then carry with them branches, logs, and other detritus…a challenge to the integrity of any timber bridge.

If the bridge were ever lost, supplies supporting the numerous artillery pieces at nearby An Hoa would then need to be ferried across. This was an unacceptable alternative.

A heavily fortified outpost had been constructed on the far side of the bridge. The position was subject to attacks, and its marines had repelled several attempts to overrun it and destroy the bridge.

Crossing at Liberty Bridge

Sentries watched the waters carefully. The flotsam was not only harmful if it hit the bridge but also could provide concealment for enemy swimmer/sappers. Enduring the seemingly endless rains they fired into the water at anything the least bit suspicious.

[133]

As we approached An Hoa, Marine artillerymen hurried to prepare their 81 mm mortar for imminent fire missions. Tanks from An Hoa, and wet and tired engineers having swept the road for mines, awaited the convoy for their escort the remaining distance.

Mud encrusted and festooned with antenna flags they preceded the trucks, protecting the convoy in the event of ambush. Rumbling ahead, the convoy trucks followed in trace under the leaden skies. The road carried them past a school and the German hospital from which the Viet Cong had abducted one of the nurses. Vietnamese pedestrians hurried to leave the roadway and the oncoming bow waves of the convoy trucks.

The artillery at An Hoa artillery could be heard long before the watch towers and perimeter defenses hove into view. The guns continued to fire as the gates were opened for the convoy trucks.

An Hoa, the headquarters of the Fifth Marine Regiment was a hectic and claustrophobic hive of soggy tents and SEA huts, duckboard walkways, and ever-present mud. Conversations were routinely interrupted by the blast of a nearby howitzer or a helicopter landing.

To use the jargon of the age, An Hoa was not considered a "garden spot" to anyone but the most hard core of the field marines.
I quickly located the commands to which I believed the subjects of my cases to be attached, and found that one had been injured and evacuated out of country to the naval hospital at Yokosuka, Japan. He was not expected to return to his command, and I would pass the case to Japan.

The subject would certainly receive a ward visit from an agent in conservative civilian attire within a few days. An NIS investigation originating in the United States implicated my second subject for importing narcotics by mail utilizing a tape cassette. Though the subject himself was then in Da Nang, his personal effects were in hooch at An Hoa. Armed with a command search authorization, it was soon discovered that the accused's locker contained traces of cannabis in several items of clothing bearing his name. He would later be interrogated in Da Nang.

Soon after completion of the command briefing on the search, the first sergeant announced that a late-afternoon CH53 flight was inbound with possible room for my return flight to Da Nang. I moved quickly to the cargo handling area adjacent the helicopter landing pad, where I was joined by about thirty-five Marine riflemen, still fully-equipped after a stint in the field. Soon, the huge helicopter appeared high above and began its steep spiral in preparation for the landing within the circular fan of the outward firing guns.

[135]

The Marine riflemen were tired and dirty. Sitting patiently and leaning against their packs, or each other, most dozed or slept.

They were well used to waiting for the Big Green Machine to tell them what to do next. Arrival of the CH53 prompted a few to shift their gaze to a young forklift driver jockeying up to the chopper rear ramp, his head only feet away from the certain death of a whirling tail rotor. Pilots always kept their aircraft running at full power.

Moments after the forklift had removed his pallet of cargo, the passengers were waved aboard. All were quickly sandwiched in as I joined the grunts, squatting on the deck as the pilots taxied a short distance and then hauled controls back to begin a steep, tight spiral climb out of small arms range. The air was cool when the helicopter leveled out, and nobody tried to speak over the rotor din...it was almost peaceful.

I was on the ground at Marble Mountain Air Facility twenty minutes later, and calling NISRA Da Nang for a ride home at the end of an eventful day.

*****

While the Fifth and Seventh Marine Regiments battled the enemy in the mountains and An Hoa Basin, their sister division, the First Marines, was fully engaged in the slice of coastal land to the east. Immediately east of the An Hoa Basin AO was a section of country the marines called Dodge City.

The First Marines were tasked with combating incursions by NVA units and the resident VC as well as maintaining effective control of the heavily populated countryside northward to Da Nang. Through it ran the Han River and its' many tributaries. This was rice-producing country, and was dotted with picturesque hamlets, paddy fields, and bamboo tree lines. It is said that an army marches on its stomach, and control of the rice harvest was a hotly contested issue between the communists and the allies. Control was maintained by civic action programs and very aggressive patrolling.

[136]

A First Marines outpost had been established at the Tu Cau Bridge, to guard this vital bridge from enemy sapper attack and to project an allied presence into the surrounding countryside. It was one of several such posts.

During the day marines and hospital corpsmen visited the villages to help implement basic improvements in health, hygiene, and security. At night they watched the roads and trails for evidence of the Viet Cong, who were anxious to wrest control back from the allies.

Marines defend the Tu Cau bridge and its surrounding countryside

Ongoing Marine ambushes and patrols paid dividends in the "hearts-and-minds" stakes at Tu Cau Bridge, as well as in surrounding villages.

Marines billeted in tents within a wired perimeter on the west side of the span that covered Song Tu Cau, and were regularly resupplied by road from Da Nang. The camp defenses illustrated the fact that pacification had been quite successful in the region, and underscored the Marine philosophy of taking the war to the enemy. Tu Cau was a small but important enclave in the strategic plan to defend vital Da Nang facilities.

On one evening in August 1969, a Marine squad led by a junior

NCO moved out of the Tu Cau perimeter to patrol down the river, and eventually establish an ambush site. The marines were hoping to surprise Viet Cong infiltrating by night into the houses surrounding the fields.

After progressing to a position several hundred yards eastward, the squad turned to the north and entered a small peanut patch. Immediately beyond their location there stood a modest two room masonry farmhouse.

They were jumpy. The squad was made up largely of newcomers, and the area was known to be rife with booby traps making night patrols unpopular. It was decided to wait out the night in a relatively safe location, sending periodic radio transmissions back to their base at the bridge, giving false positions to the operation center. A Vietnamese household had been allowing marines to use their farmhouse, and the patrol was guided there. The squad radioman set up and relaxed with a cigarette.

Not knowing other marines were nearby, a second Marine patrol approached the house. As they neared, the point man recognized the glow of a cigarette and could see the outline of the sandbagging Marine radioman through the window opening. He was certain that he had discovered the Viet Cong, and he opened fire. The fire was returned, and in the following melee, grenades were also thrown. Tragically in that instant, four Vietnamese peasants were killed and all were women and children. Miraculously, no marines were hurt.

The platoon commander arrived from his position at the bridge within a few minutes, and what he would find caused him to believe that homicide might have been committed. He isolated all of the squad members and began the gruesome task of collecting the scattered remains, struggling to calm the surviving Vietnamese. Marines secured the scene overnight, and a request for assistance from the First Marine Division staff judge advocate was sent. The Judge Advocate General (JAG) would request investigative support from NISRA Da Nang.

Assigned to lead the investigation, Special Agent Lance Arnold quickly gathered a small team of agents to assist with the most critical early periods of the inquiry. He was joined by agents Frank

Orrantia, Ed Hemphill, and me. We hurriedly left our Da Nang office in a Navy gray Dodge truck, still dressed in civilian clothes and carrying assorted rifles and equipment.

Arnold drove us through the teeming streets of Da Nang, and we finally emerged on the gravel thoroughfare that had once been the highway from Saigon to Hanoi... Route 1.

Sharing this busy road with Marine convoys could ultimately result in delays, but Route 1 was far safer than the coastal road. A few miles south, we reached our turnoff, and then drove east until a clutch of antenna masts and barbed-wire entanglements announced our arrival at Tu Cau. There, at their sandbagged command post, we were met by the sleep starved platoon commander. After his short briefing, we joined him in the walk eastward toward the village and the scene. All along the graded dirt road, and squatting in the red dust, sat members of the two patrols. All had been separated to prevent them from talking.

Children led us to the tiny Vietnamese house set back a short distance from the bridge road. We would find it at the end of a path that wandered through a field of peanuts. An inverted wicker basket sat incongruously along the path covering an unexploded 40mm grenade from the night before.

As was often the case in Vietnam curious villagers and their children would follow us. It seemed to me as though they had accepted the terrible violence of the previous night as unavoidable, another legacy of a long and painful war.

By the time NIS agents arrived, the platoon commander had methodically sifted through the wreckage and found all the victims' body parts.

Controlling agent Lance Arnold inspected the interior of the house first, noting the shrapnel and bullet-strikes in the plastered brick walls. The evidence suggested that those killed had been clustered in the small northern room and in a modest underground shelter at the time of the attack. Grenades had shattered the room and its contents, reducing it all to a collage of burnt and splintered wreckage.

[139]

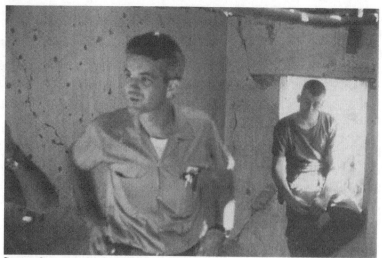

Stress shows on the face of control agent L.M. Arnold in the shrapnel damaged house

While others sifted through evidence in and around the Tu Cau farm-house, I drove back to Da Nang and met Special Agent Larry Coleman at the NSA morgue. The victims' remains had been taken to the hospital mortuary, where a medical examination had been requested.

I walked from the hot and dusty sand dunes of the Tien Sa Peninsula and through the door of the Quonset hut that housed the morgue. I was struck by a cool wet blanket of air that was clearly tainted with the scent of death. Coleman, standing over a crude red wooden coffin, turned to me with a look of overwhelming sadness. He was a man who had witnessed a great deal of death and destruction, but Pops Coleman was clearly moved.

I glanced down at the box at his feet, and it was filled with violently rent body parts. In a few seconds I had taken in the scope of the tragedy. On the top and next to a severed foot, was the scalp and cranium from a young Vietnamese woman. Her long tresses shrouded what remained of her and her family. Looking away, I walked past Coleman and the coffin and crossed the room to speak with the medical examiner. Small in stature and dapper in appearance, Dr. Bill Buck simply told me that the victims' remains all reflected the effects of modern high explosive ordnance on the human body. Little else needed to be said.

[140]

Vietnamese family members waited nearby to take the bodies back to Tu Cau for the burial that afternoon. We let them get on with their sad task.

In the meantime, interviews of witnesses at Tu Cau had begun to develop the story that we suspected. It suggested that two Marine squads had been involved in the incident, not just the squad that had initiated the attack.

Special Agent Coleman would later recall that interviews of Vietnamese peasant witnesses conducted via a local interpreter had prompted suspicions because of the uniformity of their recollection of events. Too many people seemed to remember similar and often obscure facts. Coleman closely questioned his Vietnamese interpreter and discovered that the similarity of witness statements were the product of a willingness to answer questions in a way they assumed would please the investigators. Interviews were halted, and the witnesses were re-interviewed. All testimony was then subjected to careful scrutiny by agents.

By the time interviews and interrogations were finally completed, it was apparent that the attacking squad had strayed from the area that they were to have been patrolling. The "enemy" they had discovered and fired on was actually other marines from the patrol who had approached the farm house from the opposite direction. The attack had lasted only seconds before their error was realized and hostilities halted. The defendant squad leader was not charged with murder but with a lesser offense and he was found guilty. He had taken his squad into another squad's area of operation. He had made a tragic error. It could still be argued that oversight and error had caused these civilian deaths. In the final analysis, it had been a case of negligence not malice.

But the Marine command was sensitized by then to emerging reports of a massacre by U.S. Army troops in the Quang Ngai village of My Lai, and they wanted no hint whatever that there were any Vietnamese civilian deaths that were not being thoroughly and professionally investigated. We had done a good job of investigating what was a ghastly event that never should have happened.

Weary agents and Marines trudge back to the Tu Cau Bridge from the village crime scene

*****

In May 1969 NISRA Da Nang received information from the First Marine Air Wing that the body of a Marine sergeant had been found in an abandoned bunker at the air base. It appeared that the victim had been stabbed.

SRA Don McCoy assigned the case to Special Agent Vern Oakum. An experienced investigator, Oakum was nearing the end of his tour in Vietnam and was well established with the marines at the wing. I was assigned to assist him on my first homicide investigation. The body had been removed by the time we arrived at the scene, a sandbag defensive bunker that was near a recreational area where the victim had been seen drinking the night before. The bunker was in a sad state of repair since there was little need for firing points within the perimeter area, but in it we found bloodstains and evidence of a struggle. The murder weapon had been a standard issue bayonet.

The scene was carefully processed for forensic evidence, though we assumed that contamination had occurred at the time of the discovery of the body.

[142]

Later that morning we drove to First Medical Hospital at Hill 327 to visit Graves Registration to view the deceased's remains.

Graves Registration at Hill 327 was actually located behind the hospital. It consisted of several refrigerated vans and a covered work area with examining tables. It was manned by marines from Force Logistics Command.

As one might expect, these particular marines were a different sort of individual, both in their conduct and appearance. I thought to myself that I really didn't care what anybody at the unit looked like, considering the disagreeable nature of the job they were called upon to do.

As we walked into the covered and screened area, two black marines dressed in shower thongs and shorts were finishing the processing of a dead aviator officer. His body had remained strapped into a crashed helicopter for several weeks before the site had been discovered. The sight of the aviator was neither pretty nor something my olfactory senses care to recall.

Finishing up, the men zipped the dead man into a body bag and dragged it onto a stretcher. They then jogged to the refrigerator where the bodies were stored prior to transportation to the Da Nang mortuary for final processing. "That'll be a closed coffin," the rear stretcher-bearer said. "Whew, that one stinks!"

I kept quiet while Oakum spoke to the NCO in charge and told him why we were there. The sergeant pointed to a body bag lying against the wall and said, "That's him."

After what I had just seen, I experienced a degree of dread as I pulled down the zipper on the bag not knowing what I might find. What I saw was a young black man dressed in camouflage utilities. A cursory examination showed that he had been stabbed numerous times. We hoped that a medical examination would tell us more. But for now, we took receipt of his clothing after searching them carefully. Our investigation sought to trace the victim's movements just before his murder.

Oakum was told that he had been drinking with a group of marines the previous night, and we moved as quickly as possible to locate and interview these witnesses.

The next day I would drive across the Han River to the NSA hospital opposite Marble Mountain Air Facility, to attend the examination of the victim's remains. The hospital mortuary was housed in one of many Quonset huts behind the wards, and all were similar to the others except for the signs on the doors. I parked my vehicle and entered, finding a partition with a partly opened door straight ahead. Inside, the stainless steel examination table glared under the lights. To my right, I noticed a large walk-in refrigerator that took up most of the room. The concrete floors were spotless. The strong odor of disinfectant did not succeed in covering the smell of death.

Having heard the door, a Navy hospital corpsman wearing a surgical smock entered through the partition door. I showed him my credentials and explained why I had come. "Dr. Buck will be doing the PM," he said. Then he opened the reefer door, and inside, on shelves, were the remains of Marine dead removed from the field on medevac flights. "I've got fingerprints to do, but not on this one." The bottom half of a torso lay there, the victim perhaps of a very large booby trap.

I saw the doctor moving around in the examination room, so I went in and greeted him. An intense young doctor, I would learn a great deal from him in the months ahead. My education would not be limited to just human physiology, but focused on the multitude of ways that the human body can be made to cease functioning on a permanent basis. We spoke for a few minutes about the investigation and what was known at the time about the deceased and his movements, then the corpsman assistant rolled him in from the refrigerator on a gurney.

The body bag was hoisted onto the metal table, unzipped, and the examination began. The victim was a slight, almost delicate African American. He had been stabbed many times in his torso and face. As his injuries were recorded on a medical chart, the hospital photographer arrived and began making a photographic record. Measurements of the wounds indicated to Dr. Buck that only one weapon had been used in the attack. Very few of the injuries were

[144]

defensive, causing me to wonder if somebody much stronger than him had swiftly overpowered him. Most of the injuries were on the front side of the body, and the back of the body was also carefully examined. Dr. Buck checked the anus and commented that the state of the sphincter suggested the victim had been a practicing homosexual. This was an aspect we had not yet considered, and swabs were taken for possible semen traces.

Once the body was opened and vital organs were examined, it was verified that several of a total of thirty-seven stab wounds would have been fatal.

Having survived my first autopsy, I drove back to the office in Da Nang where the other agents had been reconstructing what the victim had been doing at the club on the night of his death. They spoke to witnesses who said that he had left in the company of another black Marine NCO. Oakum interviewed the suspect who admitted that he had been drinking at the club with the victim, and that they had left the club together. He was then warned about his right to remain silent, but he told the agents that he had nothing to hide.

We began to think we had identified the murderer. He was obviously a street-smart man, but never seemed to make any attempt to hide any facts from his interviewers. When asked what he had done after he and the victim walked out of the club together, he said, "I don't know where he went, I went on a leg run to the ville. There's a place we can get through the wire."

His claim was that he had left the victim as soon as they exited the club to seek the sexual pleasures of a Vietnamese prostitute in a skivvy house near the perimeter. This was against the regulations, but it was not murder.

There were no other apparent avenues of investigation. As I had learned, the Vietnamese witnesses tended to tell interviewers what they thought the interviewer wanted to hear. But the finger still pointed directly at the big black marine.

Before this investigation concluded, Oakum had completed his twelve month assignment and was bid farewell properly by his

[145]

envious brother agents in a boozy sendoff. I would become the control agent of the homicide case. SRA Don McCoy and I discussed our options with Marine JAG staff, but the question of the NCO's guilt remained unresolved. None of the scientific evidence from the autopsy or the crime scene examination linked him to the murder. Perhaps it was time to consider a polygraph examination.

When he was re-interviewed, the suspect readily agreed to take a polygraph test. The so-called lie detector results are seldom used as evidence in court, but they can provide invaluable guides in the direction of furthering the investigation. We needed to know if this man had told us everything he knew about the victim's death.

Tom Brannon was the man who had opened up NISRA Da Nang in 1965 and acquired our office at 20 Duy Tan. He now was the Western Pacific polygraph operator, and was stationed in Taipei. We sent out a request for his services, and several days later Tom joined us in Da Nang.

Brannon was a natural as a polygraph operator, blessed with a great memory and the gift of gab, he had honed his skills with years of intense interrogation experience. We welcomed him back into the fold after more than a year away from Vietnam.

Our suspect was delivered to the office early one morning, and Brannon escorted him to the rear where the air-conditioned interview room was located with its purpose-built polygraph examination chair. He emerged less than an hour later with some startling news… "This guy is clean," he announced. We had the wrong man.

I had really hoped to be able to clear my first homicide, and we had run every logical lead to ground. But in Vietnam, where operational staff often changed daily, the environment didn't bode well for a final resolution. On the other hand, we had cleared a heavily implicated innocent man. He would never face the rigors of a general court-martial because no charges would be laid against him. We sent him back to the First Marine Air Wing. Unfortunately the case was never solved, and I have often wondered what might have happened that triggered the murderous rage that snuffed out that young marine's life.

*****

7   DA NANG, 1969 TO 1970: MAYHEM AND MURDER IN I CORPS

The summer of 1969 was a busy time at NISRA Da Nang. In addition to the usual day to day caseload of leads, narcotics, and fraud work, several incidents were of such importance that all office resources were directed toward their resolution. One such event was the murder of Australian entertainer Catherine Anne Warnes.

Miss Warnes, who used the stage name Cathy Wayne performed as a member of the musical group "Sweethearts on Parade". She was shot while performing with her troupe at the staff and officers' club at the First Force Reconnaissance Company's base camp... Camp Reasoner.

The Australian entertainers had proved very popular at earlier engagements in Vietnam, so a good crowd had assembled in the small thatched building. Sydney television personality Warnes was the featured singer. As blonde and mini-skirted Miss Warnes, who was twenty years old at the time, finished singing her last song she bowed to the crowd. As she straightened, a muffled shot was heard. Grasping her left side, Warnes spun and fell to the floor. A .22-caliber bullet had penetrated her body, striking her aorta.

The spent bullet exited the right side of her body and dropped to the floor with not even enough momentum left to puncture her dress. Her death was almost instantaneous.

The firing point was quickly identified as a fly screen to the left and rear of the victim. Seated in a row of chairs immediately in front of Miss Warnes had been the company CO, Maj. Roger Simmons, USMC. It was conjectured that he may have been the actual target of the attack. A search of the compound was begun, and Company personnel were ordered to remain in their hooches.

[147]

SRA Don McCoy received a late evening call for assistance at the 23 Doc Lap billet. It was well after curfew, a time when all personnel were expected to be in a secure, recognized compound within Da Nang City.

Marine MPs regularly manned jeeps festooned with light machine guns. After curfew, they prowled the streets watching for signs of suspicious persons.

But NISOV agents made a point of answering all calls for help, and particularly those from the Marines. The Marines seldom made requests if they were not in genuine need, nor did they take unreasonable risks with an agents' safety.

The murder scene

McCoy placed his assistant, Larry Coleman, in charge of the investigation. Tom Stallings, though near to transfer at the end of his tour, volunteered to accompany the agent team that was to drive to Camp Reasoner to conduct the preliminary investigation. They piled into an aging Chevrolet Suburban and began threading their way through the roadblocks manned by heavily armed and jumpy Vietnamese soldiers and police.

They travelled out past the air base to the western perimeter of the Da Nang enclave, where First Force Recon made its home. At this late hour, agents still carried out hasty interviews aimed at determining the whereabouts of everybody in the compound. All men had been ordered to return to their SEA huts in the minutes following the shooting.

After the first round of interviews, the agents crosschecked stories for those that did not fit or seemed implausible. Naturally Coleman and his colleagues had suspicions, but they could do little before daylight came and a more detailed search of the scene could be conducted. But the camp was buttoned up tight, and so the agents returned to their billet in town for several hours of badly needed sleep.

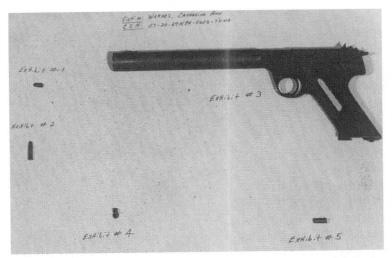

The murder weapon

The next day an alert marine assigned to search the area found a strange looking handgun in a nearby ditch.

Rusted and missing not only its grips but its magazine, it was equipped with a permanent silencer. The weapon was identified as a High Standard pistol of World War II vintage. These weapons were believed to have been manufactured especially for Office of Strategic Services operations. This was certainly not an issued weapon, in fact no .22 caliber weapons were on issue for the recon marines.

While Coleman's team aggressively pursued every potential angle
[149]

of investigation that morning, I was told to attend the victim's autopsy. They drove back to Camp Reasoner, and I made my way once again across the river to the NSA hospital and the small windowless Quonset hut that was the morgue. The body was already on the stainless-steel examining table when I arrived. Postmortem examinations of females were not a normal occurrence, and Miss Warnes' status as an international personage also added significance to the event.

That morning, the Navy had assigned its chief pathologist to conduct the autopsy. A senior commander, the graying doctor quickly put me at ease with small talk about the discipline of pathology as it applies to postmortem examination.

It was clear that he had broad experience in forensic medicine, as he spoke of examinations he had carried out on crewmembers of the USS *Pueblo* whom North Koreans had killed when the Navy spy vessel was captured on the high seas. Their remains had eventually been returned along with the survivors only after prolonged negotiations.

We knew the murder weapon was of a small caliber. The entry wound under her left armpit was minute, almost like a blemish. Opposite it, the exit wound was scarcely larger. The doctor planned to confirm Warnes' cause of death and to look for any evidence that could assist us with our investigation. He carefully removed and examined every organ in the body cavity, while taking microscope samples as he went. He asked me if there appeared to be any sexual aspect to the investigation at that point, and I answered that I was unaware of one. He said the victim was sexually active, but that there was no evidence of any trauma or unexplained body fluid.

He determined that the tiny bullet had caused her death when it had penetrated her aorta and heart. Death came quickly. Several hours later with the examination complete, Cathy Warnes was returned to her olive drab body bag and wheeled into the adjacent refrigerator.

As I walked back outside into the fresh air and tropical heat, I found myself wondering about Warnes' family in Sydney. How would they endure as they received the news of their daughter's senseless murder?

[150]

Marine combat engineers armed with a surveyor's transit, used information supplied by the Navy pathologist to determine the point from which the weapon had been fired. Agents followed the trajectory of the bullet to a parked jeep in a nearby low rise.

A search of the vehicle disclosed a spent cartridge case and a misfired .22-caliber round on the ground next to a rear wheel. Crime scene assessments led by Special Agent Larry Coleman established that the weapon had been fired from the parked jeep.

The bullet had travelled about thirty-five yards, penetrating the club fly screen before striking Warnes.

Screening the Recon Marines

Agents needed to approach the investigation from several angles. They continued checking all persons with whom Warnes had had contact. Band members assisted viewing lineups of marines. The agents also investigated the dynamics within the band to determine if any tensions had existed between its members. A major effort was continued to determine the whereabouts of all personnel within the confines of Camp Reasoner at the time the murder occurred.

Coleman identified a promising potential witness and quickly

[151]

spirited him away from the camp. The young corporal was a very capable armorer, and disassembled and serviced the entire arsenal of rifles and submachine guns to while away the hours between interviews.

Coleman had concerns about the safety of the witness and for good reasons. Camp Reasoner was home to recon marines, the eyes and ears of the force. These men regularly went into the most dangerous unsecured areas of Vietnam, particularly the border region with Laos. Contact in these areas with large North Vietnamese Army units was common.

They lived by their wits, determination, and an unsurpassed level of physical fitness. Most accepted the risk of death as part of the job description.

Special Agent Larry Coleman at the left, interviews two of the Australian entertainers while Special Agent J.F. Washko observes the re-enactment of Miss Warne's death

While the agents searched for the suspect, ongoing investigations disclosed that the murder weapon had been stolen from the company operations office the month before. It was also reported that two marines had been handling the weapon in their hooch on the night the murder occurred.

The marines had been approached by a Sgt. James W. Killen, who asked to borrow the weapon. In later testimony, Killen explained that he had wanted the weapon to shoot feral dogs, but he had found none and had returned the weapon to the marines' hooch.

When interrogated, the two marines alleged to have loaned the weapon to Killen, said that the sergeant had returned to their hooch right after the shooting. The two asked Killen why he had "done something like that". Killen had replied, "She was just winged."

As the Marine Corps prepared their case against Killen, NIS sent leads to Camp Lejeune North Carolina, the sergeant's previous duty station. The lead sheet asked if agents there could find anything out about a man who had apparently killed a woman unknown to him without any clear motive.

Their report came back while Killen sat awaiting his court-martial in the III MAF brig near the scene of the murder. It did not provide legal staff with additional ammunition for the upcoming trial, but it did contain disturbing indications that Killen had been involved in the murder of his late wife.

Killen was convicted of murdering Miss Warnes, but a motive for the shooting was never developed. He would be released from custody in 1971 after receiving a retrial in the United States. His enlistment had expired in 1969, and upon his release the well-decorated Killen was immediately discharged from the U.S. Marine Corps. He had served exactly two years and nine days for the murder.

*****

Fragmentation grenades were respected and feared by all who used them. The small M26 "frag" packed a huge wallop. Its high-explosive charge was wrapped by strands of serrated stainless-steel wire. The wire fragments traveled at several thousand feet per second upon detonation, and provided a kill radius of about fifteen meters. It was an effective weapon when deployed properly.
At Chu Lai, marines from the Seventh Engineer Battalion shared the responsibility with other organic units for guarding the base perimeter defenses.

[153]

Although later in the war grenades would be taken out of circulation in many units, in 1969 they were still being issued to sentries. Late one evening a sentry completed his watch on the perimeter and began his walk back across the bases' white sands. As he approached his hooch, he could hear what sounded like a card game going on without him. This seemed like an excellent opportunity for a practical joke.

He turned back and walked some distance away from the hooch. Taking a grenade from his pouch, he unscrewed the detonator assembly from the body. (The assembly incorporates the fuse, cap, and detonator that together initiate the grenade's main explosive charge). Without the main charge, the explosive force of the assembly is roughly equal to a blasting cap used to initiate commercial dynamite.

He pulled the pin on the assembly and carefully covered the fuse and detonator with a nearby sandbag to muffle its sound and explosive force. He then reassembled the grenade without the internal detonator. The grenade was now inert, but that would not be obvious.

With his grenade in hand the marine entered the hooch, pulled the pin, and placed the device in the middle of the table. The card players didn't wait for an explanation; they bolted in every direction, including through the fly-screens. Pleased with the reaction and hysterical with laughter, the perpetrator retrieved the grenade and walked out to find his buddies. With another dummy grenade reassembled to look and act like a live one, the jokester returned to the poker game and tried his trick a second time. But the card players didn't scatter, and seconds later there was a shattering explosion. Two marines were killed instantly and the rest were seriously injured, among them the jokester.

At the scene, agents carefully checked the perpetrators equipment. They discovered the deactivated grenade that he had used in the first ruse amongst other live grenades. It was pretty obvious that he had grabbed the wrong grenade for his second practical joke. The location where the first detonator had been harmlessly exploded under the sandbag was soon found, along with other evidence supporting what the few witnesses capable of speaking had said.

[154]

The marines in this incident had injuries so severe that they required medical evacuation from Vietnam, and were flown to the U.S. Naval Hospital at Yokosuka, Japan, for treatment.

The postmortem examination of those killed was conducted at Naval Support Activity Da Nang Hospital. The cause of death was confirmed to have been from tiny particles of stainless steel traveling at supersonic speeds, penetrating vital organs. NISRA Yokosuka agents interrogated the "grenadier" when his condition had sufficiently improved. He confirmed that he had made a deadly mistake. Manslaughter charges against him were prepared.

Old hands were occasionally heard to comment, "There are so many ways to die in Vietnam." This was a true statement that could not be refuted. Not only were there many ways to die, but many of these fell into non-glorious categories like "being stupid" or "stupid accidents."

Nobody wanted to go home in a body bag after being run over, killed by careless weapons handling, overdosing on drugs or being killed by a practical joke.

*****

The entire city of Da Nang and its outskirts were off-limits to all military personnel. Driving through the city required an authorization and once underway, stopping was not allowed. These rules made a marine's search for narcotics, contraband, and sexual favors slightly more difficult, but certainly not impossible.

Vietnamese entrepreneurs were well aware of the rules and were skilled at flaunting them if it meant improving their business with the Americans. Outside the perimeter of Hill 327 and the First Marine Division area, the shantytown called Dogpatch thrived, providing vice-of-choice options for those driving through. At several important intersections, arterials from vital tactical areas joined others. These locations saw plenty of traffic from the field, and Vietnamese hustlers and prostitutes waited.

On the southwest edge of Da Nang, one such intersection was the

[155]

exclusive domain of a ten-year-old pimp and general trader known to all as Charlie. Wiry, wily and streetwise, Charlie spoke passable English and knew how to bargain with his American clients whatever the requirement. His girls were certainly not known for their beauty, and had been imported from paddy fields far away. None of the girls spoke English, and Charlie attired his stable in black peasant pajamas, cotton blouses, and the Vietnamese peasant conical straw hat. Lipstick, rouge, and eyeliner were liberally applied in an attempt to cover a multitude of defects.

Into this domain a marine and his SeaBee buddy entered late one afternoon, after enjoying several hours of drinking at an enlisted men's club. They wanted a woman, and Charlie quickly concluded arrangements for them to share one of his girls. He took their money, and pointed out a small thatched hut away from the road where the woman was waiting. They entered the hut, and Charlie pulled a dirty curtain back across the doorway.

"Dogpatch"

The facilities were pretty basic; in fact the bed was actually a pile of discarded shipping pallets that elevated a sleeping mat from the muddy dirt floor. Having received instructions from Charlie in Vietnamese, the prostitute shed her trousers and hopped up on her "bed."

This triggered a lively discussion between the marine and the

[156]

SeaBee about who was going first. To emphasize his position on this, the marine un-holstered his .45-caliber pistol and waved it at his buddy.

The weapon unexpectedly fired, the bullet striking the SeaBee several inches below his armpit. His last words were, "You shot me, you bastard."

The U.S. model 1911 pistol had been in service for many years, and the chunky .45-caliber bullet was renowned for its knockdown lethality. In this instance, the projectile struck lobes of both the victim's lungs and ruptured his aorta before bouncing off ribs and lodging under a scapula. His death was nearly instantaneous.

His ardor now cooled by the incident, the shooter was soon in military police custody, and NIS would follow up with a thorough investigation. The accused claimed the shooting was accidental. Senseless might have been a more suitable adjective. An agent was heard to say, "Who's going to try to explain this one to the victim's mother?"

*****

NISRA Da Nang investigations did not always illustrate our investigative talents in the best light. This was certainly the case of the mysterious and obscene phone calls that were made to the nurses' quarters at the NSA hospital.

It would not be entirely correct to say that Da Nang's Navy nurses lived in a cloistered environment, but it was certainly cosseted. Like just about everybody else in-country, the nurses worked long shifts, and they worked virtually every day.

A nurse commander was in charge, and all nurses were housed together in a secure area within the NSA Hospital. They were surrounded not just in the hospital but in the geographic region, by men desperate for even a look at a real Western woman…even if she was an officer.

[157]

Marine officers stationed across the road at Marble Mountain Air Facility paid careful attention to nurses whenever an opportunity presented itself. Navy nurses did not want for attention…though some of it was unwelcome.

When nurses started receiving obscene late-evening phone calls at their quarters, their commander took the complaint directly to SRA Don McCoy. I inherited the case from him, and was frankly not particularly enchanted with the prospect of spending days identifying this perpetrator, especially given the seriousness of the rest of our caseload at NISRA Da Nang.

Special Agent Mike Quinn, a lieutenant junior grade who had been agent trained, was assigned to assist me. We began our inquiries at the nurses' quarters, where it was confirmed that nurses were getting calls featuring heavy breathing and suggestive comments. From there, we visited the Navy's telephone exchange on Tien Sa Peninsula and spoke with the duty chief about our problem.

He told us that, because the calls were being made at night, the exchange could monitor the nurses' quarters phone line. He was confident the calls were originating from within the area serviced by the exchange…because otherwise, an operator would be involved in connecting the calls. He agreed to call us and report about the activity on the line.

Two days later he did call our office, and Mike and I drove across the river to see him. "What have you got for us, Chief?" I asked as we walked into the exchange.

"Some real popular ladies in those nurses' quarters he replied."
"I can just imagine," I replied. "You got a heavy breather too?"
The chief acknowledged such a call had been placed the night previously; he had traced the call to a barracks telephone at First Light Antiaircraft Missile (LAAM) Battalion on Monkey Mountain.

This was a marine antiaircraft missile battalion positioned on the mountaintop from which they could best defend Da Nang from an enemy airborne attack. The LAAM marines had been there on standby since 1965. I could readily imagine idle minds were finding ways to create mischief.

[158]

It was time to tell the battalion battery commander he had a problem. Quinn and I returned to our quarters at 23 Doc Lap Street and there changed into camouflage utilities. Quinn put on the silver bars of a lieutenant junior grade, and I borrowed brown ensign insignia. We reasoned that we would attract far less attention at the marine outpost if we wore utilities rather than civvies.

Monkey Mountain is a conical mass situated at the northern end of the sandy Tien Sa Peninsula, a natural position both for navigation aids and antiaircraft defenses. A narrow, winding road had been built to its crest, and the drive up the road was spectacular. Below in Da Nang Harbor perhaps a dozen ships rode at anchor.

Beyond, behind the beach, the air base swarmed with all types of aircraft: helicopters, cargo aircraft, and bomb-laden fighters blazing off on their missions. Behind the sprawling town rose the Annamite Mountains and Hai Van Pass's northern blockade. Where the road finally leveled out at the top, the tail plane of a crashed Navy A4 protruded from the hillside immediately below. Stenciled across the bent fuselage were the letters, FUBAR. Quinn told me that in Navy parlance this meant "fucked up beyond all repair." I had to agree.

First LAAM had very well-established positions on the mountain crest, extending down the southern side. Barracks, messing facilities, and offices were comfortable by Marine standards and the defensive positions were carefully maintained with fresh sandbags. The barracks in which the offending telephone was located was a two-story timber-frame structure built on the very steep hillside below the administration area. A timber ladder way connected the barracks and the administration building.

We reasoned that our only possible hope for apprehending the culprits was staking the barracks out and having the telephone exchange communicate with us when the barracks phone was used to call the nurse's quarters.

The command was anxious to assist. They suggested we use a small office near the head of stairs leading down to the barracks area. This would provide us with a place in which to conceal ourselves; it had an operating telephone and was reasonably near to the barracks phone.

[159]

It looked fine to us. We said we'd plan to come back the next night. The following night we were back, concealed in the office and confident we had gained entry unseen. Everything seemed normal. It was one of those spectacularly clear nights that offered unobstructed views of the entire Da Nang area below.

Even the paddy fields to the south of the city were visible, where we could see a continuous display of pyrotechnics. At least twelve illumination flares were in the air at any one time. The afterburners of aircraft taking off on bombing missions carved blazing arcs from the air base and across the harbor waters. We could even see artillery missions being fired outward into Indian country.

First LAAM at Monkey Mountain, DaNang

Somewhere out there, marines were skirmishing with the enemy. Up on Monkey Mountain, life was far more peaceful than below. But relative peace notwithstanding, the marines lodged here were marines after all, and were not of a pacific nature.

Unfortunately for us, the LAAM decided to have a stand-to, a base defense exercise, on the night of our operation. Quinn and I heard orders being shouted and the heavy tread of men in boots running on the double. We crouched low in the office to avoid being seen in

[160]

case of illuminations. Then somebody threw a CS teargas grenade and the air conditioner began sucking in the gaseous fumes before we were able to shut it off. It became increasingly difficult to find untainted air to breathe and we were both very uncomfortable while we waited for it to dissipate.

Later the office phone rang, and the telephone exchange announced that our quarry was at that very moment doing heavy-breathing exercises for one of the nurses at the hospital. Quinn and I dropped the receiver and ran out the door and down the long ladder way to the barracks.

Ours was not a covert approach, and we were both wheezing from the effects of CS gas. The timber stair treads drummed out each of our footfalls as we proceeded down the stairs. When we burst into the barracks, the phone was not in use. Those in the squad bay feigned sleep or acted as if nothing had happened.

With the assistance of a senior NCO, we noted who was present. But we knew we had blown our chance to catch the caller in the act. I briefed command about the events of the evening. "I think we might be able to manage this," I was told.

Seeing the glint in the top sergeant's eyes as he listened to his CO, I was confident that the problem would be solved very quickly and effectively, and it was. The nurses never got another obscene phone call, or at least none that they chose to complain about. Neither Mike Quinn nor I was happy about how the case was resolved but we did manage to rationalize that we had achieved the desired result even though disaster had never seemed far away in the process.

*****

A short ferry ride across the Han from the White Elephant, III Marine Amphibious Force headquarters was housed in a picturesque former French Army compound. It was a pleasant spot when compared to other areas under U.S. military control. There were trees and even some lawn, undoubtedly a legacy of the Gallic generals who made it their home in the 1950s.

[161]

III MAF was home to the senior Marine general in Vietnam, normally a lieutenant general. Names like Lew Walt and Herman Nickerson are synonymous with the command, which included two operational divisions and logistic support. The control of the First Marine Division, defending Da Nang and points south, and the Third Marine Division positioned along the DMZ originated from here.

It was a site of many high-level briefings and conferences, and III MAF had an important intelligence component that provided information of a most sensitive nature to commanders making critical decisions about the conduct of the war. Some of that information originated from radio intercepts and other electronic warfare initiatives. These had always been the most closely guarded of secrets.

The guardian of communication intelligence for the Department of the Navy is the Naval Security Group. A close-knit body of highly proficient cryptographers and analysts, the NSG has a proud history that began in the early days of World War II when a Pearl Harbor office headed by Cdr. Joseph Rochefort broke Japanese naval codes. Their success enabled Admirals Chester Nimitz and Raymond Spruance to formulate an audacious operation plan that resulted in a defeat for the Imperial Japanese Navy at the Battle of Midway, from which the Japanese never recovered.

Much of the role of NSG in Vietnam remains classified, but we may assume that their contribution was an important one. Nothing much has ever been said about its presence at III MAF either, but it certainly was represented there.

In early 1970 a senior Marine Corps NCO working at the Army Security Agency facility at Phu Bai boarded a twin-rotor Marine CH46 helicopter for the hop south to Da Nang. In violation of security regulations governing such things, he carried extremely sensitive top-secret documents intended for III MAF. Neither the master sergeant nor his documents would make it to Da Nang. The ASA station at Phu Bai just south of the old imperial city of Hue, was a highly secure facility that carried out a range of electronic intelligence activities. Massive radio towers and high fences marked the station, but little was known about what occurred

[162]

within. With their personnel and the classified documents now unaccounted for, concerned marines launched a search for the missing aircraft.

Central coastal Vietnam is largely sandy and flat countryside. Farther inland, the Annamite Cordillera rises suddenly from the flats and paddy fields where it forms a formidable mountain barrier. Often shrouded in clouds and mist, the mountains present a serious hazard to unwary aviators, and for this reason flights from the Marine Air Group at Phu Bai normally steered a course close to the coastline and at an elevation sufficient to avoid ground fire. The only real danger point between Phu Bai and Da Nang was Hai Van Pass, north of the city but within view of the airport. Here the Annamites crowded eastward to the ocean, creating a natural barrier. It was in these mountains, that the marines began their search.

III MAF alerted First Marine Division operational staff to the possibility that the missing helicopter could have come to some grief in the Hai Van area.

As it so happened, a marine rifle platoon was in that area patrolling the pass. Hai Van had been a long time favorite location for ambushes, and it was prudent practice to aggressively patrol the ridges above the road to keep the enemy off-balance when possible. Alert marine infantry were the first to discover the crash site but the darkness mists and rain halted aircraft-borne rescuers. The grunts reported no survivors, as the chopper appeared to have impacted head on at full speed into the steep slope.

Potentially serious security implications surrounded the disposition of those top-secret documents aboard the crashed aircraft. Most important were the questions…Had the contents of the documents been compromised, and who had actually viewed them?

NISRA Da Nang SRA Don McCoy had clearance to read documents of this special classification on a need-to-know basis. Because this was clearly a NIS investigation, McCoy elected to undertake it personally, with my assistance.

McCoy and I rendezvoused to meet a CH46 that was piloted by the

[163]

squadron CO. He would personally oversee efforts to recover bodies and to investigate the crash of his aircraft. Loaded aboard the helicopter with their gear was a team of marines from First Marine Air Wing; experts in aircraft crash recovery operations.

The takeoff from Da Nang was routine. It had been raining, but the ceiling was reasonable in the low areas. The chopper made its way around the seaward side of Hai Van to the north where a distinct, heavy cloud ceiling surrounded the slopes as they reached their upper elevations.

The recovery crew was a cheerful group led by a sergeant named Brown who was in country on his second tour, having done his first as a grunt with a rifle platoon. Brown was equipped to make the first descent into the site once it was located. Bedecked in goggles, combat webbing and carrying a PRC25 radio on his back and an M79 grenade launcher in one hand, he smoked with his free hand and joked with his crew.

Don McCoy did not like to fly. He stoically endured the first minutes of the flight, strapped into his Spartan sling seat, chain smoking while he considered how the day might yet unfold. The pilot followed a bearing up the mountain slope, staying just feet below the cloud ceiling as it slowly receded upward.

Finally the "bird" hovered motionless over the jungle and below us the clouds unexpectedly cleared revealing the crash site. The pilots eased the chopper forward, hovering over the marine platoon amidst the wreckage below.

Wash from the huge double rotors overhead blew leaves, branches, and helmets from the men crouching in the jungle below, further revealing the compacted wreck, which had "accordioned" into a mass less than a quarter of its original length.

What identified the wreckage was the distinctive rear ramp and wheels, now facing skyward. Expecting the rescue crew that would assist them, marines below cleared material from atop a huge boulder immediately below the crash site, a logical landing point for the men who would be descending from above. Other marines formed an outward perimeter.

The platoon commander soon reported by radio that all bodies had been located with the exception of the two pilots, and that several had been removed. Perhaps most importantly, the master sergeant and his briefcase full of documents were there.

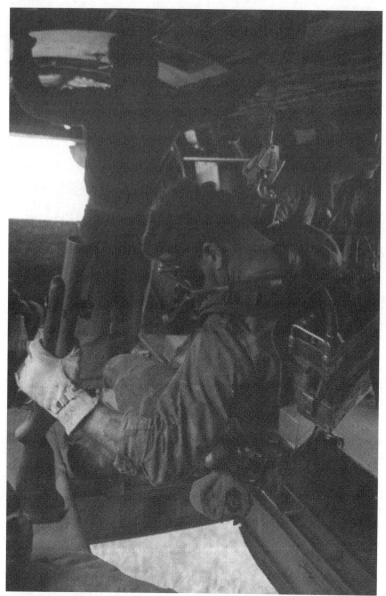

Through the "Hell Hole"

The Boeing Vertol CH46 Sea Knight is equipped with a floor hatch amidships called the "hellhole" by marines. This enables men and material to be winched in and out via a ceiling-mounted apparatus. Sergeant Brown scrambled onto the waiting jungle penetrator, (a

[166]

metal pod with folding legs that form a seat), and began his descent through the hell hole. The crew chief urged him to hurry because of worsening weather. Sergeant Brown dropped down, swinging in the wash and trying to target the large boulder.

Reaching it, marines grabbed him off the penetrator and the crew chief reeled the cable back into his winch as fast as he could to send a second marine down.

The CH-46

The weather was worsening. With the recovery team off and the penetrator back aboard, the pilots withdrew down the slope to stay under gathering clouds. Don McCoy and I had a quick conference about possible courses of action. I said I would go next, would recover the documents, and carry out the necessary interviews. Thinking for a moment, McCoy reluctantly agreed. It was unlikely that we would both get to the ground and far more unlikely that a ride off the mountain would be forthcoming in any case.

With that settled, we talked about new developments on the ground. It appeared that the platoon commander had seen the secret documents to confirm their existence, but that others had not.

Platoon commanders do not often have top secret clearances, and this one was no exception. Don McCoy smiled upon hearing this, saying, "The lieutenant is a lucky boy. He's just spent his last night in the bush, and I'd guess will soon be winging his way far to the rear where they can keep a close eye on him."

Twenty harrowing minutes passed without the cloud ceiling retreating. I sat with my gear zipped and buckled waiting to make my hurried descent, but it wouldn't happen. Low on fuel, the aircraft returned to Da Nang.

By the time it got back and was refueled, the worsening weather dictated against a second attempt. Back on the slopes of Hai Van Pass, a cheerful young marine lieutenant was packing his gear for a walk out and pick up with thoughts of hot chow, a clean rack, and cold beer on his mind. The investigation would have to be carried out from a different perspective.

Battered but intact, the papers that had sparked so much angst and concern were returned to the crypto facility at III MAF amidst sighs of relief. There was no indication that they had been compromised during the short period that they were out of Marine control. The young marine platoon commander was abruptly transferred to Okinawa and out of harm's way. McCoy and I finished up the investigation with an uneventful trip to the ASA station in Phu Bai to verify additional leads, and the case was then closed.

*****

8   THE NORTH, 1969 TO 1970: STREET WITHOUT JOY

When an international conference at Geneva divided Vietnam along the eighteenth parallel in 1954, what was formerly central Vietnam became the far north of the new Republic of Vietnam and a DMZ became the republic's northern boundary.

At the Ben Hai River Bridge where Route 1 and the railway to Hanoi crossed, communist northerners of the Democratic Republic of Vietnam faced off with their southern brothers and awaited elections that they were certain would amalgamate the entire country together as a communist state.

The elections never came… the South Vietnamese and their Western supporters believed the communists would use intimidation and other nondemocratic tactics reminiscent of the days following World War II, when the Soviet Union swallowed up Eastern Europe.

Until the DMZ was created, the country from which it was formed had been of little account to anyone but the peasants who lived on the lowlands and the tribal Montagnards inhabiting the high country.

Here the South China Sea swept onto miles of white sandy beach on both sides of the boundary, providing a source of livelihood for scattered villages of fishermen. Agriculture was difficult in most areas of the flat, sandy, and largely infertile plain that extended westward from the sea. In the hills and mountains of the Annamite Cordelera, hill tribes practiced slash-and-burn agriculture and kept largely to themselves. The Vietnamese had never been popular with Montagnard people.

The creation of a new border did nothing to change the fact that the country south of the DMZ from Quang Tri to Hue had been hardcore communist since the early 1950s. In fact, French soldiers had christened Route 1 "Street Without Joy" and with good reason. Black pajama-clad troops had sprung a series of highly successful ambushes from fortified villages along this route, causing heavy casualties amongst the French convoys.

The 1965 buildup of communist forces, which had so alarmed U.S. officials in the South, consisted of ever-increasing numbers of NVA regulars marching from their northern homeland down the Ho Chi Minh Trail. Communist leaders were confident enough to formulate a strategy that called for NVA units to draw U.S. troops into conventional battle and then inflict maximum casualties. In fact the U.S. Army in the autumn of that year faced an overwhelming

[169]

communist force at Ia Drang in the Central Highlands and beat them back into nearby Laos after fierce fighting.

The commander of MACV, Gen. William Westmoreland, was watching developments in the north closely. He believed Hue to be an irresistible target for communist planners desiring control of the old imperial city that symbolized Vietnamese unity to them. Tentacles of the Ho Chi Minh Trail extended into remote valleys in the area, supplying the means for large-unit buildup. In early 1966 the Special Forces camp in the Ashau Valley, just inland from Hue, was overrun by an enemy force comprised of at least a reinforced regiment. The surviving Montagnard irregulars and American Special Forces soldiers fought running, rear-guard actions until Marine helicopters based near Hue at Phu Bai managed to rescue the fortunate ones. This was the blatant evidence that corroborated ongoing intelligence collection in the region. The buildup of Marine forces, centered on their positions at Hue/ Phu Bai, began shortly afterward.

Although northern I Corps was assigned important U.S. Army combat elements, and was home to some of the better ARVN commands, the DMZ and points south were "Marine territory" until the end of 1969. In that three-year period, marines carried out ongoing major operations against the NVA along the DMZ and established firebases in critical areas. The marines fought the NVA and VC at Hue, and with the ARVN and US 101st Airborne drove them from the city during the 1968 Tet Offensive. They also fought a very successful campaign in the west, which culminated in the Siege of Khe Sanh. Third Marine Division headquarters ultimately moved from Phu Bai north to Dong Ha, well within enemy artillery range, and would remain there.

In these difficult and fluid conditions, NIS had a continuing responsibility to the Navy Department as well as all Marine commands needing investigative support. Until 1969 contact with northern commands and their marines was accomplished by agents doing circuits through key installations. Investigative and other lead requests forwarded to Viet Nam by NIS components around the world as well as from other federal agencies found their way to the senior resident agent's desk in Da Nang.

[170]

From Da Nang they were farmed out to the appropriate traveling agents for action. Typically when an agent was assigned a case, he would visit the Marine field element in question to brief the command and then would proceed to carry out his investigations to satisfy the requests contained in the lead. Investigating leads comprised the majority of the caseload handled by agents traveling in the far north. Requests for investigative assistance in very serious incidents also required a quick response of course, and very often became long complex investigations that were started from scratch.

The process of getting to an active combat component could prove very challenging. The agents who did this kind of "front element" work were all volunteers, as some agents would not work in the difficult field environment outside the Da Nang command headquarters. Others were just not suited for the work.

Perhaps one of the most important skills maintained by a bush agent was the comprehensive grasp of which command elements were located where, what transportation would likely be available to get him to them, and where to find that transportation.

The Marine Corps had its own fleet of C130 transports, and these with supplement from Air Force aircraft, regularly operated from Da Nang to the airports at Phu Bai and Dong Ha. So air transport was sometimes an option, weather and the enemy situation permitting.

Marine Roughrider armed convoys left Da Nang regularly for the more difficult and often dangerous trips over the ambush-vulnerable Hai Van Pass to Phu Bai. Navy and Coast Guard patrol and logistic craft plied the waters of the north, and there were the even less predictable helicopter flights from Da Nang for those who knew the ropes.

The good operators planned their work around rides they knew they could find and quickly shoved off. Typically once underway, nobody heard from them again until they turned up a week or so later. They would be tired and in need of a ride to the billet from an airport or helipad somewhere near Da Nang. In their gear would be sheafs of lead sheets and reports, most completed already, hopefully.

On the ground at forward areas, Marine counterintelligence teams often provided support to agents who turned up needing transportation, hot chow, and a place to sleep. The cordial professional relationship engendered in Vietnam between NIS and counterintelligence teams continues to this day in naval commands around the world.

There were certainly dangers present throughout these trips for the traveling agents. Enemy rocket and mortar attacks were commonplace, and it was not unusual to hear the distinctive "crack-thump" of a bullet travelling uncomfortably close. All of the traveling agents understood and accepted these risks, and they were certainly minor when compared with the daily existence of the young Marine riflemen with whom they had daily contact.

An additional danger that worried every agent who ventured out into the ever-fluid tactical world of the Vietnamese countryside was the danger of capture.

All special agents carried leather-bound credentials printed at the U.S. Mint, identifying them with a photograph and a unique number. These credentials were necessary for most official contacts and every interview. For agents on duty in Vietnam, an alternative top leaf was printed without the words "naval intelligence", and their originals were stored in a Saigon safe with the issued badge until the agent's tour of duty in Vietnam was completed.

None thought this would make very much difference if the worst happened, especially carrying a sheaf of cases and leads in their bag and a Vietnamese identity card that identified them as an agent of military intelligence. Agents thought carefully about where they took the Vietnamese identification since it was useful when dealing with difficult ARVN soldiers at roadblocks.

Fortunately, no member of the NIS command was ever captured. But credentials were lost in forward areas. An incident of this type normally sparked a detailed investigation because presentation of credentials constitutes legal authority for access to highly classified information (on a need-to-know basis, of course).

Allowances were made for the difficult working environment, but nobody at headquarters ever devised an effective means for quickly disposing of credentials in the field.

In mid-1969 NISOV directed that satellite units be established in two areas serviced by the Da Nang field office. To the south, NISSU Chu Lai was set up at the naval facility there. NISSU Quang Tri Combat Base would be accommodated by a construction battalion maintenance unit, CBMU 301, directly opposite the Quang Tri Airstrip.

With this, agent rounds men became redundant in the north. The lone agent assigned to Quang Tri was supplied with a radio-equipped jeep and an office in the plywood SEA-hut headquarters building. It had a telephone that could be patched through via a myriad of bored signalman-switchboard operators to the various major command components.

The establishment of NISSU Quang Tri was a response to a combination of factors. The first was a growing number of caseloads and the second was a desire by the command to establish a permanent presence near Third Marine Division, so that an agent could be available with a quick "serious incident" presence. The Marines had a CID section that handled misdemeanors and occasionally more serious cases, but NIS rationalized that there was less risk of legally jeopardizing a critical case if a special agent could respond immediately.

A growing caseload was symptomatic of the rot that was setting in to most U.S. commands in Vietnam. This grew alarmingly over the years until the last troops withdrew in 1972. The incidence of felonies, fraggings in particular, was rising throughout NISRA Da Nang jurisdiction, and narcotics violations became an increasing burden as well.

For an outfit of some twenty thousand men, the Third Marine Division, whose area of operation included most of northern I Corps, ran a tight ship. They were a fighting outfit, and to a large extent the field marines looked after themselves. Certainly, they were not the problem for NIS that they might have been without strong internal leadership.
Quang Tri as an established small city had sprawled along the south

bank of the Thach Han River for probably two hundred years.

South Vietnamese colors flew over provincial headquarters buildings previously built by French colonizers. The city had a railway station, (though it was no longer functioning), markets, schools and gardens. It was an important commercial center which had adapted to its war footing.

A few advisers were stationed in Quang Tri City, but the majority of U.S. contingents were in cantonments on the north of the river, connected by a fine old railway bridge with a French engineer's plaque on it inscribed with the name "Eiffel".

Quang Tri Combat Base was the antithesis of the old city across the river. It had been hastily constructed in 1967 on land between the inoperative Saigon-Hanoi railway line and the meandering river.

A U.S. Marine Air Group with utility and medium helicopters occupied the revetments of the airstrip, and other Marine units had rear-area administration housed in plywood SEA huts. Opposite the airstrip were two cantonments housing SeaBees: these were CBMU 301 and slightly north, a camp used by rotating SeaBee battalions. Westward were U.S. Army elements, including a medical evacuation hospital adjacent the SeaBees.

This supplemented the U.S. Navy's Third Med, a full-sized hospital situated to service the Third Marine Division. When further medical help was needed, hospital ships were never far away.

Quang Tri was a large base area, surrounded by wire and defensive works to protect its inhabitants from an active enemy. Roads were oiled to keep down dust, but it was always hot and dusty except when it was raining or bracing for the next typhoon. Over it all hung a pall of burnt fuel from the numerous vehicles, and of course the unforgettable odor of burning waste from the latrines.

"Shitters" were a feature of life in remote military cantonments. Waste was collected in drums, doused with diesel fuel, and burned each day. No one who ever served in Vietnam will ever forget the stench. "Not a garden spot" was an apt description, but conditions at Quang Tri were still far better than those endured by field marines living on firebases or in the bush.

Special Agent John Schlictman opened NISSU Quang Tri in 1969. He was an experienced agent who had volunteered for Vietnam duty from NISRA while in Jacksonville, Florida. A World War II veteran with twenty years of service in the U.S. Army CIC, John had retired as a warrant officer polygraph operator. He was the logical choice for SRA Don McCoy to send north.

Standing six feet six inches tall, Schlictman stood out in a crowd. He was well liked by his SeaBee hosts in the battalion wardroom where the commanding officer gathered his officers at the dining table. The wardroom was an oasis of sanity at Quang Tri Combat Base.

Showing the effects of recent storm damage, the NISSU Quang Tri Combat Base office was a typical SEA hut constructed of plywood. Special Agent John Schlictman was the first agent assigned to the satellite unit

Constructed of windowless eight-inch reinforced concrete walls, the air-conditioned building was impervious to all but direct hits, and it boasted the only flushing toilet in northern I Corps, table linen, and service by Navy stewards. Schlictman quickly learned the ropes, unit deployments, and other useful information.
Special Agent L. A. Gonzales, a former Marine infantry captain,

and I frequently assisted Schlictman. He organized a small office in CBMU 301's headquarters SEA hut which contained two desks, a small filing cabinet, a wall locker, fan – and manual typewriter. An old Vietnamese woman agreed to come daily on her rounds of headquarters to sweep accumulated sand off the plywood deck.

Agents bunked in a SEA hut at the end of the CBMU street with two SeaBee officers. By local standards it was very comfortable, with an internal shower urinal and sink. A private "two-holer" was nearby.

Because the SeaBees operated a large asphalt production plant in the base, they had an ample supply of the empty fifty-five-gallon tar drums that could be filled with sand and stood on end around the hut walls for shrapnel protection. A telephone equipped bunker for protection during rocket and mortar attacks stood a few feet away from the front door.

Most of the caseload was lead requests, most often other NIS offices asking that persons or specific information be gathered for them. Schlictman quickly learned his way around the headquarters elements at Quang Tri and at Dong Ha Combat Base ten miles to the north.

Dong Ha Combat Base housed the Third Marine Division and SeaBee brigade headquarters. Other than several forward fire bases in very hostile country, Dong Ha was the last stop before the DMZ and was within range of the NVA's hidden 130mm Soviet field guns to the north.

Working cases had become less time consuming because NISSU Quang Tri had its own new M151 jeep. For the first time, agents had the flexibility of a radio-equipped vehicle, which was serviced weekly by CBMU 301 's mechanics.

The drive from Quang Tri north to Dong Ha would take only a few minutes, but it entailed a stop at the MP checkpoint on the perimeter edge, where travel documents were checked and a quick inspection was made to ensure that flak jackets were being worn and suitable firearms carried. A radio check with either MPs or the SeaBee command post would ensure communications were available if the

[176]

worst happened out on the Street Without Joy.

A narrow two lanes, Route 1 had been widened and improved by successive deployments of road building SeaBees, who worked twelve-hour days, seven days a week, during their eight-month tours of duty.

Ammunition always at the ready, Marine artillerymen move along Route 9 below Dong Ha Mountain

Agents shared the road with tanks, ammunition trucks, and huge tractor trailers hauling armor, as well as military and civilian Vietnamese driving everything from trucks to bicycles. Accidents were a regular occurrence. When they happened, traffic stopped and drivers began to feel vulnerable.

The small arms NIS special agents carried in the north varied depending on preference and individual weapons handling abilities. They were issued the Smith and Wesson Model 19 Combat Magnum in .357 magnum caliber, but 9mm Smith and Wessons and short-barreled models were used too; it depended on circumstances. For travel in an open jeep in northern I Corps, 40mm M79 grenade launchers, .45-caliber Thompson submachine guns, and M16s were all carried.

As leads began to take Schlictman, Gonzales, and me farther

[177]

westward from Dong Ha on Route 9, the jeep took on a load of sandbags over the floorboards. This was a largely defensive step, meant to offer a degree of protection from mines. Soon after we started carrying in extra sandbags, a Marine artillery officer at Cam Lo related to agents how an ARVN officer traveling by jeep from Cam Lo toward Con Thien had recently come to grief with a VC command-detonated road mine fabricated from a U.S. 750 pound aerial bomb. "All we found was part of his spare tire. But don't worry, if you run over something that stuff on the floor will make sure you've got sand-blasted assholes." Reassurance.

The Quang Tri agents began driving to and from Cam Lo after receiving vague complaints of alleged "war atrocities." The specifics were not available, but early investigations revealed that certain SeaBees had apparently mutilated enemy dead killed by mines, then had taken photographs while posing with the corpses.

The men were part of a small detachment operating a gravel pit for road building on the banks of the Cam Lo River immediately north of Route 9. This area known as Leatherneck Square by the marines, had been the scene of large and vicious battles with the North Vietnamese Army since 1966. It was within easy range of the DMZ and NVA artillery and had seen many battalion-sized incursions by them.

The gravel pit was located at the river. It was overlooked by sharply rising hills and was largely denuded of vegetation. It was not an easy place to defend.

Bunkers had been erected at key points, where the men took turns manning .50-caliber machine guns and small arms while the others excavated and processed the gravel. Leatherneck Square was really indefensible against anything but a small-unit attack.

At a gun pit overlooking a quarry site north of Cam Lo, Special Agent L.A. Gonzales interviews a SeaBee

As their defense against artillery, the men were all billeted back at Cam Lo in large bunkers many feet underground. Interviews there implicated several men in the alleged mutilation, but also revealed that rations and other supplies were being traded away to local Vietnamese for a variety of favors including sexual ones.

This was a matter that the command itself could handle much better without NIS involvement. Ultimately we surrendered the case to them, as it involved difficult questions about the ethics of looking after homeless children in the fluidity of a war zone.

Nobody was available to feed them, even when their older sisters imparted favors to lonely sailors in return for the necessities of life.

*****

Special Agent John Schlictman administers an oath to a SeaBee witness. They are twelve feet underground in a bunker constructed as protection against enemy artillery from the DMZ

In July 1969, when John Schlictman's tour of duty was nearing its end, SRA Don McCoy assigned me to operate NISSU Quang Tri.

In my second year of service with NIS and with fewer than six months in Vietnam, I considered it a daunting prospect to be charged with the responsibility of a one man post a long way from the advice and support of more experienced agents.

Before leaving Quang Tri, Schlictman had begun an investigative lead that originated at NISSU Hong Kong, a referral from the Royal Hong Kong Police who believed a senior Marine NCO was using Fleet Post Office facilities illegally. The gunnery sergeant's activities might also have had security implications, depending on his level of access to classified material, which was unknown at that time. Schlictman explained to me that liaison had been established with the division postal officer in Dong Ha. It would be necessary to first visit the subject's command and take the investigation forward from there.

I carefully studied existing reports from Schlictman's first solo investigation at NISSU Quang Tri, which was based on criminal intelligence provided by Royal Hong Kong Police sources. The subject of the investigation had, while in Hong Kong on leave,

[180]

caused people to believe he was shipping contraband using the facilities of the Fleet Post Office at the China Fleet Club.

And sources implied he was using his military postal address in Vietnam to run an illegal commercial enterprise.

In Dong Ha, I interviewed the Marine postal officer. A watch had been kept for parcels addressed to the suspect who was assigned to the Fourth Marines operating out of Vandegrift Combat Base. The postal officer was uncertain however as to how effective their watch had been. He felt that a parcel mailed from Hong Kong might have already passed forward into the mail system. It would then become necessary to track and intercept the package as it was being delivered.

In 1969 Vandegrift was the easternmost base of the Third Marine Division. Established near a small crossroads close to Ca Lu, it supported ongoing combat operations against the North Vietnamese Army in the rugged mountains near the Laotian border. Situated in a basin and surrounded by mountains, it was the location of various battalion headquarters, and of artillery and logistics. Only fourteen miles from Khe Sanh, which was abandoned at the time, its presence was designed to keep the NVA off-balance in northwest I Corps.

I caught a ride from Dong Ha aboard a Marine CH34D helicopter and flew westward over Route 9, the highway that once led from the South China Sea across Vietnam and Laos and on to Thailand at the Mekong River.

The two Marine first lieutenants who were piloting had flown the route countless times and brightened things up on an otherwise uneventful trip by buzzing a Marine jeep. This was accomplished at an altitude low enough to make the vehicle's canvas top billow out like a yacht spinnaker and to cause its driver momentary panic. The sergeant crew chief, manning his M60 machine gun at the doorway, smiled and shook his head...crazy pilots!

[181]

Looking westward along Route 9, the road to Vandegrift Combat Base, Khe Sanh, and Laos

With the hapless jeep driver behind in the prop wash, the helicopter quickly gained altitude and out of small-arms range, tracking above the road and the mountains that it skirted. To the north, flashes on the horizon highlighted a B52 air strike. The nearby mountains were pockmarked and scarred by four years of artillery impacts and aerial bombing.

At a lone outcropping crowned by a Marine observation post known as the Rockpile, the course of the helo turned south. Then passing a battery of active 175mm guns the helicopter flew on to Vandegrift's valley location.

Touching down on the eastern side of the base I jumped off, making way for a happy group of dirt encrusted marines on their way rearward for leave or rotation home. I then began the walk toward the antenna - festooned bunker containing the battalion command post. I was surrounded by a daunting cacophony. All the sounds of war assaulted me as nearby artillery bellowed, tanks and trucks roared past, and distant helicopters clattered.

At Vandegrift the war became very real.

[182]

At the subject's battalion CP, I briefed his XO. The subject had not returned from other duties, but was expected back at any time. A record check confirmed that he had a low-level security clearance and was not handling sensitive classified materials in his assignment.

A command authorized form was signed by the XO and the gunnery sergeant in charge of postal service was then assigned to assist in the search for contraband.

Battalion senior NCOs shared open-sided tents at the base. Each man was assigned a cot and footlocker to hold personal effects. The gunnery sergeant who occupied the tent with the suspect identified his cot and personal effects for us, and the search was begun.

What I noted immediately were large numbers of letters, all carefully bundled. What became a more immediate concern was a large detonation nearby and clearly not from the adjacent 175mm gun battery. The gunnery sergeant who was already moving toward one side of the tent, directed me to a buried culvert which served as their shelter from enemy rockets.

Crowding in with some others, we sat in cramped darkness as a number of NVA 122mm rockets slammed into Vandegrift. Friendly artillery began to fire back, and after several minutes everyone returned to their duties.

Before our search had been completed, four more rocket attacks had been launched by the NVA which killed or wounded several marines. Reflecting on the nature of the circumstances that had brought me there, I was prompted to think… "I hope this investigation really is important."

The search ultimately produced letters indicating that the subject was using the mail system to transmit and acquire pornographic material from a number of addresses in the Far East and Europe as a business venture. He returned to his battalion later the same day but, as was his right under the Uniform Code of Military Justice, declined to discuss the allegations against him.

A crew chief prepares for the next flight

The Rockpile

The battalion XO was briefed on the results of our search. Command would then consider whether to charge the subject or not. By then it was too late to fly back out, and I spent a sleepless night in the empty chaplain's tent one hundred yards away from the 175mm artillery battery, which fired harassment and interdiction missions throughout the night.

First thing the next morning I walked across the base to a small hill called Charlie Med, to where the forward Navy medical detachment was housed inside the hill itself. There I found a bunker protected by ten feet of overhead earth, and doctors and hospital corpsmen wearing shorts and sandals hurrying about their duties.

Back above, a row of quiet and bandaged walking wounded stood on the helipad at the head of the ladder way awaiting the next helicopter ride to the rear. All ignored the nearby body bags also awaiting evacuation. Corpsmen told me an Army medevac Huey was expected within the hour. When it landed I crowded on with the wounded, feeling unimportant amidst the events unfolding on all sides. This was my first "taste" of the everyday existence of the combat marine. It was the first of many yet to come.

Walking wounded awaiting evacuation at Vandegrift Combat Base

[186]

*****

Suicides did occur in the stressful Vietnam environment, and it was well known that individuals compromised and then forced to commit espionage sometimes killed themselves rather than face the stigma of their acts. Because of this historical connection between security compromise and suicide, NIS took an interest in them and investigated them fully.

In late 1969 a marine stationed in a communication role at Dong Ha shot himself in the head with his M16. Witnesses said the episode occurred suddenly and without forewarning. The men who shared his hooch could offer no explanation for the death. The victim had regular access to classified material and to cryptographic equipment used for encoding and decoding messages but was not exposed to top-secret information.

The officer in charge said the victim had taken his allocated R and R leave earlier in the year in Australia, and upon his return had reported no contact with suspicious persons. This was significant because at the time, a cadre of foreign enemy agents with suspected Soviet ties were known to be befriending U.S. military personnel on leave in Sydney.

The victim's gear was thoroughly searched, and all correspondence was read for clues. He had the usual collection of photographs around Viet Nam taken with fellow marines at a weekend barbecue, letters from his family at home, and a bundle of perfumed envelopes from his fiancée.

Therein lay the likely explanation for the victim's decision to kill himself.

The last perfumed letter arrived the morning of his death aboard a mail truck emblazoned with the name "the Dear John Express". And indeed it had been. The victim had picked up his rifle and shot himself after learning his relationship had ended. Precautionary investigative leads were dispatched for confirmation by other NIS field elements in the United States, but nothing was ever developed to indicate the death had been anything other than a reaction to a Dear John letter.

It was a well established tradition in Vietnam for a Dear John letter recipient to tell those with whom he served of his misfortune. His friends were then to team up and write to the offending female, congratulating her on her nomination to a "select" club of Dear John letter writers. It was hoped that this support would make their rejected colleague feel better and help him cope with his rejection. Unfortunately this particular victim had told nobody of his plight.

*****

There were no regular days off in Vietnam, especially in northern I Corps. At Quang Tri days began at 5:00 AM at the SeaBee camp, and by 6:30 AM trucks were rolling out to their work sites along Route 1. For the NIS agent who needed to travel any distance from Quang Tri, early morning was the time to begin.

Camp Evans, Hue, Phu Bai, and Camp Eagle were all more than an hour away by road. Navy detachments, SeaBee battalions, and marines were all deployed in these areas. Requests for assistance from them required a timely response, and because telephone and radio links were insecure, agents usually visited the command concerned in person.

Weather was always an unpredictable factor. Vietnam regularly suffered at the hands of autumn typhoons, and 1969 was an especially severe season with road washouts and high winds that injured and killed both military and civilian personnel alike. The NISSU Quang Tri office was damaged by flying debris and was partially flooded. During one particularly protracted storm, I received a nonspecific request that I visit the SeaBee battalion deployed at Camp Evans, near Hue.

Naval officers at the wardroom told me that water on the road was more than two feet deep in places near Quang Tri, and certainly deeper than it was safe to drive through in a jeep.

Recently qualified by the SeaBees as a heavy-vehicle driver, I asked for the loan of a three-axle, all-wheel-drive five-ton military dump truck. Given the truck's very high ground clearance, it seemed probable that the high waters could be navigated in this way.

[188]

In camouflage utilities under a full rain suit, I started driving slowly south in the huge truck, battling driving rains and dodging Vietnamese civilians pushing bicycles and drowned motorcycles. The truck created a bow wave even at slow speeds.

A typhoon at Quang Tri Combat Base. The author in his sand-bagged M-151 jeep

Less than half way to Phu Bai while crossing rice paddy fields, a small stream in full flood brought my progress to a complete halt. The road had been washed away by the fast-moving waters. Pausing only momentarily while watching the passage of logs and other debris, I reversed my path and was safely back in Quang Tri by sundown.

Another week passed before the SeaBee command could finally be reached. Cordially welcomed by their battalion XO, I asked what the problem was and was told that a quantity of marijuana had been found in a garbage can on the main street of the cantonment.

I had expected something far more serious, but I soon realized from speaking with the engineer officer that narcotics usage was virtually unheard of within the SeaBees. Battalion personnel were skilled tradesmen and builders, mechanics and equipment operators. A high percentage of them were second-class petty officers (E5

[189]

NCOs). They expected to work hard every day of their two eight-month deployments from the United States to Vietnam.

Although there were recreational club facilities and some SeaBees were known as "hard players," the executive officer knew of no "dopers" in his battalion and was seeking advice about countering a potential problem in its early stages.

I explained that many varieties of narcotics were available just outside the gate and pointed out that the garbage can might be a "drop" that Vietnamese employed in the compound during the day as cleaners and sanitation workers used. Driving onward to Da Nang to hand-carry my completed cases, I would hear nothing further from this battalion. Unfortunately, the SeaBees were the exception and not the rule.

*****

Flying in the Jolly Green

To avoid the long and potentially hazardous drive between Quang Tri and Da Nang, I cultivated friendships with the U.S. Air Force Aerospace Recovery Squadron personnel who flew to Quang Tri every morning. They used the airstrip as a dispatch point for their extremely hazardous pilot rescue missions.

Known amongst the aviation fraternity as the Jolly Green Giants, these men routinely drove their armored H3 Sikorski helicopters into the enemy maelstrom that typically surrounded downed allied pilots.

Rounding the shoulder of the mountainous Hai Van Pass, (often by then in darkness), the rest of the flight was a straight shot, descending across Da Nang Harbor to the air base. If my luck held out, there would be a waiting ride to the NIS billet.

*****

Hue was on the route of any drive between Da Nang and Quang Tri. Route 1 passed the air base at Phu Bai and about eight miles farther, entered the southern half of the city and on to the Perfume River, which bisects it. On the southern riverbanks, some of the heaviest battle damage had befallen Hue University, Thua Thien Provincial headquarters, and other buildings along Le Loi Street during the Tet Offensive of 1968.

A year later the Vietnamese were fast rebuilding their beautiful city. Passage across the river was still via the pontoon bridge that was hastily installed to replace the adjacent demolished span originally erected by French engineers at the turn of the century. On the opposite bank, the imposing mass of the Citadel's scarred walls rose, topped by a huge flag tower from which flew the red and gold colors of the Republic of Vietnam. Beyond this was the Forbidden City and centuries of Vietnamese history.

Route 1, the "Street Without Joy", skirted the outer walls of the moated Citadel before turning due north and paralleling the rail line toward QuangTri.

Hue was a Vietnamese city in the truest sense. Considered the cultural capital of Vietnam, its religious and educational leaders had steered many critical events in the country's tumultuous history. And this tradition continued during the current conflict.

[191]

There were allied advisory units in Hue which included a SeaBee detachment, but they maintained a low profile.

It was quite unusual to see U.S. military vehicles or personnel away from the main highway, and the remainder of the city was declared off-limits.

A majestic throwback, Hue was nevertheless surrounded by the reality of the war. The Perfume River formed an important arterial for war supplies. Navy and Army personnel manned a boat ramp on the south bank from which a constant stream of landing craft disgorged pallets of artillery shells and rations. Downstream where the river empties into the South China Sea, the Naval Support Activity Detachment, (Thuan An), was situated on a sandy isthmus at the river mouth.

A year after much of Hue was destroyed during the 1968 Tet Offensive, the Noon Gate retains its majestic symmetry

A ferry had been established to carry vehicles across to the base. The surrounding countryside showed fresh evidence of conflict, with every building and wall pockmarked by bullet holes and the larger holes from other projectiles.

In early 1970 Special Agent Fred Grim and I were dispatched to Thuan An to investigate an apparent homicide. Fred Grim had just

[192]

transferred to NISRA Da Nang from Adak, Alaska. This was his first trip to the bush and his first exposure to a serious investigation under the unique conditions in Vietnam. Assessing the security situation at the time, I decided it would probably be safest to travel by sea. We arranged to go aboard a patrol craft traveling northward up the coast from Da Nang. At dawn, the patrol boat skipper standing-to off the shore and awaiting high tide, spotted a Navy LCU.

We boarded the LCU in the dark for the final run into Thuan An. The boatswain's mate chief who skippered the craft realized Grim was a newbie to Vietnam, and regaled him with stories about floating mines and the VC swimmer sappers known to frequent the Perfume River. As the morning light improved, the newbie's next surprise came as he became able to make out the black stenciled lettering on the hundreds of boxes under foot in the hold. It was a shipment of 155mm high-explosive artillery ammunition destined for Army firebases inland.

Ashore, we contacted the naval command to begin our investigation. We were told that a Vietnamese female had been shot and killed in the early hours of a previous morning as she and her family was piloting their small boat nearby.

Spotted by roving Navy sentries in their outboard-powered Boston whaler, the Vietnamese boat had been taken under fire by the vessel's M60 machine gun. The victim had been killed by a single through-and-through gunshot wound. No effort had been made to hold the body for medical examination.

Assuming the victim had been promptly buried as was customary, we began inquiring about the availability of the Vietnamese police and judicial authorities to assist us with the investigation.

We boarded a boat and went in search of the vessel the victim was allegedly shot in. We would find it several hundred yards upstream from the naval installation, moored on the riverbank.

Bullet holes consistent with those of an M60 machine gun had penetrated both gunwales. Before any efforts were made to interview the U.S. Navy boat crew, we requested copies of the rules of

[193]

engagement, which normally govern the conduct of military operations in a war zone.

Newly-arrived Special Agent Fred Grim ducks for cover as an Army Huey patrolling the Perfume River bears down on our Boston Whaler

We found that these clearly set out a so-called "no go" area for nonmilitary vessels after dark. Further investigation established that the unfortunate victim had been in a forbidden area during the predawn, when visibility was very limited. Vietnamese witnesses confirmed that the rule was common knowledge among the fishing people, who knew a breach could have very serious consequences.

At the end of the day, it was determined that no criminal act had occurred and no further investigation was warranted. It was just another sad consequence of war, and unfortunately was not an uncommon one.

*****

The people of Hue were friendly and welcoming

I managed three brief visits to Hue in 1969, always while transiting north or south. But there was never enough time to soak up its many centuries of history. Each time the experience of driving through the gates of the Citadel was as if entering another time in history.

There were uniformed men to be seen, but they were all Vietnamese. Hue Vietnamese seemed quietly confident and almost insulated from much of what was happening outside the walls. This seemed like an incongruity.

There was a well-settled community within the Citadel. Unfortunately, not only had they been subjected to abduction and execution by the communist forces that had overrun their homes just a year before, but U.S. Marine and ARVN forces had then conducted house-to-house assaults to finish removing the enemy.

The Hue people had a pleasant air of quiet self-assurance…courtesy and good manners were the norm.

I found the gates to the Citadel and the inner Purple City open and easily accessed. Vietnamese gave directions when they were asked although few people could be seen anywhere within the former emperor's living areas.

[195]

Inside the imperial throne room

On one very special occasion, an old Vietnamese care-taker removed the chain and lock from the ornately carved doors of the emperor's throne room and showed Mike Quinn and me the lacquer columned reception area from which the king had presided from his raised dais. Despite damage from stray small arms projectiles, it retained all of its grandeur…embellished with ornate gold-leaf inscriptions that had been overwritten onto red lacquer.

Outside, grand steps and a bridge across the frangipani-fringed reflecting pools led to the Noon gate and its massive central doors, intended for the exclusive use of the emperor.

From the beautiful open pavilions atop the gate, Vietnam's last emperor, Bao Dai, had abdicated in 1945 and begun a life of exile in France. Beyond the pavilion gables fluttered the Vietnamese colors from atop the flag tower built on the ramparts of the outer wall. Called the King's Knight by the Vietnamese, the flag standard stood more than one hundred feet above the Perfume River beyond.

Hue school girls at the Noonday Gate of the Hue Citadel

From here, Viet Cong had defiantly flown the NLF flag for more than three and a half weeks before their violent ejection in 1968. All of that seemed far away. Despite reminders of recent violence, the Purple City was now a small cocoon insulated from the mainstream war.

While working at Quang Tri City, I discovered there the remains of a moated inner city. But years of war and neglect had robbed it of whatever claim to grandeur it had once had. In Quang Tri, it was war as usual.

*****

The onset of the autumn monsoons brought days of drizzle and low clouds, and it was occasionally unpleasantly cool. This was a time of activity for the enemy, who was very aware that the weather the French called *cratchin* did not favor aviators.

[197]

Air support missions during which the jet pilots used bombs, rockets, and machine guns to help allied units grappling with enemy attacks, were constrained by this weather.

No pilot wanted to fly into a cloud-shrouded mountain, though many attack pilots were willing to take grave risks to help the infantry on the ground.

Helicopters weren't as fast as the fast movers, nor did they have as many navigation aids. To them the mountains were equally unforgiving. For those not flying, monsoon season was also a time of heightened awareness. Heavy rain was useful cover for enemy sappers trying to penetrate perimeter defenses planning to wreak havoc with their explosive charges and small-arms fire. Navy and Marine perimeter guards attending to normal duties during the day, were unusually alert at night and the instances of fire from the bunkers increased.

SeaBees manned and maintained a sector of the Quang Tri Combat Base perimeter. It extended along the banks of the Thach Han River, rising threateningly over the low beds of staked barbed wire and concertina emplaced before it to deter crawling sappers.

Claymore mines were carefully pointed outward "toward the enemy" as the embossed inscription on their face instructed. In late 1969 there had been no successful breaches of the Quang Tri perimeter, but the enemy frequently used monsoon rains as a screen for night rocket attacks on the base. The NVA obviously felt safer with the rain, and the counter battery radar employed by base defenders to locate launches was less effective then.

The chance that "Charles" would be accurately located and fired upon by artillery was smaller, as was the chance that a helicopter gunship could attack them in the dark and wet conditions.

Thus the men who normally enjoyed a weather-tight roof over their heads and a warm bunk within the perimeter of the base endured many sleepless nights.

Soviet 122mm and 140mm rockets would arc indiscriminately in where they produced a dangerous explosion and shrapnel effect like an artillery round. For the unprepared, a near hit was likely to be fatal. Smart men therefore leapt from their beds while donning body armor as they bolted for the nearest sandbagged bunker.

Special Agent Leo Gonzales and I experienced a number of these night time attacks, which proved more of an inconvenience than posing a mortal danger. There were other casualties from the attacks, but no near misses for us. Squatting in rainwater in the dank confines of a bunker with the SeaBee officers who shared the hooch, we waited for the all clear to come through. Two or three such interruptions in a night were not at all unusual.

Never one to dismiss the odds of being hurt or killed by a rocket attack, I had an unusual experience that boldly illustrated that the theater of war was a place where death by whatever means was never very far away.

I had met Army doctors during investigations at Graves Registration who had graciously invited me to accompany them on an overnight trip to the "rear" hospital at Camp Evans. Evans, as I knew too well, was really not much different than Quang Tri, save one important advantage...there were Army nurses at the hospital. It just so happened that they were having a party for the doctors and the medevac, (Dustoft), pilots who supported them.

An Army Huey was on standby at Quang Tri awaiting routine service and rotation, and we expected a pleasant afternoon flight of about forty minutes.

The four doctors and I loaded up in the Huey at the hospital helipad and took off, climbing on a course toward the south. Good-natured merriment abounded on the flight... none of us had had any time off, the pilots especially. We all were thirsty, and looking forward to a good time. With the Annamite ranges rising just westward and the late afternoon sun reflecting off scores of rectangular paddy dykes below, we were enjoying the cool air that blew through the doorless chopper when all forward motion abruptly stopped.

The Huey was in a hover for only a second or two when with a huge roar, an F4 Phantom laden with bombs screamed across our flight path. It was banking left with that wing pointed earthward and exposing at very close range its underside fitted with bombs and napalm tanks. It was so close that oil stains on the belly were clearly visible. Moments later, as all the chopper passengers stared in disbelief, the fighter unloaded its bombs from a lower altitude, aiming at an "enemy target" on a nearby range. It arced up into the skies above and was gone.

Now with much more sober passengers, all once more aware of the dangers of modern warfare, the chopper continued on the remainder of an uneventful flight to Camp Evans. After landing, the chopper pilot said he had reacted to a flash of sunlight off the fighter canopy, slowing as much as possible just before seeing the fighter on its bombing run. He was certain the pilot had never seen the "Dustoff" thumping through the airspace.

Camp Evans was home to important elements of the U.S. Army's 101st Airborne Division. Spread out over low foothills west of Route 1, its metal airstrip was home to a large gaggle of olive drab Hueys and Cobras. All were parked in protective sand-filled steel revetments designed as protection from enemy rocket and mortar attack. Helicopters were the workhorses of the 101st Airborne, then operating as paratroopers without parachutes. Helicopters had changed combat tactics irreversibly in Vietnam and had allowed infantry to rapidly deploy to remote locations. As we walked from the Dustoff chopper toward the hospital, a group of recon soldiers practiced hot extraction exercises. Dangling high in the air from their individual ropes affixed to a Huey, they practiced life-saving tactics designed for small groups needing to get out of the jungle in a hurry.

At the hospital, a large maintenance tent erected on hardstand was being readied for the nurse's party. A pair of soldiers began by wheeling a jeep trailer into the tent and then filling it with ice and cans of beer. A barbecue barrel was fired up, and with dusk fast approaching, the festivities began.

Evans was in a combat zone. The Navy had no nurses stationed ashore in northern I Corps, but the Army took a different approach. The few nurses wore the same battle dress as their male counter-parts, and all showed signs of the fatigue that endless days in a forward hospital created. Amid hamburgers off the barbecue fire,

[200]

many beers were consumed and a rosy bonhomie developed among partygoers.

When enemy rockets later began cascading onto the adjacent metal strip at Evans, no one rushed for cover. Exhausted and now inebriated partiers sat and watched the fireworks nearby and eventually crawled off to find a spot for a few hours of sleep. The return flight to Quang Tri on the following morning was subdued, but without any of the alarming elements of the flight going down.

In the midst of the insanity of Quang Tri Combat Base, there was a small oasis of peace and tranquility in the form of a very old Buddhist monastery. When the SeaBees built their two camps on the west side of the airstrip and Route 1, the camps were carefully laid out to provide a buffer of space around the grounds. An entry road was all there was to indicate what lay beyond, and established trees and shrubs shielded the Vietnamese from the rush and roar of the American war effort around them on every side.

The walk to the monastery from NISSU Quang Tri was short and provided an idyllic break. The monks were gracious hosts, and seemed to appreciate the genuine interest of their visitors. The lotus pond, (behind which stood a canopied statue of Buddha's mother), screened the entrance to the monastery itself. It was said to have been build about 1820, and the shrine and artifacts within were carefully maintained.

Because of its position within the perimeter of the combat base, it could not have enjoyed many Vietnamese visitors and even fewer Americans. The lotus pond and its ever-present butterflies were always a pleasant relief from the press of war.

*****

9   POLITICS AND VIETNAM, 1970: DISSENT AND SABOTAGE

The late 1960s were turbulent times in America. It was inevitable that this unrest would spill over to Vietnam when men taken from the politically and socially-unsettled United States were inducted or chose to enlist into the armed forces. Race riots, beginning in the mid '60s, had set America alight especially after the Reverend Martin Luther King was assassinated in Memphis in 1968.

President Lyndon Johnson had refused the politically unpopular measure of calling up reserves to meet the growing requirement for troops in Southeast Asia…instead, draft quotas were increased.

To achieve quotas, the standards for inductees were reduced. Perhaps the most infamous of programs designed to get the numbers whatever the cost, was Secretary of Defense Robert McNamara's "Project 100,000". This initiative targeted uneducated young men who otherwise might not have met the usual standards, and were frequently the disadvantaged living in America's ghettos. Along with genuinely good recruits who served with pride and dignity, the Army in particular received a raft of delinquents and other ne'er-do-wells.

The Marine Corps too was not immune to the effects of McNamara's plan. The proud force had built a legacy of honor and tradition based largely on volunteers who wanted to be marines and who were dedicated to the mission. The "new" draft had a definite negative impact on that tradition.

For a segment of poor American blacks plucked from the ghettos, Marine Corps discipline meted out by an NCO corps of predominately self made non-blacks was a source of friction. In the later years of the war, some black Marine malcontents made it known that their aim was the disruption and destruction of the corps. Encouraged and sometimes supported by extremists in the United States, they made a mission of proselytizing other blacks, enforcing segregation by coercion and urging violent acts to achieve their aims.

[202]

Just as Ku Klux Klan members had earlier been carefully investigated and monitored, now extreme black organizations like the Black Panthers were a concern for U.S. agencies.

NIS participated in intelligence collection programs to assist in the monitoring. It was discovered that extremists in the United States were encouraging young men to select the Marine Corps as their branch of service as a means of acquiring weapons training and other military skills useful in an impending domestic revolution.

Information was gathered about a militant black organization in both the First Marines and Force Logistic Command (FLC), which called itself Maw Maw. The organization was presumably named after the black insurgent group Mau Mau that was pivotal in the overthrow of the white British rule of Kenya in the 1950s.

The Maw Maw aims remained nonspecific other than to destroy the war machine at any opportunity and gain revenge for perceived misdeeds against "the brothers". Members wore a small plastic device removed from satchel charges.

Aggressive information collection allowed command to preempt some destructive Maw Maw activities that were then in the planning stages. Transfers from Vietnam and administrative discharges effectively served to defuse the worst of these tensions.

An increased consciousness toward racial sensitivities extended clear to the desk of the commandant of marines. Commandant, Gen. Leonard Chapman, USMC, set out guidelines designed to illustrate recognition of the issues and to instruct Marine Corps leaders that racial differences were to be managed in prescribed ways. Issues such as regulation haircuts, jewelry, diet, and the music in entertainment areas were found to be topics of frequent discussion in malcontented groups.

A future commandant of the U.S. Marines, then Col. P. X. Kelly, commanded the First Marines during the Maw Maw inquiries. The most senior member of the command, he could well have been the most vilified by rebellious blacks…but he was not. "The man sees only green" was a universal comment by angry malcontents who were not shy about talking of plans for death and destruction in their blacks-only meetings. "Doing some beasts [white Marines)" was not an infrequent topic of discussion.

From time to time, their plans were taken from the planning and haranguing stage to actual action. An alleged plan to destroy an entire fire base by placing demolitions in artillery ammunition storage areas, was discovered and effectively neutralized by the break-up and transfer of members of the group. But in some instances, radical group activities were learned of only after the fact.

In February 1970 overt signs of racial tension at Force Logistic Command, Da Nang were noticed. Black marines had formed groups exclusive of whites and were holding regular meetings to discuss perceived grievances. When a three-girl Australian group calling themselves the Chiffons was scheduled to play at Andy's Pub, (the maintenance battalion enlisted men's club at FLC), several hundred marines crowded into an open patio area near the stage.

The area was fenced and much of it was paved with concrete for tables and chairs. As the performance progressed, some troublesome black marines were asked to leave. As the Chiffons neared the end of their performance, an unidentified object was thrown over the fence from outside. This was followed by an M26 fragmentation grenade that exploded an instant later. The grenade had landed on the sand adjacent to a concrete slab after bouncing off the seven foot perimeter fence. Its blast hurled hundreds of fragments of wood and metal into the packed audience.

Sixty-two marines were injured and all but ten would require hospitalization. Cpl. Ronald A. Pate, a decorated marine who had the misfortune of being next to the fence and was killed.

Upon realizing that the incident had not been a random attack by the enemy, Marine authorities directed Marine Corps CID to begin an investigation. They requested assistance from NISRA Da Nang the following morning. SRA Don McCoy assigned the investigation to Special Agent Fred Grim.

Grim left the office alone and drove through the city. As usual, Route 1 was crowded as he headed north in the direction of Hai Van

Pass and toward Camp Brooks at Red Beach. His first stop was the office of CID investigator Sgt. Joe Bean. Bean and his colleagues had developed information during the night that was moving the investigation toward the black extremists. They had not yet developed any firm leads, but the FLC's black extremist group seemed a good starting point.

As a priority, Grim requested that an immediate inventory of defensive ammunition and grenades be conducted, and the agent soon discovered that someone had broken into a CONEX storage container and removed a quantity of M26 fragmentation grenades.

Grim called McCoy for help and every available agent in Da Nang was rounded up and dispatched to FLC armed with crime scene equipment and fingerprinting supplies.

In the meantime, Grim had located and interviewed a young Hispanic marine who confirmed that he had seen several black marines, whom he identified by name, enter the CONEX and remove grenades. These had been placed in a sandbag and buried nearby. At last Grim had suspects, and arriving agents began assembling the pieces of the puzzle to determine the whereabouts of suspects and witnesses before during and after the incident. A search of the area resulted in the recovery of the stolen grenades; and with the grenades entered into evidence it became apparent that fingerprints could play a crucial role in the investigation. The grenades would be sent to the FBI laboratory in Washington, D.C., to allow their highly qualified specialists to develop evidence of human handling.

The dispatch of grenades from Vietnam to Washington, D.C., was in itself highly problematic. While FLC officers arranged a courier, Fred Grim approached the Marine explosive ordnance detachment (EOD) for assistance in rendering the explosives safe for the airborne journey to the States.

Grim recounted… "A gunnery sergeant turned up and said the detonator/ firing assemblies could be unscrewed from the top of each grenade. This would make them impossible to fire without a sympathetic detonation. I sat there nervously with the gunny, watching him unscrew firing assemblies from each of twelve grenades, while he carefully avoided touching the round grenade body which we hoped had finger or palm prints on them. That done, I decided we should take his finger and palm prints too, just to facilitate the process of elimination. To my dismay, the gunny's workingman fingers and palms were so hard and horny I was unable to get usable prints from them."

Meanwhile, a group of agents had set up shop in the maintenance battalion chow hall and were fingerprinting and palm printing scores of potential suspects.

Assistant SRA Carl Sundstrom remembers, "At one time, we had everybody and his brother out there."

A happy Marine captain whose wife was a resident of Washington, D.C. got orders to hand-carry the evidence to the FBI. That meant that to preserve the chain of evidence, custody of the grenades had to be under his exclusive control at all times. He was almost certain to be asked under oath during a future trial whether there had been any times when the grenades were not with him and would have been available for tampering.

Said Sundstrom, "Although the courier's orders were carefully written and personnel along the way alerted, the air carriers went berserk when this guy turned up with a box of grenades."

To the credit of the young officer, the evidence was duly delivered to the FBI laboratory. Unfortunately, usable prints could not be developed on any of the grenades.

Meanwhile Grim and his colleagues had conducted interviews of both key witnesses and potential suspects. In an effort to assemble all of the facts surrounding the killing as well as any inconsistencies, several marines were interviewed more than once in the interrogation room at NISRA Da Nang. The scenario was definitely developing, but there were no confessions and key witnesses were giving little away. In a further set back, the witness who had observed the grenade theft admitted without prompting to heavy narcotics abuse, thus diminishing his value as a credible witness.

To date the investigation had established that on the night of Pate's

[206]

murder, a group of between twenty and thirty black marines assigned to the maintenance battalion had met on the basketball court. This had been a regular meeting place for the group, which used the courts as a forum for grievances about a variety of issues ranging from haircut regulations to the perceived mistreatment by NCOs and officers.

One witness said that on the night of February 5, Lance Cpl. Joseph L. Jones had complained that he was being framed after "pep pills" had been found in a surprise search of his gear. Jones allegedly had told the group he intended to kill some white marines and advised all present to stay away from the USO show that night.

Jones and three other suspects, Cpl. Ronald E. Gales, Cpl. James B. Addison, and Lance Cpl. Andrew M. Harris Jr., were arrested under charges of premeditated murder, conspiracy, and assault with intent to commit murder.

Trial counsel for Corporal Gales sought immunity for his client in exchange for his testimony against the other three marines. In a controversial move command granted Gales immunity from prosecution. He subsequently furnished a detailed statement in which he admitted breaking into the ammunition storage CONEX with Jones and Addison.

Gales told agents he had accompanied Jones, Harris, and Addison to the enlisted club and Jones had entered the fenced open entertainment area to warn the blacks present there to leave. Gales testified that Harris lobbed a grenade over the fence, but the grenade failed to explode because the tape had not been removed from the striker lever.

Gales then implicated Harris as the man who threw the second grenade, though evidence seemed to indicate that Gales himself might have actually been responsible himself.

Harris was arrested in California two days before his discharge date and was returned to Vietnam to stand trial. Meanwhile Gales had been sent to the brig in Iwakuni, Japan for his own safety while awaiting the trial. Several other witnesses were also transferred abruptly to Okinawa, out of range of any possible retribution.

[207]

The prosecution case was dependent almost entirely on testimony. The process of successfully filtering through conflicting recollections and the outright deception was a daunting task. Central to the prosecutions success was polygraph operator Special Agent Tom Brannon. Patient and methodical, Brannon was given carte blanche by his controllers in Washington to conduct his interviews interrogations and polygraph tests.

Brannon would recall… "This was the first time headquarters had not insisted on a case-by-case authority to conduct polygraph exams. They basically understood that I would need to use 'the box' on short notice, and this was the case." Brannon interviewed and confirmed the testimony of two witnesses on February 24, while working in the tiny windowless interrogation room at NISRA Da Nang.

Both marines were found to be truthful in what they told the examiner, and on February 26 Brannon conducted two more witness interviews and polygraph examinations. Significantly, the second witness after several hours of fruitless conversation opened up and corroborated a number of important elements of the case.

"This guy was a decorated, squared away Marine NCO with a fine combat record. He just wasn't going to dime on other black marines. In the end, an appeal to his honor and loyalty to the corps convinced him to reconsider," Brannon recalls.

Da Nang agents assisted Brannon in his interviews, and Carl Sundstrom remembers the long hours with the witnesses and of reducing their statements to writing. "We worked our fingers to the bone both day and night. The longest statement I ever typed in my entire career was written during this investigation."

Lance Corporal Harris was the first of the trio to stand trial, and Gales was called as a prosecution witness. Gales would identify Harris as the person who threw both grenades in his sworn testimony.

Harris took the stand in his own defense in rebuttal to Gales. Ably assisted by his counsel, they undermined the credibility of Gales based on the witness's previous disciplinary record. The court felt that they could not convict Harris based on the evidence presented, and he was found not guilty on all charges.

Addison's trial came next, and again, Gales was called as a key witness. He provided essentially the same testimony as he had presented at Harris's trial. In his rebuttal, Addison swore that he had run away from the co-accused at the club when he realized what was about to happen. The court chose to believe Addison in preference to Gales, and he too was acquitted.

Twice rebuffed, the Marine Corps prosecution decided not to proceed with the charges against Jones, and he was administratively discharged on the grounds of his alleged drug abuse.

Years later, a Marine major approached Special Agent Brannon who was then conducting investigations at Naval Air Station, Lemoore.

The major, a member of the JAG Corps, asked Brannon if he was the same agent who had investigated the killing of Corporal Pate in Viet Nam. Brannon said that he was. The major thanked him, and then explained that he had known and respected the combat decorated Pate, and had visited his family after the major had returned from Viet Nam as an enlisted man.

He had attended law school on the GI Bill, and his deceased friend was never far from his thoughts. A request under the Freedom of Information Act had identified Brannon to him. Tom Brannon recalls, "I was really touched that this guy sought me out to offer his thanks after all those years."

The travesty of the trials that followed Pate's death will never fade from Brannon's memory.

*****

Fragging seemed to beget more fraggings, and they were usually very difficult to solve. In an atmosphere approaching near-anarchy in some military organizations, their incidents spread like a disease.

Pvt. Ronald McDonald, USMC, may well have been the "Project 100,000 poster boy", Defense Secretary Robert McNamara's unfortunate experiment.

His was a social engineering plan to fill vacancies in the armed forces by lowering the entry standards. McDonald was assigned to FLC at Red Beach, near the site of the original marine landings in 1965. FLC itself sprawled over acres of white sand, and was situated back from the beach with the Annamite Mountains and Hai Van Pass towering behind it.

Most of the buildings were of the SEA hut design, with a smaller version of it for living that was known universally as a hooch. Dozens of hooches stood in rows, back from sandy streets. Many had sandbags or sand-filled barrels pushed up against the lower walls to act as protection against rocket or mortar rounds, but the hooches were still vulnerable to ground attack.

When Ronald McDonald decided to retaliate against a perceived affront from a career NCO, fragging was his technique of choice. Finding a grenade for this purpose was problematic at FLC because offensive ordnance was carefully secured and controlled in the wake of previous incidents. He had decided that he was going to frag the gunnery sergeant, but didn't know what he was going to use to do it. Finally, when he couldn't find a frag for this purposes closer to home, his search took him out into the Vietnamese village beyond the FLC perimeter wire.

There was very little that could not be purchased in these settlements, which had survived in large part by dubious commerce just like this with nearby base occupants. McDonald went to a shanty built out of pressed beer cans and bought himself a drink.

Next he asked the Vietnamese woman where he could buy a grenade. Because of language difficulties she didn't understand him at first. Once she did, she told the marine he was *dinky-dau* (crazy). Still, recognizing the sales opportunity, she sent one of her kids off with a burst of Vietnamese and soon, McDonald's grenade arrived.

What the woman produced was a fragmentation grenade unlike anything McDonald had ever seen before. It was a British 36 grenade better known as a Mills Bomb.

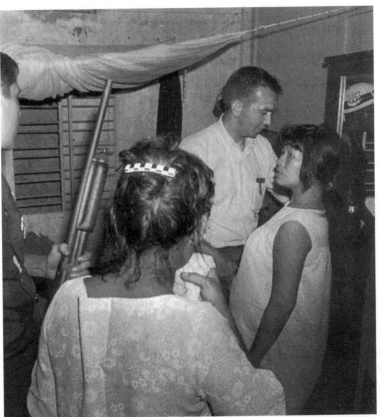

Pursuing a deserter Marine wanted for murder, Special Agents Joe Washko on the left, and Ed Hemphill search a Vietnamese home where the suspect had recently been sighted

Bigger than U.S. designs, the British grenade had a cast-iron striated casing designed to break up into large and very lethal chunks upon detonation. A removable threaded base plug allowed the weapon to be disassembled and cleaned in the field and was also the access point for installing the fuse/detonator assembly. The grenade contained a substantial explosive charge.

[211]

The source of the British grenade can only be guessed at. British forces entered Vietnam after the August 1945 surrender of the occupying Japanese forces. Perhaps the grenade had been left by them when the French returned to reclaim their Indochinese empire. It was old ordnance to be sure and had been armed for many years, but it still worked just as its British designers had intended.

In the cover of darkness, McDonald approached the gunny's hooch and opened the door. He rolled the grenade across the plywood deck toward the sleeping NCO. It detonated with a roar, sending its chunks of cast iron in all directions. Fortunately for the gunny, he made a habit of standing his helmet and flak jacket next to his bunk for easy access. The body armor absorbed much of the shrapnel, and both hooch occupants survived the attack.

Special Agent Ed Hemphill of NISRA Da Nang took over the investigation, and Assistant Senior Resident Agent Carl Sundstrom assisted him.

Sundstrom recalls; "I remember the crime scene was a little different than other fraggings. There were fewer shrapnel strikes, and the holes were bigger. I particularly recall a neat round hole about the size of a fifty cent piece, penetrating the center bulkhead in the gunny's SEA hut." Likely, the threaded base plug common to the 36 grenade design had made that hole.

As was typical in these investigations, there was virtually no useful physical evidence to assist in building a case. Agents relied heavily on witness testimony, poring over statements and revisiting conflicting statements.

Through painstaking work and an excellent nose for clues, Hemphill identified McDonald as the probable perpetrator. He received little help from the witnesses who he believed had knowledge confirming McDonald's guilt. In desperation, assistance was requested of polygraph operator Tom Brannon, who flew into Vietnam from his Taiwan office.

Brannon and Hemphill, with assistance from other Da Nang agents, methodically interviewed and then re-interviewed the witnesses. Brannon then took over with his polygraph. The accused had little

[212]

interest in speaking with agents, but the witnesses finally talked...
with confirmation of their stories by the polygraph results.
McDonald was court-martialed and found guilty, and in an
extraordinary move, the court awarded the maximum sentence
available under military law...eighty-eight years in a federal
penitentiary.

Brannon recalls, "They led this guy away in handcuffs, but he was
still giving the black power salute."

*****

Brannon and Grim teamed up for one last case in June 1970. It was
a nonfatal fragging at a Marine aviation detachment perched on the
crest of Monkey Mountain, overlooking Da Nang Harbor. An
officer thought by his less-than-enthusiastic troops to be
overzealous, was targeted and warned by means of an exploding
grenade. This was clearly an act of intimidation and would not be
tolerated.

SRA Ed Fitzpatrick teamed Grim up with Special Agent Walt
Focht. Focht had been a second-class petty officer in the Navy
before entering service with the Huntington Beach Police
Department, where he achieved the rank of sergeant. He was a
tenacious investigator who was liked and respected by his peers.

Fitzpatrick, Grim, and Focht, were called out late one night. They
navigated the narrow winding road up to the top of Monkey
Mountain and immediately began asking questions.
Not surprisingly, there was virtually no physical evidence to point
them toward those responsible, but they soon identified malcontents
who may have had a reason to throw the grenade. Witnesses
cooperated up to a point. Suspects, warned of their right to remain
silent, gave up as little as they could. Grim and Focht were
confident they had the perpetrator, who, despite a series of
interrogations, continued to maintain his innocence.

Again, Brannon's services were requested, and the accused decided
he would talk to him. He admitted his guilt, which was confirmed
by polygraph, and the next day he reconstructed the fragging for
agents and a photographer.

[213]

*****

Aviation has been a vital component of the U.S. Marine Corps since the 1920s, and successive commandants have embraced its importance. In Korea Marine aviators earned respect and admiration for their air strikes flown in support of the men on the ground. They were expert at dropping explosives and napalm "danger close", just in front of the friendly lines with uncanny accuracy.

The Marine Corps had evolved the concept of close air support, and they were proud of it; nobody did it better. Marine pilots deploying to Vietnam were well schooled and ready to carry on in another aviation role if required. They did this very successfully.

Unlike those in other services, Marine pilots are multi-disciplined, and it was not unusual for a C130 Hercules pilot to later train and attain great proficiency piloting transport or attack helicopters. It was the common scuttlebutt among grunts sandwiched in the rear of a C130 in the midst of a gut-wrenching banking turn to say, "Skipper's carrier-qualified," and receive a knowing nod in reply. Some Marine pilots flew four-engine cargo aircraft like they would an F8 Crusader…with élan one might say.

Marines repair, maintain, and crew all their aircraft. This means enlisted men assigned to aviation are highly trained and motivated. Marine aviation units did not, therefore, seem to receive as many visits from NIS as others did.

In 1971 with the "Vietnamization" in full-swing and allied units being systematically withdrawn, it was common to hear men say, "I don't want to be the last guy killed in Vietnam." Morale was not what it had been, and neither was the quality of enlisted marines filling the lower ranks. Discipline is a way of life in the Marine Corps, but the cracks were beginning to show.

At Marble Mountain Air Facility, home to Marine helicopter squadrons, two acts of sabotage within days of each other rattled commands and starkly illustrated internal problems. First a critical retaining nut on the primary servo of a CH53 had been tampered with. The maintenance NCO who discovered the condition as part of a preflight inspection described it as a completely foolproof

[214]

means of ensuring that the aircraft would spin out of control and crash at some point after takeoff. Normally the nut was carefully torqued down and wired to prevent its loosening. There was no doubt, the wire had been removed on purpose.

Cobra gunship at Marble Mountain

NISRA Da Nang SRA Charles M. Bickley headed the investigation into the incident. As was common, there was virtually no forensic evidence at the scene, and sentries and flight line personnel recalled no unusual activity. Bickley began the inquiries aimed at discovering any clashes, conflicts, or motive for revenge, and sent leads to other NIS components requesting interviews with personnel already rotated.

Agents doggedly pursued every avenue of inquiry available and tried to develop new ones, but it was an uphill battle. A week later, and shortly after the aircraft had been returned to service, it crashed into the water south of Hue. There were no survivors and no witnesses to the crash, and crash site investigations were inconclusive. The event left a bitter taste and more than a few marines wondering what was happening "to our Marine Corps."

A few days later in a Marble Mountain aircraft shelter, a crudely built bomb assemblage using a taped M26 fragmentation grenade, a gasoline-filled coffee can, and a seventeen pound high-explosive rocket warhead, was discovered adjacent to a metal shipping container packed full of explosives. The bomb was meant to detonate when the electrical tape wrapped around the striker lever dissolved in the gasoline in which the grenade was immersed. That explosion was meant to initiate the rocket warhead immediately alongside which would set off the contents of the rocket locker.

Agents arrived at the scene just before a Marine Corps EOD disposal unit. The Marine MP, the first to respond when the device was discovered, met them at the scene. The concrete aircraft shelter was vacant except for the steel ordnance storage box, the untouched explosive device and the normal stored equipment. The danger from the fragmentation grenade was still uncertain. A cursory inspection revealed that the tape securing the striker lever appeared to have loosened. Deactivating the explosive clearly would be a job for EOD At this point whatever forensic evidence might have been present was of secondary importance.

This EOD "Gunner" was a cool customer. Here he drinks coffee while being interviewed by Senior Resident Agent Chuck Bickley in an ordnance revetment storing aerial rockets

A salty Marine "Gunner" (Warrant Officer) headed the two-man EOD team. Not surprisingly this man, a veteran of at least two wars, took a very direct approach to the problem. Ordering all a safe distance away, he walked alone into the shelter, plunged his hand into the can of gasoline and firmly grasped the grenade while holding the striker lever safely against the grenade body.

Walking back out into the open, he was met by his sergeant assistant who forced a piece of wire into the holes where the pin had been removed and they took it away.

For the EOD it was a fairly routine incident, but it illustrated the daily danger in their lives and the professionalism with which they approached it. The NIS agents who had seen ample evidence of what explosives do to human bodies, were uniformly impressed.

The investigation into this incident would go nowhere however. No worthwhile forensic evidence could be developed, and there were no witnesses other than the marine who made the discovery. Clearly, there were internal problems within the unit but no tangible leads could help identify any suspects.

*****

In the hills south of An Hoa and the Arizona territory was a mountaintop fire support base known as FSB Ryder. From Ryder the marines had a clear view of the enemy from all sides. But it was their view of the large An Hoa Basin to their north that underscored the base's strategic value. The North Vietnamese Army units moving into the Arizona, into Go Noi Island, and their favorite rocket-launching sites situated closer to Da Nang had to pass through Ryder's artillery fan.

The Twelfth Marines and their Marine engineers had turned the hilltop firebase into an impressive bastion. The perimeter was both heavily wired and mined and was interspersed with strategically sited defensive bunkers which had considerable overhead cover in the form of sand bags. Their resupply was by regularly scheduled helicopter lifts.

[217]

The cannon-cockers on Ryder were a proud bunch who knew they were doing a good job providing artillery support to fellow Marine infantrymen operating in the large valley below them. They routinely sniped at the small enemy groups with their 105 and 155mm howitzers when the unwise Northerners attempted to cross the valley. When laser-sighting gear arrived, NCOs claimed they were getting first-round kills on individual targets, without the need for bracketing.

There were a few troublemakers chaffing over the "old-fashioned" style of Marine authority imposed by senior NCOs, and there was a growing concern that a narcotics problem was developing. Nobody slept well on an isolated mountaintop that was surrounded by the enemy, knowing that the marines on guard duty might be impaired.

Threats were being made against various NCOs and a fragmentation grenade was found attached to the NCO latrine door. The NCO thought to be in the greatest danger of attack was quietly moved off of the mountain and to the rear. Special Agent Carl Skiff traveled to Ryder to investigate, where his inquiries implicated several marines involved with marijuana usage. But as the investigation proceeded, sinister evidence of a much more serious nature was uncovered.

It seems that a small group was planning a reprisal by detonating the central artillery magazines on the small mountaintop. Given the size of the ammunition caches, the massive resulting explosion would ensure the complete destruction of the entire installation. Satchel charges had been assembled and a date to carry out the attack had been set.

Alerted to the threat, command moved quickly to transfer the suspected conspirators away from the base in advance of the attack, and disaster was averted.

*****

In this growing atmosphere of uncertainty and turbulence, military commands were exceptionally sensitive to every overt expression of discontent. The Marine Corps was certainly not the only crucible of dissent, as illustrated by an incident involving a five-inch naval gun aboard a Navy destroyer. Underway and being replenished by the ammunition ship USS *Pyro,* command would find themselves in the midst of a situation that required a call to NISRA Da Nang requesting urgent assistance.

USS *Blue,* a Fletcher-class destroyer, had been assigned to fire naval gunfire support missions from its position off the coast of I Corps. Naval gunfire assistance was often called for from units in trouble. Renowned for their accuracy, Navy ships on the gun line routinely fired their batteries at shore targets all night long, in the mornings the magazines would often need refilling.

The crew would get very little sleep at night as the batteries "banged away" with terrific reports. When daylight finally came, it was then time to clean and service the equipment, and get ready for the next mission. This could come at virtually at any time. The crew of a warship employed on the gun line faced chronic fatigue and stress. Special Agent Lorne Hamilton was assigned to this case, and he brought with him an excellent knowledge of onboard ship fire control systems from his own service at sea. He was flown to the gun line by helicopter, where he immediately began his inquiries aboard the two ships.

He quickly determined the facts that were central to the incident had taken place as *Pyro* had come alongside to pass ammunition to *Blue* for replenishment of their magazine. To access the forward magazines, the five-inch turret had been turned to the side and with muzzles depressed. The crew aboard the ammunition ship had begun rigging lines and other equipment for the operation when one of the guns, now pointed directly at the supply ship, was fired. There had been no secondary explosion, in fact no projectile penetrated the supply ship as the gun had been fired without a projectile.

One of the *Pyro* crewmen who had been standing only a few feet from the muzzle when the gun went off had been blown over and had received burns. He seemed to be shell-shocked from his near-death experience. How could something like this have been an accident?

Hamilton was known for his methodical approach toward investigations. When he interviewed the key players aboard the

[219]

destroyer, he learned that a fire control petty officer had been showing a new crewmember the guns.

The petty officer admitted to grasping the pistol grip used for firing them and pulling the trigger. The resulting detonation had been entirely unexpected and no one admitted to knowing how the gun had come to be loaded.

The interviews of the turret crewmembers that were responsible for loading and servicing the guns were not initially productive. Hamilton was now suspicious, and digging further he learned that the crewmembers did not always fully secure their gun turrets between missions. In this instance, he found that the gun turrets had not been secured the night before.

Destroyers are narrow vessels built for speed, not comfort. They buck and rear in large seas and lean dramatically when making the sort of underway turns they're known for. Hamilton knew this.

He patiently reconstructed the events that he envisioned by demonstrating that when the destroyer was underway at high speed and heeled over in a hard turn, a round left sitting on a loading tray could possibly have slipped into the self-closing breach. This scenario was a recipe for disaster, but it was not sabotage.

*****

10   SAIGON AND CAM RANH, 1969 TO 1970

Saigon was the gateway for all agents assigned to Vietnam, and their arrival at Tan Son Nhut Airport and the subsequent introduction to the city were unforgettable experiences for most.

By 1969 a large percentage of passengers to and from Vietnam were being flown in by contract carriers on commercial passenger jets. Travis Air Force Base was not far from San Francisco California, and remained a favored departure point for the flights. These were usually aboard Boeing 707s or DC8s configured to carry as many passengers as possible. When meals were served, they were spartan. The service was certainly not commercial grade either, but the stewardesses were considerate of the lot of the young men heading to their uncertain destinies.

Stops at Hickham Air Force Base Hawaii, and Clark Air Force Base in the Philippines allowed the lucky ones not traveling the full distance to the war zone the opportunity to disembark.

Normally about sixteen hours or so after the beautiful California coast had faded away the passengers stared down at a red and barren coastline. An announcement from the cockpit was usually made that the aircraft was coming over Vietnam at this point.

Pilots maintained altitude until they were quite close to Saigon, then began a rather un-civilian like and steep approach to the strip. Few passengers said anything when the wheels touched the tarmac as a cheerful stewardess welcomed everyone to Vietnam.

Even men familiar with Far Eastern tropic climes were taken aback when the passenger door opened and the humid mantle that covered Tan Son Nhut wafted in, smothering the last vestiges of Western hygiene. The olfactory cocktail of burned jet fuel, excrement, rotting vegetables, and humanity, was unforgettable.

Some new arrivals compared the exit from the aircraft to a passage from one world to another, and entering customs hall in the old airport terminal reinforced this impression. Faded Air France posters printed in the '50s announced destinations like Angkor Wat and Paris, while Vietnamese officials scurried around under slowly turning ceiling fans.

With immigration formalities completed, tired newly arriving agents who had been looking forward to finally finishing their journey, then faced the Vietnamese telephone system for the first time. The system was comprised of a series of overlapping exchanges operated by Vietnamese women, and a caller needed to know what exchange the number was a part of before a connection could be made.

The Naval Investigative Service Office, Vietnam was located in the southern Chinese quarter known as Cholon. The Tiger Telephone Exchange serviced Cholon. Once they had been connected to the Tiger Exchange, callers needed to tell the operator they wanted Tiger 3967. Even a friendly Air Force security policeman might have trouble getting through the Tiger switchboard, but eventually a voice on the other end told the new guy to sit tight and wait. Somebody would be on the way.

Beyond the airport gates Saigon festered. Grossly overtaxed by the war's refugees and opportunists, few of the city's basic amenities such as water, electricity, or sewerage were fully functional. Those that worked still weren't dependable.

An agent's first exposure to Saigon would be the drive from Tan Son Nhut through areas of the Gia Dinh District, hastily thrown up in the false boom of the war. The traffic was always chaotic since there were no rules of the road other than "the largest has the right-of-way." The battered Navy sedan shared the street with pedicab drivers (called cyclo in Vietnam), farmers pushing carts loaded with produce, buses, pretty Vietnamese girls on Honda 50 motorcycles, and military vehicles spewing clouds of diesel fumes.

Along street verges and sidewalks, the commercial panoply was everywhere… repairers of tubes and tires were set up beside cigarettes and bread loaf vendors. People were everywhere. Fecal matter stood in the gutters. Every now and then, a bare backside was thrust over the curb to deposit more of it. It was not a bad thing that prudence dictated that car windows be rolled up when Westerners drove through the streets. Open windows might attract a grenade, and if not that, certainly some well-fed flies.

Street verges that were once broad sidewalks were cluttered with humanity now, but many graceful tamarind trees still remained casting their afternoon shadows over narrow storefronts and the dwellings above them. Where no building front faced the street, high walls topped with glass or barbed wire did.

NISOV and the NISRA field offices were situated behind just such a wall. Cholon, the scene of grim street battles and considerable damage during the Tet Offensive the year before, was well mended a year later. Successive generations of Vietnamese had become

[222]

skilled at plastering bullet holes and shrapnel chips in the masonry walls. One surrounded an entire city block, enclosing the premises of the Army Post Exchange, a military post office, and the Chase Manhattan Bank.

"Saigon street scene" portable soup kitchens opposite the Cholon office

The old home that housed NISOV had been built on a corner and behind a seven foot wall. In more peaceful times it must have provided its owners with a quiet refuge from the city beyond. Now, a permanent sentry in a guard post adjacent to the steel entry gate monitored the street, guarded Navy vehicles, and controlled all entry. Clutching a well-worn M1 Garand, his smiling face greeted every new arrival, who by then were seriously wondering what their next 365 days in Viet Nam would bring.

[223]

Inside the gate a covered walkway lead to the front entrance…large
mango trees provided shade. Inside the door was a small waiting
area, decorated with a collage of photographs of those staff and
agents that were assigned. The clerical staff was situated beyond,
and the CO's office was to the immediate left. It was here that the
Navy yeoman accepted orders and arranged for flights onward to up-
country if this was required.

NISO Vietnam was co-located with the Cholon PX.

The XO and the adviser to Vietnamese counterparts were quartered
in what had been a single bedroom, along with the supervising
agent and the NISRA senior resident agent and his assistant. The
agent offices were in the servant quarters immediately to the rear.
The agents, themselves arriving hot and dirty at the end of the day,
typically welcomed the new arrivals and then got them settled with
a bunk for the night.

Later in the afternoon at the end of the day, the migration from the
office would begin preceded by the sound of security containers
being slammed shut and combination dials spinning. In small
groups the agents would leave the office compound and cross the
street. Dodging cyclos and motorcycles, they headed for the
opposite corner where semi-permanent street vendors were established just outside a walled eatery known to everyone as Fuji's
Restaurant. Many believed that Fuji had been a holdover from the
Japanese occupation of Indochina, but no one knew for sure.
Travelling north, a second street was crossed and then the
abandoned railway tracks were negotiated before the Five Oceans

[224]

BOQ came into sight. Army BOQ managers assigned three men to each of the two-cubicle rooms, and agents assigned to Saigon had passed their room assignments on to successors for years.

Room number 4 was the epicenter of NISOV social life. Its bar with refrigerator chairs and coffee tables, was the after-work gathering spot for agents, assigned naval officers, and quite often their supervising agent.

"The mystery man" was permanently assigned the bunk behind the bar, meaning a bed could always be found for transit personnel. "Newbies" often spent their first night in the bunk, in this most popular room in the BOQ. If they were lucky, they were treated to a meal up on the rooftop first, followed by a few drinks afterward before lapsing into an exhausted sleep.

Room number 4 not only had a well-equipped bar, it also had a very large resident rat that lived in its primitive shower drain. Shower water, definitely non-potable, was not carried away from the tiled shower by a central floor drain as normally happens. Rather, it collected and drained out a hole on one side through a gap about the size of a common brick.

Quite regularly, room number 4's rat became alarmed as water began pouring through his home. He would make a rapid foray into the shower and run several quick circuits around it, scampering over the feet of the "showerer", before exiting back to his lair. Newbies found this experience especially disconcerting, and there were amused and knowing looks when room 4 drinkers heard yells from the shower area. It was all part of the initiation process.

For both new arrivals to the Saigon office and agents in transit to Da Nang, breakfast at the Five Oceans hotel was always an eye-opener. As was the case in most buildings of its vintage, the roof area of the old hotel was intended to be a service area. When the Army took over its management, the roof became the logical location for dining facilities. Bar facilities were available, a small stage could be erected for the entertainment, and barbecues were popular.

Rising several stories behind temporary huts erected by Saigon refugees on the abandoned rail line, the Five Oceans BOQ was a short walk away from the office

When the weather cooperated, an evening on the rooftop could be very pleasant, with a cool freshening breeze carrying away some of the dust and fumes of the day. The whole visual array of Saigon could be seen off in the distance.

Breakfast there however, was devoid of all charm. The tropical sun rises early, as did the patrons and merchants of the market immediately adjacent to the BOQ. It was served in a timber-framed and fly screened SEA hut erected on the roof. This effectively served as a shelter from the rain and to a lesser extent from the insects, but all the inescapable odors of rotting produce, fish, garbage, and waste wafted through.

*****

The term "Vietnamization" has been referred to in earlier chapters and it deserves further explanation at this point. By 1970 it was much more than a catch phrase, and had in fact become a policy that changed the lives of everybody living in the Republic of South Vietnam.

President Johnson, before his March 1968 decision not to run for re-election, entertained several strategic options for pursuing the war.

[226]

He had not been a vigorous supporter of the military strategy to "punish the enemy until meaningful negotiations occurred". The Tet Offensive, undoubtedly a military victory for the United States and its allies, had been perceived in the United States as a stalemate...or worse.

Bowing to growing domestic pressure and dissent, President Johnson decided upon a new strategy. This would over time, turn the responsibility for the prosecution of the war over to what proved to be an ill-prepared South Vietnamese force. Not surprisingly, the president did not consult America's Vietnamese allies before initiating his plan. In reality Johnson's strategy was a means of finally extricating the United States from the war, whatever the cost.

The newly elected President, Richard M. Nixon, waited until the middle of 1969 to embrace Vietnamization himself and a policy crafted by Secretary of Defense Melvin Laird got the ball rolling.

By the end of the year, the United States was to withdraw some of its troops and the South Vietnamese were to assume certain new military responsibilities.

Ironically, the Vietnamese did not recognize this as an American cut-and-run strategy, but saw it as an accelerated equipping and training program for their troops. The war was a long way from over in 1970, but by then it was being fought in a different way.

With an increased emphasis on pacification and joint operations with the South Vietnamese, a larger portion of their country was rendered safe. Killing still occurred every day to be sure, but the large-scale military movements had decreased from the previous years. This was largely due to more than a decade of hard work, sacrifice, and investment in South Vietnam by the U.S. government and its people.

In 1970, as I neared the end of my first year in Vietnam, I decided to extend my tour. Most of 1969 had been spent in far-north I Corps. My new assignment was that of another one-man satellite unit, this time operating out of Cam Ranh Bay. While not exactly a backwater, Cam Ranh was known as relatively pleasant duty, both because there had been very little enemy activity on the Cam Ranh

Peninsula and also because naval elements there had been relatively law-abiding.

Cam Ranh Bay itself is a magnificent natural harbor, situated in what was then II Corps about midway up the coast between Da Nang and Saigon. The U.S. Navy had visited it during World War II, and the French armed forces had made use of the anchorage for many years, so it was logical that the United States would choose to transform the sandy isthmus and bay into a huge logistics facility. With the aid of civilian contractors a massive air facility was completed, fuel storage tanks were built, and substantial ammunition and logistic storage parks were constructed there. As a bonus, topography rendered much of the base, especially the Navy at the southern end, relatively immune to enemy rocket attack.

In 1970 the U.S. Navy elements at Cam Ranh were evenly divided between the aviation elements located at the air base and the personnel supporting the patrol vessels and communications located farther down the peninsula on the water's edge.

I had visited Cam Ranh Bay earlier, during a weekend away from Da Nang in late 1969. A school friend was serving as the officer in charge of an Army military intelligence detachment set amid sand dunes with sweeping views of the South China Sea. My weekend away had been a quiet and very pleasant change from the more hostile atmosphere farther north. The base was a city made up of hundreds of SEA huts set in individual cantonments and was notice-ably devoid of Vietnamese civilians. Only one fishing village was located within the base area. This had been entirely fenced off and had military police assigned to make sure that U.S. personnel were excluded.

When I arrived in Cam Ranh to take over the Naval Investigative Service Satellite Unit in March 1970, I was looking forward to having my own office once again. The office was furnished with a desk, chairs, and a security container. It was located at the Navy base amongst spaces previously used by the U.S. Navy patrol craft, fast (PCF or swift boat) support personnel. The Vietnamese were then taking over the "swifts", and it was anticipated that the VNN would soon have the entire office building to themselves. As a result, a move became essential. I could not comply with security regulations governing the storage of classified material when my safe was located in an office space controlled by non-U.S. personnel.

Fortunately, the U.S. Coast Guard detachment there had a single room available in a small office that was built overlooking the beach. I quickly arranged to have my office furnishings moved across the sand to the new building and quickly grew to appreciate my Coast Guard hosts. In time, with other moves afoot in the Vietnamization program, the Naval Intelligence liaison officer (NILO) would share the same building.

And I knew that I was one of the lucky ones. With a magnificent view of the sweeping white-sand beach and the beautiful azure waters of the South China Sea less than twenty yards away, my workspace could not have been improved upon. Sleeping quarters were nearby…a simple private cubicle, screened and louvered, provided just enough room for my cot, table, and fan. Its previous owners had built shelves from ammunition boxes to hold a collection of paperback novels. Obviously, my predecessors had also learned that reading was one of the safer after-hours pastimes in Vietnam.

As more Vietnamese were moved onto the base, the U.S. Navy sailors became unsettled. Shower and toilet blocks had to be designated for the two different nationalities. Peasant Vietnamese had, what was to us, an unpleasant habit of standing on the toilet seats and squatting while spraying excrement in places other than the bowl. Fixtures were broken. Security of personal effects, which was always an issue, became more of a problem. Any theft was blamed on the Vietnamese, and in many instances this was justified.

Now settled into my new routine, I began learning the ins and outs of how Cam Ranh worked. The base was under the command of a U.S. Navy commander, a helpful dynamic leader who unfortunately was burdened with an aging reserve executive officer who had a pronounced talent for putting both feet in his mouth.

A short distance northward on the beach was the Naval Communication Station, a large facility of considerable importance. Still further away at a massive concrete airstrip, Naval Air Facility

(NAF) Cam Ranh occupied the western edge of the taxiway. NAF shared its hangars with a detachment of Army P2V Neptune aircraft, there in support of an Army Security Agency unit. And it was here that the senior naval officer in II Corps, a naval aviator captain, hung his hat. Here too was the II Corps Navy legal office…a key point of contact for me.

It soon became clear that changes were afoot! Young enlisted men were not privy to the guidelines that directed the conduct of the war, but they were certainly attuned to the changes brought about by Vietnamization.

When an infantry unit was withdrawn, those who did not see it read about it in the next day's edition of *Stars and Stripes* newspaper or heard via Armed Forces Radio. It wasn't envy that unsettled people, it was the realization that the United States was pulling out of Vietnam. There was nothing glorious about the prospect of being killed or wounded when all anybody, (especially people at home), could think about was bugging out. The men began to think about little other than the day they were due for rotation out of country.

In the first month or two, my life as Cam Ranh's naval intelligence agent became almost a routine. Lead cases came to me from my SRA in Saigon. Trusting neither the post office nor sailors at the communication station who might be tempted to read my message traffic, I began catching the Navy's Friday Cl17 flight to Saigon, hand-carrying my file folders with me. I was back at Cam Ranh again on Monday.

I met many more members of the command and learned more about what was happening at the grassroots level than ever before. With a growing concern about the menace of drug abuse that by then was sweeping Vietnam, commands asked me to conduct drug awareness programs, mostly for senior COs.

The troops seemed quite knowledgeable about the narcotics then in circulation, but I soon learned that most chiefs could not recognize the distinctive odor of burning cannabis. I burned old marijuana seized as evidence on a Bunsen burner, passed around opium, and showed them illustrations of heroin.

[230]

It was at about this time that, SRA Bernie Taylor gave me a classified case that was unlike any I had thus far encountered.

A "confidential informant of known reliability", (i.e., another agency in the intelligence community), had intercepted a letter mailed from NAF Cam Ranh and addressed to a Soviet governmental division in the USSR. The mail was from a Navy officer with whom I was acquainted, who had expressed an interest in traveling to the Soviet Union.

My first course of action was to carry out discreet checks to determine the officer's current access level to classified material. Then during several informal contacts with him, and using my own personal interest in international travel as a catalyst, I learned that he hoped one day to ride the Trans-Siberian Railway and that he had even written for information and a brochure. This provided an explanation for what was most probably an innocent indiscretion. The Navy had a very real and legitimate concern about any member, contacting by any means, a hostile enemy power… the Soviet Union in particular. Mine was, I'm sure, only a facet of what was a much fuller investigation.

I began to notice that more of my time was being devoted to narcotics investigations. A new Navy padre had reported aboard, and straight as an arrow, the chaplain looked men who asked for advice about narcotics problems in the eye and told them they had a duty to report it. I soon had sailors turning up at my office, with many signing confessions implicating others. Barracks searches and interrogations were to follow.

Concerned commands naturally would take the most expedient option when ridding themselves of these people, none of whom were model sailors, either by means of military justice or the ad-ministrative discharge process. Admin discharges were on "other-than-honorable" terms. Selfishly, I was glad to see them go quickly since I was billeted among a growing group of recalcitrants and was very aware of my vulnerability to an attack by fragmentation grenade.

Despite the distractions caused by "the dopers," life at NISSU Cam Ranh was reasonably pleasant. The officers' club that was adjacent

[231]

to my office provided good company and a huge verandah. Occasionally the Army veterinarians (known as "dog mechanics") would gather up a group of Air Force nurses from the large evacuation hospital at the air base and take them down to the beach. There was always considerable competition for the attention of any American woman in Vietnam, perhaps even more-so in the hothouse atmosphere of the Cam Ranh enclave.

About August 1970, Cam Ranh became less isolated from the war when rockets fell on the naval air facility. Bunkers were then quickly repaired, extra barbed wire was erected, and patrols were increased. The aerial attacks were soon followed by sapper attacks led by North Vietnamese Army regulars.

Aircraft were always a favorite sapper target. On one occasion during my tenure there, a breach was made of the perimeter during which several of the sappers involved were killed and one was captured. I met the prisoner the following day when he arrived at the portion of my office I shared with the NILO. He was wearing an empty sandbag over his head and was being escorted by a young Vietnamese Navy officer whom I recognized to be a member of the Vietnamese Naval Security Bloc. Small dark and wiry, the North Vietnamese sapper looked remarkably fit for first having survived the privations of a march down the Ho Chi Minh Trail and then after living in the rugged, mountainous terrain inland from Cam Ranh. The interrogation was very much a Vietnamese affair. The sapper was secured to an office chair and blindfolded, facing his interrogator.

Never raising his voice, the young officer kept firing a string of questions at his captive, periodically prompting a response with a sharp smack on the bare inner thigh with a ruler. I was told that later a field telephone was produced and electric shocks were applied, but I had left long before that. I learned that valuable information had been obtained, and the wiry young sapper was on his way to the POW compound on Phu Quoc Island "for the duration."

By mid 1970 the Navy facility staff at Cam Ranh was beginning to act more like a group of naval advisers, which in many ways was what their roles had become.
Vietnamese officers and soldiers needed a good deal of follow-up

[232]

advice before they could be expected to effectively operate the fleet of patrol vessels given to them by the United States. The "swifts" and gunboats were a crucial element in halting the flow of contraband being transported by sea from North Vietnam. The U.S. Navy with the assistance of the Coast Guard had set up an effective blockade of the coast, and now it was time for Vietnamese to take the reins.

The Navy SEALs had been active in the Vietnam War from the very earliest time. Their Vietnamese counterparts were called the LDNN, an abbreviation that translates roughly to "soldiers who fight under the sea".

VC prisoners disembark

LDNN units had played important roles in early covert operations in North Vietnam, and it was perfectly logical that a SEAL detachment should play a role in training the new LDNN recruits. Cam Ranh was an ideal location for this purpose.

The training camp was a rough conglomerate of hooches and scrounged material and was located immediately outside the perimeter. SEALS were ostensibly an element of a Vietnamese command and this suited their purposes well. They were expected to observe normal military rules and courtesies while at the base but were largely free to act independently and travel where they wished.

The SEAL detachment commander, Lt. Richard Kuhn, USN, was a powerfully built officer with a penchant for unconventional approaches to the daily challenges of command.

He was ably assisted by petty officers led by Chief Churchill, a salty master chief hospital corpsman who had begun his combat career on August 7, 1942, with the invasion of Guadalcanal. Churchill wore among his many other decorations, the Purple Heart Medal with five clusters: "four of the six wounds were to my head," he was heard to say.

With more than two decades experience in treating combat injuries and a range of maladies, troops preferred his basic approach to medicine, in part because it did not involve a medical record entry. The standard treatment for chancroid involved immersion of the infected member in an open beer can filled with a potent, colorful solution of silver nitrate. His results were "guaranteed".

The hooch that was used for meetings and planning also had a bar built into the central partition. This plywood wall was adorned with a variety of trophies including captured NLF flags, a portrait of Ho Chi Minh captured in a cross-border raid, photographs of various personalities (including those undergoing Doc Churchill's renowned chancroid treatment), and a number of badly torn skivvy shorts. "Skivvy checks" are a long-standing SEAL tradition.

SEALS do not wear underwear, and unwritten law dictates that skivvies are not to be worn. Visitors to SEAL premises might be subjected to a skivvy check and offending garments removed forthwith…normally by reaching behind the waist of the outer garment, grasping the undergarment and tearing it off. All of Lieutenant Kuhn's men had served multiple tours in Vietnam under the most intense combat conditions. They were every bit as unconventional as their secret missions were.

Vietnamese SEALS in training

I enjoyed their company, watched with interest as they polished each group of Vietnamese recruits, and observed with awe the brutal punishment of the recruit's final test.

US Navy SEALS return

During "hell week", the quiet nights were shattered by squads of chanting LDNN aspirants running down the sandy streets carrying rubber boats over their heads. Each no-doubt wondered if they had what it took to survive the nonstop week with virtually no rest.

*****

[235]

In 1970 a Navy presence still remained at the port of Qui Nhon at its location north of Cam Ranh Bay. Qui Nhon had been a particularly important base in earlier days of the war when most supplies for the war in the Central Highlands were funneled across its docks.

The Army maintained important logistic facilities to support military initiatives in the highlands and northern coastal areas of II Corps.

The harbor was buffered by a seaward island of considerable elevation, so Qui Nhon was well protected but heavily congested with military and merchant shipping.

This traffic, combined with scores of Vietnamese coastal and fishing junks, made it easy to understand why a great deal of shipping in support of the war went elsewhere.

The Navy detachment was situated on the island, facing the protected harbor and the city of Qui Nhon. An LCM regularly traveled between the city and the base and was the source of logistic supply.

One of my trips to Qui Nhon was in response to a command request for assistance after irregularities were noticed in the small fleet post office. These post offices supplied most of the services then associated with civilian postal service, including mail order purchase and insured parcel service. Good mail service was a critical and morale-sensitive issue since receiving a letter or package at mail call was normally the only link service personnel had with the outside world during their yearlong tours of duty. When I received the call, the telephone link from Qui Nhon was not a good one and the details of the problem were not clear, but I agreed to travel the following day.

Agents wishing to take advantage of the comprehensive air transport system being operated by the U.S. Air Force, required patience and a set of orders. We regularly carried a set of mimeographed orders authorizing us to travel to wherever… whenever we deemed it necessary. As long as the Air Force received two copies of these and agents checked in at least two hours early, a sling seat would be reserved on the regularly scheduled C130. I avoided Air Force flights whenever possible because of these two-hour check-in policies and the regular delays.

For flights between Cam Ranh and Qui Nhon however, I had no options available. Arriving mid-afternoon, I was met by a Navy jeep and then treated to an afternoon LCM trip through the busy harbor. That evening, I interviewed several witnesses about their suspicions regarding the post office. Initial indications were that the postal clerk was simply stealing various items of value through the mail system.

Everybody in Vietnam, at one time or another, used the mail-order catalog service provided by the huge PX in Japan. It offered everything from stereo amplifiers to Mikimoto pearls. The items that were ordered were often delivered by mail to Vietnam within a week or ten days, but could also be delivered to a U.S. address if desired. Customs declarations were prominently displayed on all of these orders, so the mail clerk knew what these parcels contained.

I decided to test the clerk's honesty by making up a parcel with its attractive contents prominently marked, and put it in the mail. Not long after the package was dropped off, both the post office and the clerk were searched. Unmistakable evidence of postal theft was discovered, and the subject of the investigation quickly confessed to a number of offenses. The mail and other related stolen items were recovered, and eventually found their way to their rightful owners.

The once-quiet Cam Ranh office grew progressively busier during my tenure there. In late 1970 I was transferred to Saigon and turned the operation over to Special Agent Anderson T. Lambert.

Lambert's caseload would skyrocket, and a deteriorating situation at the southern end prompted him to relocate the office to the naval air facility. Soon after the move, a 122mm Soviet rocket plowed through the roof of the officers' club only moments after he had left it. There were numerous casualties as a result and Andy Lambert was seriously shaken by the loss…it haunted him the rest of his life.

*****

[237]

11 SAIGON, 1969 TO 1970: POW RESCUE AND THE *EAGLE* MUTINY

In mid-year of 1969 NISOV came under the inspired leadership of commanding officer Lt. Cdr. Thomas A. Brooks, USN. At that time, Tom Brooks already exhibited the hard-charging brilliance that characterized his ultimate rise to directorship of Naval Intelligence. He quickly learned the ropes in Saigon, set his goals, and started making things happen. Junior officers soon learned to make a note when the CO made a request or gave an order, because Tom Brooks never forgot.

Troop levels had reached their peak with more than five hundred thousand Americans assigned to commands within the Republic of Vietnam. U.S. Navy forces too were at a record level, and NISOV special agent staffing reached its high-water mark of twenty-one.

These men were distributed among the two resident agencies and four one-man satellite units then in operation. In harsh contrast, the Army had literally hundreds of criminal investigators and military intelligence agents in Vietnam. The Air Force OSI was also very well represented in country.

Commander Brooks has said the quality of his all-volunteer agent force permitted his command to do far more with fewer resources, but he acknowledges that five times the number of special agents could have been usefully employed in Vietnam.

"The special agents were uniformly outstanding. All were volunteers. They were dedicated, hard-working professionals, and we had great admiration for them. The two men who were my supervising agents, Don Schunk and Allan J. Kersenbrock, were two of the finest men I have ever worked with. When I returned to the United States, I commented to the then-director of Naval Intelligence, Rear Admiral Rex Rectanus that I wished that the naval intelligence community at large possessed the level of professionalism and dedication that I found in the NIS special agent corps."

The reality of a twenty-one-man agent force was simply that the NIS agents could not take every request for assistance that came their way.

In the field, it was prudent for agents on the scene to consider carefully the sometimes fine line between war-induced incidents and those involving overt criminal acts before agreeing to investigate. NIS accepted no requests for help with non-felonious criminal investigations, and by 1969 the sheer volume of serious criminal cases had every agent involved in investigations of this type anyway. The historical emphasis on counterintelligence operations changed to criminal investigations.

In Da Nang, Tom Brooks exploited his successful relationship with the Vietnamese Naval intelligence officers there by formulating and implementing a program to recruit civilian informants from those employed within U.S. Navy installations.

In coordination with the U.S. Army's 525 Military Intelligence Group, the mission objective was to utilize informants to identify Viet Cong sympathizers and other internal problems in general. The initiative was eventually expanded to the recruiting and running of agents in areas near Navy and Marine Corps facilities in I Corps to report movement of VC in the area. These collection efforts were designed to produce information about graft, theft, and intimidation rather than identifying an "enemy within".

Naval counterintelligence requirements were satisfied through this in a variety of ways. U.S. Army counterintelligence personnel were distributed throughout South Vietnam and shared their information. So did well-established CIA resources. The Vietnamese Navy Security Bloc, to which a full-time adviser from NISOV was assigned, also provided information on a regular basis, and was more than willing to assist when they were needed. And the VNNSB would be asked for their help in the case of the VC's capture of naval intelligence officer Lt. Cdr. Jack Graf, USN.

As one would expect of a career intelligence officer…prior to his assignment to South Vietnam Graf had been exposed to very sensitive, but compartmentalized, information. His capture, the only such case for the Navy in the Vietnam War, was viewed seriously and with alarm by senior naval intelligence officers. They wanted Jack Graf back immediately, whatever it took.

Graf's Vietnam assignment had been as fourth coastal zone intelligence officer, and his area of responsibility encompassed most of the Mekong Delta. This was the most densely populated region in the country, and included riverine areas in which Viet Cong forces remained a potent force.

It was over the coastal mudflats of Kien Hoa Province where the tributaries of the Mekong flow into the South China Sea, that Graf was lost. He had been flying in a U.S. Army Mohawk on a routine intelligence collection mission, when his aircraft came under fire. Both Graf and the pilot survived the crash but were captured by Viet Cong troops.

COMNAVFORV senior intelligence officer Capt. Robert Pyle, USN, requested most urgent assistance from the U.S. Army's Joint Personnel Recovery Center (JPRC). He asked Tom Brooks to travel to Honolulu to see Mrs. Graf, and assure her that everything possible was being done to find her husband. Brooks found a seat on an Air Force C141 on its return leg to Hawaii, and flew into Hickham Air Force Base just a few days before Thanksgiving Day 1969.

His first stop was the Commander in Chief Pacific Fleet (CINCPACFLT) Chaplain's Office to get the name of the casualty assistance coordination officer (CACO), a Marine lieutenant colonel. He was not there at the time.

Brooks got Graf's address and drove over to their house. Graf's wife was no longer living there and neighbors were unable to provide any useful information as to where she had gone. Walking through the neighborhood searching for anybody who might know, he spoke to an old man who was sitting on his front porch…his daughter had the new address.

The Graf's had no children. Mrs. Graf and her German shepherd dog lived alone in a new housing development where they had moved just before Graf had been deployed. She had no relatives on the island, knew very few people, and was a lonely and very worried lady. Incredibly, though she had been notified about her husband having been shot down weeks before, nobody had been by to see her.

Brooks recalls, "I mentioned the CACO's name, and his name meant nothing to her. I assured her of our efforts to recover Jack, left her my name and address, and set out to find that CACO. I found him at his CINCPACFLT desk and angrily accosted him demanding to know why he had not done his duty with regard to Mrs. Graf."

"He turned beet red and was about to dress me down for talking disrespectfully to him as a senior officer. I suggested that we go see the chief of staff if he had a problem, but if not to then answer my question."

The Marine Officer turned defensive, saying he had tried his best to see Mrs. Graf, but that she had moved and he had been unable find her. Brooks provided him with her address and telephone number, and some unsolicited words of advice.

The next day when he called Mrs. Graf, she said the CACO had been to see her the previous afternoon and had been pleasant and very apologetic for not finding her earlier. She characterized him as a nice and helpful man. "I didn't tell her about our meeting, but I expressed my pleasure and wished her well."

There was no Thanksgiving in 1969 for Tom Brooks. As luck would have it, he lost the holiday when he crossed the International Date Line on his way back to Saigon.

Back in Vietnam, the effort to recover Graf was not going well. None of the U.S. elements had intelligence capabilities in the area and the closest South Vietnamese presence was fifty miles from the crash site. It was increasingly clear too that the Army staff at JPRC was incapable of formulating any imaginative operation or of implementing a prompt reaction of any kind to the crisis at hand. It fell to Tom Brooks and his Vietnamese counterparts at VNNSB to rescue Graf before it was too late.

Of primary importance in the early planning stages of the operation

[241]

was dependable intelligence about the situation at and around the crash site. What enemy units were present, where were they, and were there any stories in circulation about captured Americans?

Commanders Nguyen Nhu Vy and Nguyen Do Hai of VNNSB set about locating any dependable Vietnamese with knowledge and connections in this lonely, hostile area of the delta. They found a VNN junior-grade lieutenant with relatives in the area who volunteered to assist.

This brave Vietnamese officer set off alone aboard a Honda 50 motorcycle into Indian country dressed in civilian clothes and with full knowledge of the consequences should one of the many Viet Cong sympathizers in the area identify him.

He covered a good deal of country in his efforts to acquire information. Ultimately, his relatives provided the first tangible intelligence about the crash and its victims. In return, his family expected the Americans to evacuate them by helicopter and resettle them at a location well away from VC influence.

Armed with the intelligence, U.S. Army officers at JPRC proved a model of bureaucratic inertia. Alternative operational plans were drawn up and debated as valuable time ticked away. Their final plan envisaged floating 155mm howitzers down the river on barges and using Laotian Montagnards to conduct the rescue attempt in the swamps of Kien Hoa. To put this rather astonishing plan together would take "several weeks". Clearly Jack Graf was not going to get any meaningful help from them.

Finally the Navy took the matter into its own hands. Tom Brooks visited the province chief's senior American adviser, a retired U.S. Army lieutenant colonel, in Ben Tre (Kien Hoa City).

The senior adviser immediately volunteered to help and went to work to make a team of U.S. SEAL advisers and their South Vietnamese SEAL counterparts available for the operation. But the plan met with JPRC resistance and it was concluded that he could only use assets that belonged to him and over which U.S. headquarters in Saigon had no say.

Thus Lieutenant Commander Brooks and VNNSB adviser Lt. Ron Lodziewski were given two squads of Vietnamese Regional Forces militia, known as RFPFs (or ruff-puffs), and a handful of Kit Carson scouts, who were Viet Cong deserters. They all piled into two overloaded Hueys and set out for the tip of Kien Hoa Peninsula.

Here the Kit Carson scouts interrogated villagers and learned that a white man...(perhaps Graf) and a black man, (the Mohawk pilot), had been taken down the river by boat about twelve hours before. The teams climbed back into the helos and tried to reconnoiter the river on the way back, but the jungle canopy was so dense that boats could easily hide at the sound of any approaching helicopters. Tom Brooks remembers the Graf episode as a crushing disappointment, "On December 11, 1969, I was sitting in Ben Tre with my adviser to the VNNSB, Lt. Ron Lodziewski, waiting for a ride back to Saigon after our operation had failed to locate Graf and his pilot."

"It was obvious that American incompetence was central to the failure. I will never forget that brave Vietnamese lieutenant junior-grade who got nothing more for his efforts than a rather emotional thank you from me. It seemed to be enough for him."

Returning to Saigon, after the abortive rescue attempt, Brooks and Lieutenant Lodziewski debriefed Captain Pyle. Brooks was careful not to reveal too many details, but it quickly became clear that the two had been much too closely involved in the operation, including going out into Indian country with the RFPFs.

Brooks remembers, "This got me a sound chewing out for my second offense at traveling places where I was not allowed to go because of my clearances. The first time was for driving my jeep from Quang Tri to Da Nang down Bernard Fall's famous *Street Without Joy*. It was a very interesting trip and totally uneventful, but very much against the rules and in retrospect not too smart".

A number of months later after most of the Kien Hoa Peninsula had been pacified, a U.S. Army helo pilot observed a man waving his shirt from a clearing and landed to investigate. It was the pilot of the Mohawk who had managed to escape his captors. He confirmed that the NISOV rescue team had just missed them by hours and related the sad news that Jack Graf had been killed attempting to escape.

Subsequent interrogations of a VC defector revealed that Graf's body had been buried in a bridge embankment, but that spring flooding had washed away both the bridge and embankment. Jack Graf received the burial at sea he would have wanted in the nearby downstream waters of the South China Sea.

Brooks relates, "I have often thought about Mrs. Graf and wondered how she made out. I still feel sorrow for her. More importantly, I can still feel anger for that CACO. Brave Vietnamese risked their lives to try to rescue a man they had never even met, and the CACO couldn't take the trouble to track down Mrs. Graf's new address."

*****

Historically, a cornerstone of the NIS mission has been to protect sensitive information that if compromised, could result in serious damage to both U.S. interests and personnel. Proper procedures for the safe custody of classified materials were drummed into every person who was exposed to it.

Especially in a war zone, it was expected that all material classified "for official use only" through to "top secret" would be carefully maintained under lock and key and kept in a designated secure area.

When reports NISOV received from an informant indicated that a Vietnamese street vendor was selling baked goods wrapped in official Navy documents, it could be safely said that it caused considerable concern. The informant said that a Vietnamese employee of COMNAVFORV who had access to the burn bags used to store discarded classified documents awaiting destruction had been selling the documents to the street vendor.

The Cookie Lady, as she was soon christened by those working the case, was a Vietnamese street vendor identified as a possible low-ranking element in an enemy espionage operation. NISOV's Vietnamese case officer was sent to the Saigon street corner near the premises of COMNAVFORV, where the Cookie Lady was known to operate. He first engaged the entrepreneur in conversation then bought three cookies from her. The Cookie Lady obligingly wrapped each in an official U.S. Navy document, classified confidential.

Investigation quickly determined that neither the Cookie Lady nor her friend the enterprising Navy employee who had supplied the "used paper" could read English. Nor did inquiries give rise to suspicions that either had connections with enemy personnel or sympathizers. The glaring deficiencies in security procedures at COMNAVFORV were quickly addressed to be sure!

*****

NISOV maintained an interest in activities in and around Saigon's waterfronts, as it had from the earliest days. Under Tom Brooks, a network of informants was activated who targeted Viet Cong activity in the vital maritime commercial hub. Executive officer Lt. Norman Idleberg, USN, served as the case officer.

Because vast quantities of war supplies moved across the docks, it was important to know whether the VC had any influence among the longshoremen, deck hands, local boatmen, and merchants working there. The network, using civilian informants of various nationalities produced interesting results…though perhaps not what was expected.

It turned out that the commercial opportunities for the dockside underworld organizations were so attractive that the enemy had been unable to establish a toehold. Chinese and Vietnamese criminal societies and families carefully guarded their interests at the Port of Saigon.

As a result, they were well aware of activity in the area, and they were willing to cooperate and share their information as long as there was no disruption to their own operations. NISOV did not ignore reports of criminal activity at the docks entirely, so it became necessary to consider the best interests of the Navy in these cases. As Maynard Anderson had discovered four years earlier, the presence of so many Americans in South Vietnam created new

[245]

opportunities for criminal enterprise.

A staggering volume of materiel that was not limited to weapons, was required to sustain more than five hundred thousand military personnel and the system that supported them.

U.S. personnel had access to military commissary and post-exchange facilities that were in some ways superior to the supermarkets and department stores back home. South Vietnam was an economic backwater, a country of agrarian peasants unaccustomed to the merchandise Americans took for granted as daily necessities. Naturally, when this material was offered for sale to the Americans in stores that the Vietnamese could not access, opportunities were created for all sorts of illegal activity.

In the years before, entire shipping containers had been stolen en route to U.S. supply stores in Viet Nam. In 1970 the increased volume of material and numbers of troops with legal access to stores created opportunities for more sophisticated black marketing. GIs were not supposed to buy supplies at the PX for Vietnamese friends, and they were forbidden from reselling the merchandise.

Profit margins for this type of activity were attractive, and the po-tential gains for enterprising Vietnamese entrepreneurs were staggering. More sophisticated underworld elements in Saigon quickly learned that there were easier ways to get U.S. merchandise than taking chances with overt criminal activities such as robbery and theft. They would turn to a growing community of U.S. deserters, and the fringe-dwelling civilian technical representatives and support contractors who enjoyed legal access to the military supply system.

Saigon supported the largest deserter community in South Vietnam. Already a very large city, and growing more overpopulated every day, it offered hundreds of places where a deserter could hide from the authorities. While the runaway Americans money lasted, they could maintain a certain amount of independence from criminal elements of the Vietnamese community.

Bar owners and the Vietnamese women who managed them, kept a sharp lookout for men with no money and those with serious drug habits. Once recruited, these men represented immediate access to the U.S. supply system. The Vietnamese criminals ran cribs of deserters, furnishing them with forged and stolen identification that facilitated access to stores. Especially if they were supporting a drug habit, these men could be relied upon to return with the merchandise that they'd been sent out to purchase.

South Vietnam's fragile domestic economy precluded conversion of the local currency to a foreign exchange which could be traded internationally. Viet Cong elements continued to devise schemes to acquire U.S. currency to purchase internationally the materiel required for its war against the non-communists.

The domestic demand for the dollar, (known in-country as green), was so strong that authorities withdrew all U.S. currency from circulation, and introduced military payment certificates (MPC) as a substitute.

In theory MPC was valid for transactions within South Vietnam alone, and Vietnamese civilians were not supposed to possess it. In reality MPC was freely exchanged everywhere from bars to tailor shops for piasters. This behavior prompted authorities on several occasions to secretly change MPC types. By locking up the Americans in their compounds overnight, contacts with Vietnamese holding old MPC was limited. In this way the old MPC issue was rendered valueless unless a Vietnamese could find a way to get it into the compound and to a compliant American who would be willing exchange it. Attempts at this were rarely successful. Unless MPC could be converted into saleable merchandise such as tobacco, liquor, or stereo components, it was of little value to the Vietnamese criminal element. What was most desirable was MPC safely converted into U.S. dollars and deposited in a Hong Kong bank.

What the criminals needed was a negotiable instrument, and the U.S. postal money order suited this purpose perfectly. Deserters armed with false or stolen identification could legally purchase money orders at the unit post office. When this ruse became widespread, MACV installed a massive IBM computer to counter it by tracking money order purchasers by name, date of purchase, and the amount of money involved.

NIS and sister organizations regularly received the multi-paged

[247]

computer printouts showing that illegal currency manipulation had occurred. In Saigon, these often led agents into the heart of "deserter communities".

NISOV's mission required that careful scrutiny of these deserters be maintained. This was especially true if there were any indications that the man might defect to the enemy.

Lieutenant Idleberg recalled being involved in a mission to recover one such serviceman:

"I became involved because of my role as point of contact with the Vietnamese Navy Security Bloc. We received information from VNNSB that initiated the plan to extract him from his hideaway near Dalat, in the Central Highlands. I flew aboard a U.S. military aircraft to Dalat dressed in civilian clothes with a team of Vietnamese. After dark we moved in close to the hut where this guy was supposed to be. We hid behind an earthen berm, then charged in together and apprehended the American and his Vietnamese consort. She was released and he was returned to the naval brig on Plantation Road in Saigon. I recall that he made good an escape before we could talk to him again. This he accomplished without any clothing, and it was reported that he ran stark naked down Plantation Road before losing himself in one of the myriad back streets. Despite this, he was eventually recaptured."

Although NIS was always on watch for potential defectors, Norm Idleberg believes few deserters ever actually contemplated defection, "Most of those guys were either scared or disenchanted with their lot in the war. Some had found the girl of their dreams...someone of the opposite sex who paid attention to them, or they were just plain disgruntled."

There were never sufficient resources in any allied organization to seriously attack the deserter problem. There was certainly no political will to undertake an operation that would have pitted American MPs against American soldiers. Some deserters were very well organized, armed, and effectively shielded by sympathetic Vietnamese. NISOV never discovered indications that the VC was using the document-forging capabilities of the underworld to further their aims. Our belief was that the criminal elements were not

[248]

interested in such an arrangement because little commercial advantage would be derived from it.

*****

Jurisdictional issues exacerbated NISOV's problems dealing with illegal activities in the U.S. civilian community. During the early years of the Vietnam War, courts had held that civilian employees of the U.S. government were not subject to the military legal framework afforded by the UCMJ. The Vietnamese National Police was seldom genuinely interested in alleged offenses by U.S. civilians, unless the offenses had potential for extortion or their help was specifically requested by a U.S. agency.

The U.S. military initiative in the Republic of Vietnam was highly dependent on civilian contractors not only for construction of critical infrastructure such as bridges, roads, and airfields but also for special projects such as aircraft maintenance and reconditioning. President Johnson had encouraged several prominent American contractors, lead by companies from his native Texas, to assemble the world's largest construction consortium, RMK-BRJ.

The consortium employed hundreds of U.S. citizens with specialty construction skills to tackle huge projects such as the massive military facility at Cam Ranh Bay.

The civilian contractors formed a separate stratum in the mélange that comprised the U.S. presence in Vietnam. Attracted by generous salaries, tax breaks, and the spirit of adventure, they lived on the Vietnamese economy. They often survived by their wits in insecure areas, with their only protection the goodwill of neighbors. Many stayed for several years, and most had Vietnamese mistresses or wives. A kindly appraiser might have labeled them as "pioneering stock."

RMK employed many thousands of both Vietnamese and expatriate Korean personnel, as well as Americans. Other U.S. construction and maintenance organizations included Pacific Architects and Engineers (PA&E).

Also in-country were many technical representatives representing aircraft companies, communication manufacturers, and helicopter maintenance companies.

Few but direct-hire U.S. civilian employees enjoyed full access to PX, ancillary banking, and military post office facilities, but the majority had at least partial privileges. Anyone who needed something badly enough could always find service personnel to buy it. This resulted in strange anomalies in the PX supply system as it tried to adjust for the strong domestic demand for such basics as laundry detergent.

On the other end of the value spectrum, the latest in Japanese refrigerators, stereo systems, radios, fans, and jewelry were much sought after in the Vietnamese civilian economy.

All were stocked in the larger post exchanges, and if an item was not actually in stock, it could quickly be ordered from the main Pacific exchange warehouse in Japan. Where there is demand, there always exists financial opportunity, and many in the civilian community abused the PX system for personal gain by making purchases and selling at inflated rates to Vietnamese clientele. One such man had been the subject of prolonged investigation in both Saigon and Japan.

A former U.S. Navy enlisted man with aircraft maintenance expertise, the civilian employee had missed very few opportunities to turn a dollar in the hotbed of Saigon's underworld. He was first linked to a major narcotics importation scheme after NIS agents intercepted kilo bundles of opium. He was also alleged to have been involved in a scheme to steal platinum from critical helicopter components during maintenance inspections. He was linked to illegal trade in gold and had been arrested and imprisoned by Vietnamese authorities for complicity in car theft and fencing schemes. There was also compelling evidence that he had been involved in a variety of illegal currency manipulation scams.

Other than encouraging the Vietnamese authorities to act, NIS agents had little recourse against the man and he knew it. But Special Agents Don Webb and Mike Jones were very patient men. They began accumulating reports on the suspect's activities, and a small Vietnamese police group with a name that translated roughly to Treasury Fraud Repression Unit showed interest.

Funding for the organization was founded predominantly on the assets it was able to seize and they also provided potential legal means for arrest and remand of the subject.

By the time the Treasury Fraud Repression Unit agreed to help with the case, Webb and Jones had pieced together the details of the suspect's latest scam. He had traveled to Japan where he purchased large numbers of electrical components and other high-demand, high-value items. Next he made use of the military postal system to ship these to himself for sale in Vietnam without the involvement of Vietnamese Customs officials.

The checks presented to the exchanges as payment had all been written against an account opened at the Saigon branch of Chase Manhattan Bank. The account had been established using identification stolen from a serviceman months earlier, and the minimum of $50 was the only amount ever deposited. Of course all of the checks that he had written had bounced. NISO Japan agents documented in considerable detail aspects of the purchases, banking, and postal transfer and forwarded these to NISSU Vung Tau resident agent Ben Johnson.

Johnson remembers, "I received a lead from Japan requesting that I check the military post office for parcels mailed by the suspect from the Yokosuka Navy Exchange. At the post office, I found two parcels, one of which contained about five pounds of pachinko balls such as the Japanese use in gaming machines. As instructed, these were seized and returned to Saigon as evidence. While I was there, I checked with my contacts at Vietnamese National Police and was able to locate the house in Saigon where the suspect was living."

Further evidence would surface, and Special Agents Webb, Jones, and Johnson went to the house in middle-class Saigon in the early hours of the morning in an attempt to locate their quarry.

Jones recalls: "There were no guards in the neighborhood, however the homes were protected with heavy metal gates and barred windows, and frequently the residents had dogs freely wandering

[251]

about the premises. On this particular morning Webb and I were driving an International Scout and we were adequately armed."

"I had my NIS issue .357 Magnum and a small caliber backup in my waistband. Webb was wearing his model 19 in his John Wayne holster. We arrived at the residence and began banging on the metal gate. Shortly a Vietnamese female, who appeared to be a maid, approached."

"Upon seeing that we were armed and displaying Vietnam Military Security Service cards she decided to allow us entrance. Once inside the two-story house we observed the suspect, fully clothed, asleep on a couch in the living room area. We woke him up and properly identified ourselves. Still being very unsure of our legal jurisdiction, we assertively invited him to accompany us to the Cholon Office."

"During the course of this conversation we suddenly noticed he had a Russian K54 automatic in his waistband. With each of us having a grip on our model 19s we asked him to slowly remove the automatic."

"He responded, dropped the magazine, and pulled back the action showing that there was no chambered round. After the tension eased, he agreed to accompany us."

The suspect was interviewed at length at the NISRA Saigon office. Well aware that he was out of the legal grasp of the agents, he made partial admissions about his activities. He was eventually released but agreed to keep regular appointments with Jones. In the course of several months, he actually provided the agent with useful intelligence about black market activities in Saigon.

The agents were certain that they had proved the man had been involved in important violations of U.S. federal law. At that time though no established legal mechanism could bring the man to trial, nor did a legal precedent exist for trying him under U.S. law for offenses committed in Vietnam or elsewhere outside U.S. boundaries.

Representations were made to the U.S. attorney in Honolulu to determine whether federal prosecutors would consider a ground breaking case. Exchanges of messages followed between Hawaii and Saigon requesting the particulars of the investigation. Finally, the decision was made that the accused would be tried under U.S. law if he could be delivered to U.S. marshals on American soil.

Anticipating this development, agents had carefully orchestrated with Vietnamese police the arrest and detention of the accused, on a range of offenses pertaining to violations of immigration law. He was remanded to the notorious Chi Hoa Prison in Saigon as the wheels of South Vietnamese justice ground ahead, albeit very slowly.

When news was received of the U.S. attorney's decision, secret negotiations were begun with Vietnamese authorities to secure their cooperation in the plan to return the man for appearance in U.S. courts. Ultimately, they agreed to formally deport and deliver him to a place of our choice.

In the meantime, the NISOV CO and supervising agent were seeking transportation assistance from the U.S. Air Force. What was needed was a cargo aircraft returning to Hawaii without any personnel aboard. After assurances that an agent assuming responsibility for the prisoner would accompany the accused at all times, the Air Force command at Tan Son hut Air Base agreed to help and arrangements were begun.

Military Airlift Command officers soon contacted NISOV to advise them that a certain C141 Starlifter had been scheduled to fly into Tan Son Nhut, unload, and return the next day to Hickham Air Force Base in Hawaii. Kadena Air Force Base, Okinawa would be the midway fueling point. In Hawaii, NIS Pacific special agents liaised with U.S. marshals, providing them with aircraft arrival times.

For reasons of security and to help keep the accused in the dark as to his impending travels, Vietnamese police and prison authorities were the last to be told of the plan. Webb and Jones had contacts at Chi Hoa Prison who monitored the prisoner's activities. Those sources said it was apparent that the man had no idea of what was in

[253]

store for him. No longer with a disposable income, he was living on bananas and complaining to anybody who would listen to him.

On the day of the flight, NIS agents drove out on the flight line at Tan Son Nhut, where the C141 was in the final stages of preflight preparation. The flight was under the command of an Air Force Colonel and his copilot was a young first lieutenant. The crew chief was a senior NCO who was busy checking stowage aboard the aircraft.

SRA Fred Givens and Special Agent Art Newman stood by, anticipating the arrival of Vietnamese police with the prisoner. As prisoner escort I was attired in a new, never-worn linen tropical suit. I looked sharp but was not comfortable in the growing heat and humidity of the Saigon morning.

On time, two green and white jeeps loaded with National Police drove up alongside the parked aircraft. In the rear of the second vehicle sat the prisoner, handcuffed and manacled.

His captors helped him to his feet, out of the open-air jeep, and onto the tarmac. Clutching the waistline of his beltless trousers, he was obviously taken aback by what was happening to him. Givens and Newman, ignoring his whining protestations, hustled him up the lowered aircraft stairway and into the sling seat that awaited him. The crew chief fastened the seat belt for him.

The Colonel lost no time in getting under way. I said good-bye to the other agents, who wished me well on my trip back to "the world."

The crew chief closed and bolted the hatch, and soon we were taxiing and then taking off in a steep climb eastbound. Every Air Force crew chief I have ever met has been a consummate professional whose first worry is the airworthiness of his aircraft and consequently, any potential threat to its well-being. The master sergeant on this flight was clearly such a man, and he was uncomfortable about my prisoner.

After his no-nonsense installation in the seat by Newman and Givens, the prisoner decided to test me. First, he ignored safety

[254]

instructions about his seat belt and then, after the aircraft had reached cruising altitude he announced that he was going to get up and move around. I ordered him to remain seated and moved to refasten his seat belt but he resisted my effort, lashing out with his manacled legs and arms.

I pushed him back and refastened the belt with the assistance of the crew chief. Just moments later he made another attempt and again I turned to the crew chief for assistance. After an impromptu conference in which the crew expressed concerns about the welfare of the aircraft, we removed the still-resisting prisoner from the relative comfort of his sling seat and secured his handcuffs and manacles to the deck. Things became much quieter after that.

At Kadena, Okinawa we landed to take on fuel and were met by two very large air police who took the prisoner in charge while we attended to business on the ground. Soon, we were on our way once again.

Even seasoned air travelers seldom have the opportunity to observe the splendor of the Pacific Ocean that pilots see from the flight deck. Flying eastward through the night at very high elevation, we were treated to a sunrise of such magnificence as to be almost surreal with the glorious colors filtering over and through the fluffy bed of white clouds far below us.

We arrived at Hickham Air Force Base in Honolulu soon after dawn on a Sunday morning. Two U.S. marshals were alongside soon after the engines were shut down and moments later they had taken my prisoner away. Monday morning's edition of the *Honolulu Tribune* devoted several columns of space to an interesting story about a man allegedly kidnapped by federal authorities. I was not mentioned by name.

Months later, my prisoner was tried and convicted in federal court. The conviction was upheld on appeal, and a valued court precedent, which spelled the end of automatic immunity for U.S. civilians committing offenses against their country in offshore locations, was successfully established.

[255]

Similarly vexatious legal issues would surface in March of 1970 when a civilian crew aboard a vessel chartered by the U.S. government seized her as an act of political demonstration against the Vietnam War. SS *Columbia Eagle* was enroute to Thailand with a cargo of napalm and bombs when mutineers took control of the ship and forced most of the crew into lifeboats, casting them adrift in the South China Sea. The mutineers then set sail for Cambodia, believing delivery of the vessel to a neutral port to be an effective means of voicing their condemnation of the war to the international community.

On the night of March 14, 1970, a passing freighter named the SS *Rappahannock,* also en route to Thailand, but with a load of munitions for the U.S. Air Force, saw flares fired by the castaways and hove-to to investigate.

The *Columbia Eagle* crewmembers had been adrift for seven hours. Their master and other crucial officers and crewmembers were still aboard her.

The senior officer identified himself as *Columbia Eagle's* second mate, Robert W. Stevenson. He related to *Rappahannock's* Captain Lignos that there had been an abandon ship alarm the day before at about 1:30 PM. When the men realized that the alarm was not routine, they had proceeded to their boat stations where they asked the mate on watch whether the alarm was genuine. Herbert Gunn, standing on the wing of the ship bridge, told them that there was a bomb scare and that they should man the lifeboats.

Following Gunn's orders, Stevenson shepherded all but fifteen crewmembers into the boats and awaited instructions to cast off. Gunn had withdrawn into the wheelhouse, but returned to the bridge wing where he yelled orders to Stevenson. They were ordered to cast off immediately and were told that the nearest land was about a hundred miles to the north of their current position. The boats took to the water and pulled away. About an hour passed before a plume of smoke from the stack signaled that the *Eagle* was getting under way, and soon the men were bobbing alone in the open waters of the Gulf of Thailand.

The castaways were made at home aboard their rescue ship and

[256]

were safely delivered to nearby Sattahip, Thailand. There they would wait for several weeks while events surrounding the mutiny unfolded.

Responding to urgent requests from senior naval authorities, NISOV commanding officer Lt. Cdr. Tom Brooks dispatched special agent Don Webb to Thailand. Webb was a well respected man who had served two tours in Vietnam. He would be accompanied by executive officer Lt. Norm Idleberg, USN.

They were instructed to first interview the *Columbia Eagle* crewmembers. After meeting at the U.S. embassy in Bangkok with U.S. advisers and a U.S. Coast Guard investigative team that was headed by a Lieutenant Commander Spiker, Webb and Idleberg traveled to the port town of Sattahip. It was there that they began their interviews with the full expectation that *Eagle* would soon be released and that the remaining crewmembers would then be available to them.

Idleberg dispatched regular reports from the embassy to his head-quarters in Saigon. Ultimately, he and Webb completed their interviews but would have to wait to speak with the remaining crewmembers. By late March, Idleberg was getting anxious. "I was scheduled for R and R to see my wife in Hawaii and as the date for that travel neared, I expressed these concerns to Tom Brooks." Brooks ordered Idleberg and Webb back to Saigon. Lieutenant Idleberg was soon boarding his R and R flight and Webb returned to his normal duties, while awaiting news of *Columbia Eagles* movements.

The mutineers had managed to navigate *Columbia Eagle* to Kompong Som; Cambodia's main seaport. The ship's master, Capt. Donald Swann, had set a circuitous course in the hopes that U.S. Coast Guard patrol vessels operating in the Gulf of Thailand would intercept them. At Kompong Som, *Columbia Eagle* was anchored a safe distance from the port, due to its dangerous cargo of bombs and napalm.

The two mutineers, Fireman Clyde McKay and Bedroom Steward Alvin Glatkowski accompanied by ship's master Swann, were soon taken ashore and were then flown to the Cambodian capital of

[257]

Phnom Penh. Upon their arrival, McKay and Glatkowski declared themselves to be political revolutionaries and were granted asylum by Prince Sihanouk. They "gave" *Columbia Eagle* and her cargo to the Cambodian government, renounced their U.S. citizenship, and soon were extolling revolutionary messages to Phnom Penh's overseas press corps.

Two days later the Sihanouk government, which had tried to maintain a nonaligned political course, was overthrown by a pro-U.S. faction headed by Gen. Lon Nol. The two mutineers were incarcerated while the new government decided what to do with them.

Three weeks after the mutiny, Captain Swann was returned to his ship. Following inspection by Cambodian naval authorities and a contingent of foreign journalists, he was finally permitted to sail *Columbia Eagle* from Cambodian waters. U.S. Coast Guard Lieu-tenant Commander Spiker, who had been dispatched to conduct investigations into the incident, boarded the ship as she departed Cambodia and they headed directly to Sattahip, Thailand.

With her castaways finally repatriated, *Columbia Eagle* set sail for the giant U.S. Naval base at Subic Bay in the Philippines where its munitions cargo was to be offloaded. U.S. Coast Guard cutter *Chase* accompanied her enroute. During the weeks following the seizure of *Columbia Eagle,* the media had enjoyed reporting on many facets of the story, including profiles of the alleged mutineers.

Back in Saigon, Idleberg and Webb utilizing typical NISOV ingenuity, rushed to join *Columbia Eagle* as she steamed across the Gulf of Thailand. They boarded an unscheduled Air America flight to An Thoi, a Vietnamese village on Phu Quoc Island in the Gulf of Cambodia. From there, they took an Army helicopter to a U.S. Coast Guard cutter on patrol. On April 8, 1970, the U.S. Army helicopter landed them aboard the cutter *Chase* in the Gulf of Thailand, from which they transferred by boat to *Columbia Eagle.*

When Webb and Idleberg approached *Eagle* as she lay in open water, they noticed that the old ship's sides were festooned with crudely painted white peace symbols. Uncertain what they faced aboard, the men clambered up a swinging Jacob's ladder where they were greeted by Coast Guard investigator Lieutenant Commander Spiker.

They soon found the reunited ship crewmembers to be unsettled and distrustful of each other. The NISOV and Coast Guard teams began an investigation designed to determine the facts surrounding the rebellion as well as whether any conspirators remained aboard.

Idleberg who was also NISOV's counterintelligence officer was keen to learn what he could about affiliations the mutineers might have had with subversive U.S. and foreign organizations. There were unconfirmed allegations that the pair had been supported in some manner by U.S. anti-war elements, including the Students for a Democratic Society (SDS). At the time, the SDS was allegedly involved in violent attacks against targets within the United States.

Working in the captain's stateroom investigators systematically interviewed crewmembers, profiling the role each person had played during the mutiny. In the four days it took to traverse the seas to their destination in the Philippines, no complicity was discovered between crewmembers and mutineers. Glatkowski surrendered to the authorities at the American Embassy in Phnom Penh in December of 1970. McKay escaped from custody that same year and found his way to communist Khmer Rouge positions in the Cambodian countryside.

Several years later, Lieutenant Commander Idleberg who at the time was assigned to attaché duty at the US. Embassy in Rome, was called to testify. The case was convening in Seattle, Washington, over a different matter entirely…*Columbia Eagle's* owners were suing the government. They had not been paid for their part in the ill-fated voyage since their cargo was never delivered, and they never were.

*****

12   SAIGON 1970 TO 1971: FRAGGINGS, AND HEROIN ARRIVES

By 1970, Saigon had become familiar turf for me. I had a permanent bunk at the Five Oceans BOQ situated next door to our gathering spot and watering hole. Special Agent Bernie Taylor was SRA, and was my immediate superior. NISOV was under the able leadership of commanding officer Lt. Cdr. Thomas A. Brooks, USN, and Supervising Agent Allan J. Kersenbrock.

Al Kersenbrock had begun his career in his native Hawaii, where he had served in the Honolulu Police Department. An extremely capable investigator, his powers of alternative thinking helped to resolve a number of cases which had had previously uncertain outcomes. He was my mentor and adviser, and a good friend to me.

Eschewing the predictable Army fare on the BOQ roof, we would often venture across the street to Fuji's Restaurant or down to the corner where a Chinese Vietnamese family ran a well-patronized soup kitchen. There groups of Asian men in white singlets sat around well worn round wooden tables, clutching bowls of steaming *pho* and rapidly shoveling the mixture into their mouths with chopsticks.

Though our technique with the chopsticks was not nearly so accomplished, we enjoyed the mixtures of noodles beef, and coriander every bit as much as the locals. Certainly we never knew with whom we were sharing lunch, and the others may have thought that we were becoming complacent about the enemy threat. But we were always armed, and we used common sense to pick our table. Eating at the soup kitchen for us was a risk worth taking.

Opium trafficking had always been a problem, and Cholon was well known for its opium dens. Small quantities of liquid opium were always available in the city's underworld market, and NISOV had made several important large seizures. One was particularly memorable, because the opium blocks that were stored in a converted closet that served as our evidence locker, melted during an especially warm month. The office janitor, Mr. Ngau, was quick to clean the tarry substance from the locker floor. Taking it outside to add to a smoking fire, he grinned at us and assumed a body builder's stance. "All-same tiger!" he said…He knew very well what opium did.

When heroin came to Saigon it was very sudden, surprising us all. NISOV's offices were incorporated into a compound housing the Cholon PX, the Chase Bank, and an Army post office. It was a natural gathering place for military shoppers.

Heroin vendors began stationing themselves under the trees at the compound gate, where they could easily accost potential purchasers and show their wares. The women sold souvenirs, drinks, and pornographic photographs in a roaring trade, which continued for as long as the exchange stayed open. As military police and the Vietnamese National Police became aware of this, vendors entrusted heroin vials to the younger and more agile kids. They were far more likely to make a successful getaway from the police.

The problem was clearly getting out of control. Special Agent Clayton Spradley while standing in a check-out line behind a young soldier at the Cholon PX, was shocked to see a vial of heroin fall out of the soldier's breast pocket as he reached for cash to pay for his purchases. We assumed that the heroin was coming from the same single source because it always seemed to be sold in the same small plastic vials, but its point of origin was a closely guarded secret and was one that I was never privy to. Once this high potency heroin hit the street, overdose deaths immediately began to occur. Often 97 percent pure and with users typically inhaling it, those who overdosed died quickly and with heavy hemorrhaging from nasal passages.

Heroin that was this pure also had the potential to earn exporters large dividends if it could be safely "moved" back to the United States. Before long military police had to be assigned to the mortuary in an effort to halt shipments in the remains of men who had been killed and processed through the facility.

Overdose deaths would increase the frequency of our trips to the Army-operated Saigon mortuary, and Special Agent John Morgan and I arrived one morning to inspect the body of a sailor who had died while on liberty in Can Tho. It was a quiet day for them…none of the dozen or so preparation tables that lined the walls were in use

[261]

by any of the civilian morticians on the Army staff. A cheerful young Army NCO greeted us, and after we explained our business, he rolled out a gurney with a zipped body bag on it and left the room.

I unzipped the bag to expose the deceased…a young black male. His age was about twenty-two. His heavily muscled arms were crossed over his chest, and I had some difficulty unbending them to inspect for needle marks.

My initial inspection was inconclusive, but I knew the pathology report would tell me more when it came through. I zipped the bag back up and washed my hands in the nearby sink.

In an adjoining area, an MP was looking into the open thoracic cavity of a soldier who had been recently run over by a forklift on the Newport Docks. "Enough of this shit," Morgan said as I thanked our escort, and we walked out again into the fresh air.

Not long after this trip to the mortuary, another sailor who was billeted at the bachelor enlisted quarters along Plantation Road, on the way to Tan Son Nhut Airport, was discovered dead in his bunk. Morgan and I went to the scene to carry out a detailed search…part of the investigation designed to verify the cause of death. His body had been removed, but little else appeared to have been disturbed. The victim's pillow was indented from his head and was soaked with blood. A magazine now bloody and crumpled, rested on top of the pillow. What appeared to be heroin powder was on the sheet, and an open vial lay nearby.

Curious, Morgan stooped down to see what the victim had been reading. Snorting, he turned to me and said, "It's some hippy magazine which sings the praises of discovering your inner self with drugs." Turning back, he said, "Blow your mind, baby!" I stood on the bed with my Navy Leica and took an unforgettable photo with all the key elements clearly evident: heroin, the magazine article's exhortation, and the blood of an unfortunate young man who wasn't getting a second chance. The photo found its way into drug education lectures, but it didn't make much of a difference.

In another incident while returning to the office from the nearby PX, Morgan arrested a soldier assigned to the Army post office just as he was buying heroin from a street vendor. The soldier's coworkers witnessed his arrest and became belligerent about it.

Under normal circumstances their reaction would not have worried John Morgan in the least, but the Cholon Army Post Office handled all of our NISO mail each day. It was always hard to get Morgan out on the street until after morning mail call while he waited expectantly for sweet-smelling envelopes from his love far away.

After the arrest took place, the postal workers would receive harsh words if Morgan's daily letter wasn't there. Mail was a very serious part of his life in Vietnam, as it was for most of us.

*****

In many ways working out of the Saigon office was quite different from the experience of working up north. Most days the Saigon agents were able to wear their civilian clothes to work. Civvies were hardly a cover for anybody who knew what to look for however. Every agent carried a credential case in his breast pocket that was maintained in its place by the distinctive money clip that all Vietnam agents wore as a badge of honor. Agent side arms were often worn outside of shirts, depending on individual preference and the circumstances.

In Saigon, investigations most often centered around areas where Navy personnel passed en route to their field elements. Transit facilities and barracks were located along Plantation Road which was an area characterized by a high density of bars and massage parlors. A pall of dust, diesel smoke, and rotting garbage hung over Plantation Road-except when rain showers cleared the atmosphere and transformed the road verges to mud. Aside from having fewer opportunities to meet Vietnamese women (on a strictly commercial basis), sailors were often in better surroundings at their distant forward duty stations.

Logistic support bases, known as LSBs, had been developed in key river locations for the benefit of the riverine navy, better known as the Brown Water Navy. At their bases, maintenance was done on

[263]

the many small craft that allowed the U.S. and Vietnamese navies to prosecute the war in the densely populated Mekong Delta. There were the fast alloy-hulled PCFs, armored Monitors bristling with heavy weapons, fiberglass-hulled riverine patrol jet boats (PBRs), amongst others. This work required a skilled maintenance staff and accompanying dry dock facilities. The important Nha Be Logistic Support Base was nearest to Saigon, less than an hour from Cholon by road. The drive to the base was an easy one through the center of Saigon, to the bridge near the Majestic Hotel that led to Nha Be's gates.

Nha Be supported the patrol forces that kept the river to the port of Saigon open. It was also a useful jumping-off spot for operations into the nearby Rung Sat Special Zone. Infamous as a hideout for Viet Cong over the many years, the Rung Sat was a labyrinth of dense mangrove swamp that was extremely difficult to patrol.

The base itself was a series of timber-framed barracks, workshops, and warehouses that was largely surrounded by the water. As was typical the little town had grown up outside the gates, coming as close to the base as the authorities would allow. Commercial enterprises of every description from mechanics to coffin makers, grocers, bars, and fishermen's huts were found there. When in Nha Be, the SEAL teams frequented an establishment known simply as the Green Door. Their post-operation scenes there were legendary, and wise men stayed clear.

With the advent of Vietnamization came the accelerated handover of Navy assets and materiel to the VNN. As I had observed at Cam Ranh, the handover program also provided temptation and opportunity to Vietnamese with criminal intentions. The incidents of burglary and theft increased. We had a low resolution rate for these, although when VNNSB could spare a man to assist with interrogations the odds of finding the perpetrator jumped dramatically. Vietnamese recalcitrants did not respond favorably when interviewed by men who treated them like the hardcore enemy insurgents they were usually extracting information from.

Large-scale thieving of Navy goods was not a regular event, but it did happen. One scam was operated by a fuel-hauling contractor who had built false baffles in his trailer tank…the baffles would retain fuel after the tank was "emptied" at the Navy's fuel farm. The U.S. Navy became the unwitting supplier of fuel for a large portion of Saigon's private vehicles.

One morning in late 1970 I drove to Nha Be with a lead case, intending to interview a sailor assigned to a ship I believed was anchored there at the river. After I'd parked my vehicle within the base perimeter, I glanced at the river but saw no ship. Nearby, a cheerful boatswain mate was sweeping up aboard his LCM. I asked him if he knew where the ship was. "Sure," he said. "Six miles or so downriver she's anchored." He would be delivering mail and other supplies and said he'd be glad to have me along. He was expecting two more passengers, and about a half an hour later we were under way.

This was my first up-close look at the Soi Rap River. I'd flown over its broad muddy tract several times and enjoyed this opportunity to view the Vietnamese river life up close. The sailors transiting to their ship found places in the vehicle where they sacked out. I stood with the boatswain next to his rail-mounted M60 as we burbled downstream, passing sampans and fishermen hauling in their nets. Several miles downstream the river split, and dead ahead on a spit of land overlooking the junction stood the ramparts of an old French fort.

I commented as I inspected the fortress with field glasses that the only thing that appeared to be missing was a detachment from the Foreign Legion. Noting my interest the boatswain said he would stop on the way back…that a detachment of Regional Force militia was in fact still there. Minutes later we rounded a bend and saw two Navy logistic ships anchored in the river.

The coxswain swung his boat in a wide arc and pulled alongside the vessel I was visiting. I clambered up a swaying Jacob's ladder, holding my file folder in my teeth. Once aboard the XO greeted me and introduced me to the master at arms who had arranged a private office for my interview.

Soon after this, the boatswain mate chief delivered my witness. He proved cooperative, and I had what I needed from him in less than an hour. After lunch in the wardroom I waited while materiel was loaded on the LCM for delivery upon our return to Nha Be. We were under way an hour later and headed upstream for our stop at the French fortress.

The French military engineers had built a substantial reinforced-concrete jetty and a small railway to deliver supplies to the fort. Several Vietnamese who were fishing on the jetty jumped to their feet when they noticed the LCM heading toward them. Picking up their rifles and other gear, the militia personnel waved at us, standing by to take the lines. We were soon alongside.

Although they did not speak English and we did not speak Vietnamese, we gave them some rations and indicated to them that we had an interest in visiting the fort. They seemed happy to have us and helped us onto the crumbling wharf.

I always carried my Rollei 35 with me on all my travels in Vietnam. It was a fine quality compact camera and I certainly wanted an opportunity to record this site. I was certain that it had witnessed many important events in the contemporary history of Indochina.

The Vietnamese led us up following a well worn foot path where the narrow-gauge rail line had once been. To one side of us, a narrow steel cylindrical observation tower, (what must have been a claustrophobic post for the soldier assigned to it), had been toppled by some type of high explosives, perhaps an aerial bomb.

About seven hundred yards up from the jetty were the gates to the fort. An inscription in French and the date from the late nineteenth century were embossed on the keystone.

I climbed the staircases above the monsoon flooded courtyard to inspect the massive eight-inch guns that had once protected Saigon from any seaborne invasion by France's enemies. I would later learn that the fort had been used by the Japanese during the occupation of French Indochina in World War II, then by the Viet Minh in the first Indochina War, and even briefly by Viet Cong forces.

At the old fort

I mused that the tiny militia detachment would have been unable to do much more than call for help by radio if they had been attacked. With my pictures taken we thanked our Vietnamese hosts, returned to the LCM, and started off once again toward Nha Be.

Soon after our departure, and noticing my concern that the day had almost passed, the coxswain swung the boat into a side channel explaining it was a shortcut. I said nothing, but nervously watched the increasingly narrow mangrove inlet for signs of human activity.

I knew who could be found in the Rung Sat Special Zone and was not keen to surprise the enemy on an LCM carrying one machine gun. Several minutes later as diplomatically as possible, I pointed out that the channel showed no signs that it would widen and suggested perhaps we had taken the wrong turn from the river.

In good humor the coxswain slowed and then began to reverse until a turnaround was possible. I grew even more nervous, knowing the noise of the boat diesels had resonated all over the flat country. I was hoping that non-friendlies weren't at that very moment racing along a track to the mangrove banks to ambush us. Fortunately that did not happen. As did happen at several other easily remembered points during my Vietnam tour, I felt I had taken some unnecessary risks.

[267]

These all could well have exposed me to a non-glorious death…the kind nobody wants their family to hear about. The photographs that I took did turn out well, however.

*****

The French had officially pulled out of Vietnam after their defeat at Dien Bien Phu in 1954. Though the colonial government had gone, various commercial arrangements remained that tied France to Vietnam. By 1970 few overt signs of either the French or French businesses remained, except in places like the huge Michelin rubber plantations.

I was not privy to intelligence about French activities in South Vietnam, but it seemed apparent that the Europeans were still pursuing activities very much in their own interests. I had heard rumors about cash protection payments to the Viet Cong by plantations anxious to save their trees for the day when rubber production could be restarted anew. It followed that it was quite often not in their "French best interests" to cooperate with U.S. forces and their allies.

One day on the flight line at Tan Son Nhut near the Air America terminal, I looked at a hangar whose door was partially open. Curious, I moved to where I could get a better look inside when my presence was noted and a surly man of European appearance pulled the sliding door closed. Inside had been a new twin-engine Beechcraft, festooned with unusual antennae. It was a French plane, obviously configured for an electronic intelligence/ intercept role. And who was there to spy on in South Vietnam other than the Americans and their allies? I was uncomfortable with the thought that French intelligence might be aiding our enemies as part of a French initiative to protect their investments in South Vietnam. But there was no way that I could prove any of this in any event.

Other suspicions were raised in 1971 when a NIS technical counter-measures team visited Saigon from Honolulu. They brought with them several mysterious metal boxes containing equipment that could be used to sweep for any evidence of enemy intrusion-gear.

[268]

The team was there to sweep the premises used by the commander of Naval Forces Vietnam. Both the intelligence division and the admiral's own office and conference areas required periodic sweeping. The technicians, who were both special agents, began their work the next morning but nothing was found. Having been in Vietnam for more than two years, one of the agents asked me what I knew about COMNAVFORV's neighbors. I told him that the French diplomatic mission maintained consular premises opposite and diagonally from the main entrance to the naval headquarters. Further, I commented that the admiral's office had large, old-fashioned windows, which were within view of the French buildings. I was not privy to the world of the techies and I had no need to know that type of information.

I had however been briefed about Soviet initiatives to gather information within the U.S. embassy in Moscow involving powerful external radiation and listening devices. There was little reason to doubt that the French would have an interest in knowing what was being said in Adm. Robert Salzer's office, and I felt quite certain that they had access to the state-of-the-art technology necessary to carry it out. I do not know whether any evidence of intrusion was discovered, but countermeasures were most certainly suggested.

I wasn't alone in my feelings of disgust at the threat posed by French self-interest. Fair weather allies could quickly flip if opportunities arose. Given the amount that the United States had invested in France's efforts to counter communism in Indochina, I remained unimpressed.

*****

Saigon had its share of mayhem, to be sure, but it was not on the scale of what the I Corps agents in Da Nang had become accustomed to. Fraggings had not become a problem in Saigon, likely because the commands had taken measures to limit access to offensive ordnance. There were shootings and serious assaults, but no fraggings until late in 1970. One evening after work, several of us had gathered in room 4 for a few beers when a call came through for the duty agent…That was me.

[269]

When I took the call, I was told that a grenade had just been thrown into a room occupied by two enlisted Navy advisers at a downtown BEQ. Both men were seriously injured and were being rushed to Third Field Hospital for treatment.

I requested that U.S. Army military police establish a cordon around the BEQ and that all personnel be confined to their rooms. I then rushed across the street to the office, where I assembled the crime scene equipment. All available agents quickly turned out to help. We got to the crime scene about forty minutes after the explosion.

The Le Lai BEQ was situated in central Saigon, and was a typical drab former Vietnamese hotel of indeterminate age. It was surrounded by security wire, barricades against vehicle attack, and security bunkers. The MPs had had no difficulty in shutting access to and from the premises down as had been requested.

Agents spoke to the MPs who had been the first on the scene, then began interviewing other witnesses. No one had actually seen the act being committed. After the initial round of interviews, agents began rechecking stories and digging deeper to learn who the victims had been with that evening. I walked upstairs to begin processing the crime scene.

On the seventh-floor landing, I noticed that a pool table had been used as an emergency treatment area to stabilize the victims before rushing them away. Several items of clothing were recovered, and all exhibited evidence of injury from shrapnel.

The room was the narrow rectangle typical of cheap Vietnamese hotels, with a toilet at the back. The two victims, whose beds had been on opposite walls, shared the room. Another door opened onto a balcony above the street.

The windows, taped to reduce the effect of flying glass in the event of enemy attack had been shattered by the overpressure created by the explosion in the room. The wooden entry door bore marks of numerous shrapnel strikes from the exploding grenade.

Against the rear partition wall, fan shaped powder stains and more fragmentation strikes identified the actual site of the explosion. The grenade had been thrown into the room and had rolled against the wall before detonating.

An M26 fragmentation grenade produces a fearsome explosion out in the open. When contained in the space of a brick and concrete structure vented only by an open casement window, the blast must have been incredible. With thousands of minute fragments moving at high velocities, I had always considered the fifteen-meter kill radius estimate conservative.

That the victims had not been killed outright seemed nothing short of miraculous. The room contents had been reduced by the blast to pieces littering the floor. Everything seemed to have holes in it. Carefully searching and photographing the room, we could find nothing linking the victims with the attacker.

Soon other interviews had provided information about what had happened in the room before the incident. The two victims had been drinking with an outsider since that afternoon. The binge had continued in the victims' room and had been accompanied by noises, but no one was willing to say that an argument had taken place. One person suggested that the third man did not appear to be an engine-room rating, as had the victims.

Special Agent Clayton Spradley issued orders to teams who were to begin looking for the victims' drinking partner from the day before.

The day following the fragging, a man came to the NISOV office in Cholon. He had heard that we were on the lookout for the person who had been with the two victims.

Clayton Spradley and I interrogated him. A first-class petty officer in the SeaBees, he waived his right to remain silent. He admitted that he had been with the victims and though he became increasingly uncomfortable as the interview continued, he did not terminate the interview. We continued to go over the details of his story.

"Frag" devastation

Spradley and I made an effective interrogation team. We had several successful confessions behind us and had developed a close rapport and an ability to read each other. Spradley was a quiet Floridian, was a few years older than me, and had a soft voice and pleasant manner.

Some may have thought, (to their ultimate detriment), that he might be easily duped. Spradley however, had an amazing memory for minute facts and could call these up effortlessly when the time was right. I worked as an opposite to him to keep the interview flowing.

After two hours, the suspect was well aware that a comprehensive investigation into his activities on the evening of the attack had taken place, and his alibis were systematically disproven. Spradley and I were at the stage of illustrating the inconsistencies in the alibi that a court-martial would hear.

[272]

The author interviews a US Army military police officer during the post-blast investigation

Spradley finally said "Why don't you just tell us and get all of this behind you". After a long pause, the suspect nodded his head and said, "OK. I threw it."

Special Agent Clayton Spradley

He then related how they had started drinking late in the afternoon after coming in from the field. He was ready to relax after the "bush-time" and had joined them with a friendly spirit. The victims were both engine-room petty officers, while he was a SeaBee, part of the Civil Engineer Corps. There had been the expected gentle banter about SeaBees compared to fleet sailors.

After they had been drinking for several hours, the victims suggested they go to the room and continue the party there.

The suspect said that once up in their room, the victims' moods had turned surly from their drunkenness. The banter had then become vicious. It culminated in the two victims' attacking and then ejecting him from their room after he had accidentally disturbed the cards during their poker game.

Angry and bleeding after his beating, the SeaBee had gone to the room where his field gear was stowed. He removed a fragmentation grenade, and returned to the room where he heard the victims talking and laughing about what had just happened. He pulled the pin, threw the grenade through the open window, and bugged out. We reduced the suspect's account to a statement, which he signed. By this time, he and Spradley were talking about hunting and fishing experiences.

Both victims eventually made full recoveries, but they had paid a heavy price. Spradley vividly recalled watching medical personnel at the Army Third Field Hospital as they extracted dozens of grenade shards from their wounds.

When the time came for the court-martial, an excellent service record and character references were of little help. The Sea Bee was awarded a dishonorable discharge with forfeiture of all pay and allowances, and was returned to the United States with a felony conviction hanging over him. I've often wondered what became of him.

*****

Spradley and I would inherit another fragging, this time at Logistic Support Base Ben Luc. At first the incident was reported as the

[274]

possible result of enemy attack, with personnel injured while in their quarters by shrapnel penetrating the plywood hooches. But there seemed to be inconsistencies in these reports. Supervising Agent Al Kersenbrock, not convinced by our preliminary investigations, ordered us back to Ben Luc to do some more digging.

Ben Luc is a village situated on one of the many river tributaries over which the road from Saigon to the Mekong Delta traverses. Near the north side of the bridge the U.S. Navy built the base to support the monitors and patrol craft of the Brown Water Navy, used to fight the enemy on the inland waterways.

A hardstand area on the riverbank facilitated the haul-outs necessary to repair any battle damage and to perform the maintenance required to keep the sophisticated machinery operable in the harsh tropical climes.

Here were docking facilities, a headquarters building, SEA huts for the troops, and newer concrete masonry houses that had been erected for Vietnamese Navy personnel and their families. Vietnamization was an active proposition at Ben Luc. Many of the vessels had by this time been turned over to the VNN, and they were playing a larger part in riverine patrol and offensive operations. Vietnamese families were settling into the modest dwellings built by SeaBees, and there was considerable command focus on how well the assimilation was working.

Thus, both COMNAVFORV and VNN headquarters were concerned when these "attacks" occurred. NISOV turned to its VNN counterparts in the VNNSB, to see what information had been developed through their sources. VNNSB personnel were similarly unconvinced that the explosions were a result of enemy action.

Clay Spradley and I drove south out of Cholon early one morning and after battling unusually heavy Vietnamese traffic, pulled into Ben Luc about an hour later. At the headquarters building we were escorted down to inspect where the latest of the four explosions had occurred. We made note of the signature fan-shaped spread of grenade shrapnel on the plywood siding of the SEA hut. There seemed to be little doubt that a U.S. grenade was used, but this fact did not by any means implicate an American in the attack.

[275]

Vietnamese allies used our ordnance, and so did the Viet Cong when they had it. The delta was a heavily populated region, and the grenade could have come from just about anywhere.

We conducted several grenade throwing trials in an effort to isolate areas from which they might have been thrown. But the extreme height of the perimeter fence ruled out any throws from having come from outside the wire.

We reviewed all of the rosters to determine who was on duty and where they should have been at the time of the incidents. Off duty status was also confirmed. Sailors were asked where they had been and what they were doing at the time that the grenades had exploded. VNNSB officers carried out their own inquiries on the Vietnamese side of the base to determine whether VNN witnesses would be able to assist in the investigation. There was no evidence of friction existing between any of the U.S. and Vietnamese personnel. Spradley and I agreed that the VNNSB investigator would certainly turn up this information if it existed, so we began to focus more on the U.S. Navy personnel.

We investigated the possibility that command problems might have sparked retribution against those nearest the blasts, but there were none. Returning to the results of our grenade-throwing trials, we took a new approach.

Elevated watchtowers overlooked the wire at several key points around the perimeter. With this kind of a vantage point, we wondered why the sentries had not been more help to us in our investigation to date. We re-examined the names and found that one sailor had been on duty on both of the nights when attacks had occurred. Although he had seemed helpful initially in the early hours of the investigation, we began to wonder if he was telling us everything that he knew. We found that the young man had recently transferred from the United States. He had volunteered and had left a wife and new baby in California.

We discussed the case on the way back to Saigon that afternoon, and in the office we talked to Supervising Agent Kersenbrock about our findings and feelings about the investigation. A great lateral thinker, Kersenbrock felt certain that we had isolated the Ben Luc fragger and urged us to interrogate the suspect more fully.

Spradley and I agreed that an interrogation was necessary but were not quite so certain that the time was right to conduct it. We were concerned about how little we would have to go on if our suspect exercised his right to remain silent, as so many do when confronted by federal agents searching for facts.

But the next morning we were back in our Navy gray Dodge pickup and heading south to Ben Luc. We had decided that we would do the interrogation, and we would go into it trying to learn as much as we could about the suspect before broaching questions about his movements on the two nights in question.

At Ben Luc we were given a private office, and the suspect arrived soon afterward. Warned in accordance with article 31 of the Uniform Code of Military Justice, he cheerfully waived his right to silence and signed the waiver. He would be glad to assist us with our investigation and was soon explaining why he had volunteered for Vietnam. Being in a combat zone was a rite of initiation into manhood for him, and he was proud to stand watch over the sleeping inhabitants of the base at night.

Spradley and I had serious suspicions about this man and his story. We let him know that we genuinely respected his desire to serve and explained that we too were volunteers. "You must have seen them coming through the wire that night?" I said. He was surprised, and hesitated without answering. "We know you were just trying to do your job," Spradley quickly followed up.

The subject visibly reacted to this but still said nothing. Spradley changed the subject, and since I had provided most of the pressure during the interview, I got up and left the office. When I returned about ten minutes later, the suspect and Spradley were showing each other the wrinkled family photos from their wallets. I said nothing, staying in the background and letting them talk.

Eventually, the conversation lagged and I looked at Spradley. He said once again, using the suspect's name, that he knew he had done his best to defend the base. Nobody had died, and we needed to understand exactly what had happened.

[277]

The suspect began to hedge, and I urged him to take the honorable option…he would be respected for that. "Just tell us what happened," I said. "You saw them coming through the wire, didn't you," Spradley added in an effort to push the suspect toward coming clean. "You threw the grenades?" I said. Staring into his lap, he paused then nodded his head in affirmation. "I threw them," he said.

The interview thus ended on a low key. We shook hands, wished the man well, and then we walked over the headquarters where we explained to the man's CO what had been said. "He's your man," I said.

Later, on the road and heading north, we talked some more about him. "If there is such a thing as a John Wayne syndrome, this man could have it," Spradley volunteered.

As it happened, an Army psychiatrist in Saigon agreed that the man was likely experiencing delusions when the phantom attacks occurred. He was hospitalized and then returned to the United States.

COMNAVFORV, VNN chief of naval operations, and even CINCPACFLT gave kudos to NISOV. Al Kersenbrock rewarded us with something a little more tangible, a chance to travel to Thailand to pursue leads on a large-scale larceny investigation.

*****

For agents assigned to Vietnam, all opportunities to work in Thailand were eagerly sought after. Thailand was a very important bridgehead in the fight against communist North Vietnam, and although there was probably not enough work for NIS to justify a full-time presence in Bangkok, enough work accumulated that a trip each month was necessary.

Agents from both Da Nang and Saigon shared the Thailand caseload. For Clayton Spradley and me, this was an "extra". For any agent in the Vietnam war zone, Thailand's relative safety, modern hotels, and restaurants were something to look forward to. We were given an investigation that had originated with the officer

[278]

in charge of construction (OICC), Thailand. The senior SeaBee believed a certain Thai national had stolen many thousands of dollars in construction materials by diverting and selling them. Other agents had already conducted the preliminary inquiries, and it now fell to us to conduct the several remaining interviews and hopefully to wrap the case up.

With buoyant spirits, Spradley and I boarded a regular Navy Scatback flight, (a C117 on the "beer run" to Bangkok), and two hours later we were walking across the steaming tarmac at the military side of Don Muang Air Base in Thailand. Dressed in civvies, we decided to check into our hotel and then visit OICC Thailand that afternoon.

Thailand's senior SeaBee greeted us courteously at his high-rise Bangkok office, then briefed us with his suspicions and concerns. He told us the suspect was a Thai national employee assigned to the Vientiane, Laos detachment.

Examination of documents associated with the granting of service contracts to civilian contractors in Laos had created a strong suspicion that the suspect was rigging the process for kickback payments. Witnesses and records were all to be found in Vientiane. The captain suggested it might be most effective to pursue the investigation in Laos, and we had to agree with the logic of his argument. I telephoned Al Kersenbrock to tell him of our intention to travel to Laos. He seemed less than enchanted with the plan but assented. Next, we visited the American embassy to explain our mission to the security officer. Everything seemed to be in order as we boarded the overnight train to north Nong Khai. Fortified with several cold quarts of Sing Ha beer, we sat back in our Pullman bunks to watch the Thai countryside go by until it became dark.

The next morning a SeaBee lieutenant dispatched from Vientiane to assist us with the investigation met us at the train station.

Nong Khai was the end of the rail line to the north, beyond was the sweeping expanse of the mighty Mekong River, and the towering mountains of Laos. Neither of us knew at the time the extent of the bitter and very secret war being waged in Laos against the North Vietnamese by the CIA and its hill tribe allies. But we would soon

[279]

pick up some none-too-subtle hints.

At the Thai border post, we learned that our travel documents were not in order because we had entered the country on a U.S. military transport. Therefore, the ferryboat to dockside Vientiane was not an available option for us. Our SeaBee escort was clearly anxious to get us across the river to complete our investigation. "Don't worry about it," he told us. "We go back and forth across the river in private boats all the time."

Spradley and I looked at each other knowing full well that we had probably already violated Thai law, but not wanting to go back empty-handed, we agreed to go. A few minutes later we three big Americans were in a small motorized sampan with only inches of freeboard, "puttering" across the Mekong. I was relieved when we got to the other side and immediately taken with the quiet beauty of Vientiane as our host drove us to the office. Laos was truly a step back in time where young saffron-clad Buddhist monks with heads shaven, walked in line for their rice ration, as did herds of ducks. Cars were few. Buildings were a fascinating mixture of French colonial architecture and the sweeping gables of traditional Lao structures.

At the OICC office we quickly identified the records we required, and who was needed for our interview. We decided that we would continue the inquiry after checking into our hotel. A phone call from the security officer at the American Embassy in Vientiane reached us soon after our check in. In no uncertain terms, the officer told me that although the ambassador was as yet unaware of our unauthorized presence, if we did not depart from Laos immediately he soon would be.

I assured the ambassador's security officer that we would be leaving as soon as we could, but we weren't in that big of a hurry. After having come all that way, it seemed foolish not to carry the investigation as far as possible, even if the spooks didn't want us around. We did what we could, arranging for records to be shipped to Bangkok, and then made our way once again back across the expanses of the muddy Mekong to Thailand.

Staying well away from Thai officials, we boarded the next train to Bangkok. Several days later, any remaining questions had been answered and the case was completed. OICC Thailand was directed to conduct some badly needed housekeeping.

In Bangkok, I immediately telephoned Al Kersenbrock in Saigon to tell him about our brush with the American Embassy in Vientiane.

At the end of the call, I had the feeling that the whole matter would remain in a holding pattern until our supervisor knew a little better what repercussions he could expect. Clayton Spradley and I began to think that the initiative that was encouraged and had previously earned accolades might lead to some unpleasant form of disciplinary action.

Weeks later, and back in Saigon, we asked Al Kersenbrock if we were going to be in the clear. We breathed a collective sigh of relief…our excursion was determined to have been warranted, and we finally were able to put the worry of our diplomatic gaffe behind us once and for all.

*****

To support their riverine forces, the U.S. Navy deployed two aviation attack squadrons to the Mekong Delta. These were comprised of VAL-4, a fixed wing squadron flying OVI0 Broncos, and HAL-4 (Helicopter Attack Squadron Four), called the Sea Wolves. The chopper gunship squadron used aging UHIB Hueys configured as gunships, and carried side-mounted rocket pods and flex M60 machine guns.

Sea Wolf helicopters were stationed away from the squadron base at Binh Thuy, near Can Tho. The Navy reasoned that nearby gunships could save lives in the sort of heavy contacts riverine forces frequently encountered on the rivers and canals.

The gunships were stationed aboard barracks ships that had landing pads constructed on their upper decks. Helicopters were sometimes sent to forward bases when there was an operational need. Thus it was that a pair of Sea Wolf gunships stationed at LSB Ben Luc was flying missions upriver on the Cambodian border in the area known as the Parrot's Beak.

Flying in tandem at several thousand feet, the choppers were returning from a mission one evening. The lead aircraft reported one-to-one vibration from the overhead main rotor and said he was reducing revolutions. The following aircraft acknowledged this and reduced speed to stay in formation. There was more discussion about the problem by radio when suddenly and without warning, the rotor assembly and transmission broke away and the helicopter crashed into the mud of the Plain of Reeds.

The next day Navy recovery teams went to the site to recover the bodies and critical pieces of the crashed aircraft to help in the investigation that would follow. The rotor assembly and portions of the main rotor were extracted from the mud and returned to their squadron headquarters at Binh Thuy. At Binh Thuy, experts would pore over the pieces searching for an explanation for the cause of the catastrophic failure.

After a thorough cleaning their work began, looking for inconsistencies in the badly mangled machinery. The pilot's last broadcast mentioned experiencing a vibration each time the main rotor turned, so the examiners began by looking at main rotor remains. On the end of one of the two blades, marks were noticed on an internal component. They should not have been there. Had this crash in fact been a case of sabotage?

The experts concluded that the imbalance caused by one rotor suddenly losing part of its length and becoming unbalanced would be more than sufficient to cause the transmission and both blades to separate from the aircraft.

NIS is mandated to investigate all acts of sabotage, and Command was quick to ask for assistance in the investigation of this crash. There were also concerns that other aircraft might have been tampered with.

Special Agent Bill Worochock was then the Binh Thuy resident agent. He came to Saigon and joined me for preliminary investigations at Ben Luc, where the fateful mission had originated.

[282]

Worochock and I normally didn't get much chance to see each other. Binh Thuy was a busy office with Worochock having responsibility on his own for the entire southern delta region.

He flew to Saigon periodically to deliver cases and consult with the SRA, but this was far from a regular occurrence. We used the driving time to Ben Luc to discuss what we knew about the incident. At this point, I was still uncertain why the aviation experts thought sabotage might have occurred. How could somebody climb up on a parked Huey and cut the leading edge of a main rotor without being seen? And assuming such a thing was a possibility wouldn't the preflight examination have discovered even the smallest cut? Was it possible to make a cut and fill it with something?

Compounding my curiosity, Worochok explained that the alloy rotor surface metal showed signs of tearing, rather than a clean cut. To cut the rotor, it would have been necessary to cut through the outer skin to reach internal components. Scientific examination would be necessary to verify whether this had occurred.

At Ben Luc, we pulled into the compound, told headquarters we were there, and walked over to the helo pad where a Sea Wolf Huey sat on stand-by status. No crew was present at the time. Worochock and I walked around the helo pad, considering the possibilities of a night intruder successfully evading sentries to take a hacksaw to a parked helicopter. We considered it possible but it seemed highly unlikely. It remained a possibility that we could not yet dismiss completely.

As we finished inspecting the area, the chopper crew chief arrived to begin his preflight check. We watched carefully to see what he did and how he did it, with special interest when he ran his bare hand along the leading edge of the main rotor blades. He explained that gunship maintenance people were especially careful of critical mechanical components because the aircraft came under fire regularly. He assured us that all crewmembers were equally as fastidious as he had been. "They're careful if they want to stay alive," he told us. Our next question was an obvious one… "What kind of a crew chief had the man been who had gone down?" "One of the best," he said.

[283]

It was a typical morning in the delta, already hot and getting hotter, accompanied by soaring humidity levels. The crew chief unzipped his flight suit and pulled it off his shoulders, sweat stained his torso. Soon we noticed the pilot and copilot walking toward us, around the blast revetment. This was the crew that had witnessed the crash, so we took this opportunity to interview them.

The day of the crash they had been on a support mission. As those missions usually came when somebody was under attack, there was an air of urgency as the flight inspection proceeded and the rocket ordnance and machine guns were checked and rechecked. All confirmed that the flight had been routine. Neither of the aircraft had been under enemy fire during the mission and when it arose, the vibration in the other helicopter was thought to be just a minor mechanical problem.

They all were young men, and each had his own way of coping with the loss of close friends and comrades. Theirs was a very dangerous profession and this was not the first time they had lost wingmen, but that didn't make it any easier. They had no idea what had caused the crash. Each seemed to attribute it to either fate or bad luck. Minutes after the interview concluded and with the turbine screaming, the Huey lifted off amid the heat waves from the metal matting and climbed out over the river en route to another rescue mission. We stood and watched the chopper as it flew away from us and finally out of our sight. After a pause, Worochock said, "If this was sabotage, I don't see any way it could have been carried out here in Vietnam." We would have to wait for the results of the scientific inspection of the rotor before knowing which way to take the investigation next.

The FBI crime laboratory assisted us by examining the recovered rotor blade. Their findings were definitive…the end of the leading edge had been cut at the point where the blade failed. But the metal covering over the leading edge, which must be a single and unified piece of metal to retain strength and integrity, was not cut. The FBI concluded that the U.S. aviation maintenance company that had reconditioned the blades had used two pieces of material in the leading edge.

As hardened as we had become to the vagaries of war, Worochock and I were both shocked at the implications of the examination. The contractor had put their bottom line ahead of the lives of a helicopter's crewmembers. They had used a leftover and a scrap to achieve the blade length that they required, and then covered it with metal skin. Five Navy men had paid for this with their lives.

There was a somewhat happy ending to this story. The case was referred to the FBI, accompanied by our investigation showing who the blade reconditioning contractor was and when the work had been done. None of us were asked to testify, but we later learned that a successful prosecution against the contractor had been made in federal court.

*****

Cdr. Donn T. Burrows, USN, replaced Tom Brooks as CO NISOV in 1970. He was well-liked by the men, and kept up the forward momentum on a number of programs he inherited in his takeover from Brooks.

COMNAVFORV was situated in Saigon, and not far from the CO's villa. Traditionally NISOV's CO wore a second hat as an intelligence officer of COMNAVFORV's intelligence section, N-2. Thus NISOV had a ready conduit for intelligence and investigative support. N-2 was under the command of a navy captain, with an intelligence designator. In other words, he was a career intelligence officer. Being N-2 could be a particularly thankless job if command initiatives were not running favorably or if the admiral was a taskmaster.

N-2 was the man expected to know the answers, sometimes even when the required information had yet to be acquired. He depended on a network of NILOs posted in key areas whose duties essentially involved acting as information sponges from all available local resources. He would refer the gathered information to Saigon for assessment and evaluation. N-2 relied on these junior officers and if one of them let him down, he could find himself in a vulnerable

[285]

position at the admiral's infamous working breakfasts. These occurred promptly at 6:00 AM every morning.

Commanders Brooks and Burrows, with Supervising Agents Schunk and Kersenbrock, often called in to brief the N-2 before the breakfast meetings. This routine provided interesting insights into the operation of the command, and doubtless occasionally caused them to reflect on their good fortune, being quartered well away from the pressure cooker of the command headquarters.

V.Adm. Elmo Zumwalt, USN, had built Naval Forces Vietnam, into a substantial fighting force over several years of dedicated service. In 1969 he was promoted and transferred to Washington, D.C. His replacement was V.Adm. Jerome H. King, USN.

King was a dynamic leader and a great friend of NISOV, but he was a tough and ruthless taskmaster who regularly gave his staff early morning indigestion at the dreaded breakfast meetings. Years later, Al Kersenbrock recounted the sight of glassy-eyed Navy captains staring at their office walls after facing their commander's caustic criticism at one of the breakfasts.

These were interesting times to be sure, in the N-2 shop. Ever the opportunists, the Intel officers at N-2 were always looking for ways to further the allied cause against the Viet Cong and North Vietnamese. One such opportunity came in the form of a near-dead carrier pigeon. It had landed exhausted on the deck of a patrolling U.S. Navy vessel that was assigned to coastal surveillance duties under Operation Market Time. The crewmembers rescued the bird, feeding and caring for it, and considered making it a pet before Asian characters and numerals were discovered tattooed inside its wing.

Realizing that they might have stumbled upon something important, they turned the bird over to the shore-based intelligence staff, which conveyed it to Saigon and the compound of COMNAVFORV. The intelligence staff there quickly realized the bird was a trained carrier pigeon of the North Vietnamese Army.

While N-2 was considering his options, the pigeon was left in the care of a young sailor from the Deep South. A pigeon fancier with an aptitude for birds, quarters for the bird were found in the attic area of one of the compound buildings.

All were fine examples of French colonial architecture replete with spacious attic areas. N-2 staff and a curious Al Kersenbrock, watched the pigeon's rehabilitation with interest and visited the pigeon loft regularly.

Ultimately a plan was hatched in which the bird would be released with a radio homing device attached to its back. There seemed to be a reasonable probability that the bird would return home to its enemy staff installation somewhere deep in the jungle of II Corps. The pigeon trainer began affixing small parcels to the bird on in-house training flights to build up its stamina for the mission.

The radio homing device was large, about half the size of a deck of playing cards. It was no small cargo for a pigeon. But over the next several months, the bird increased its fitness to a point that allowed the N-2 to put his finishing touches on an operational plan and start thinking seriously about the pigeon's release.

The pigeon had originally landed at a point off II Corps and Cam Ranh Bay was the nearest naval facility. When the bird was finally released, it was in this same general area. The hope was that it would quickly find its bearings and continue its flight back home. Fixed-wing and rotary-wing aircraft and the "observers" with their appropriate radio tracking equipment were organized to chase the pigeon. The plan was to follow the bird's flight home and then conduct a huge aerial attack on the elusive enemy complex.

There was considerable excitement and anticipation in the confines of N-2 office spaces in Saigon when the Vietnamese pigeon was finally released. It began winging inland with the homing transmitter on its back.

The assigned aircraft struggled to keep up with the bird's flight, and ultimately they were unable to. Soon he was out of their range, and no amount of searching could find the bird with the beeper on its back. The operation was a washout, and the speedy bird was never found…nor was its elusive NVA headquarters home.

An incident in early 1971, which first reports suggested was simply another of many enemy attacks on shipping, would lead NIS agents to discover important information surrounding communist Chinese off-shore intelligence operations.

Registered in Somalia, captained by a Dutch national and with a crew of mainland Chinese seamen, the SS *Yellow Dragon* came under fierce attack while sailing up the Mekong River. Destined for the Cambodian capital, the ship came under fire at a point close to the international boundary between South Vietnam and Cambodia. It was assumed that Viet Cong forces had carried out the attack. Panic-stricken, the Chinese crew abandoned the ship and took to the river in a lifeboat. The swift currents swept the crew downstream before the leaking boat lodged itself on a mud bank and the crewmembers were able to make their way ashore. The captain knew that he had a responsibility to the crewmembers but that he could do little to save the vessel without their assistance, and decided to leave *Yellow Dragon*. He gathered up his sailors, who were without even the most basic identification papers, and led them to a nearby township. Vietnamese Navy personnel had assisted with the evacuation and then had demanded payment in U.S. currency from the crew for their help.

The abandoned ship then triggered an orgy of looting by Vietnamese Navy personnel, who enjoyed unfettered access to the *Yellow Dragon* for about three days. They began by stealing the cargo and then the crew's personal effects. The paneling, fittings, and major engine components were next. When the ship's master reached Saigon, he alleged his vessel had been subject to acts of piracy by the South Vietnamese, and implied complicity by U.S. personnel.

Though it was known that the captain was married to a woman from Shanghai and maintained a residence in communist China, COMNAVFORV was nonetheless disturbed to hear his allegations against Vietnamese allies.

It was a particularly sensitive period in the Vietnamization process as well. NISOV was asked to begin an investigation of the incident

[288]

immediately and furnish a report to the admiral as a matter of urgency. Special Agent Clayton Spradley was assigned the case and began his investigation by contacting the VNNSB to determine what it knew of the incident. Spradley was surprised to receive "friendly" advice from VNNSB that his investigation might prove fatal, a warning that provided later direction in establishing VNNSB complicity in events following the attack.

Undaunted, Spradley and his interpreter Sergeant Trieu flew by Navy helicopter to a logistic support base near the site of the attack, and from there they traveled by boat to the sunken *Yellow Dragon*. The vessel had been systematically stripped, not unlike an animal caught in piranha-infested waters.

Spradley and Trieu established that the weapons used in the attack on *Yellow Dragon* were of U.S. manufacture, and they were soon satisfied that the attack had indeed been launched by the South Vietnamese Navy. Understandably, the case became one of considerable sensitivity. Examples of lawlessness by allied forces were not helpful to the Vietnamization process, particularly if word ever reached the journalist corps sitting atop their bar stools back in Saigon.

Further discreet investigation in the nearby riverside town confirmed Spradley's suspicions. Luckily, he had thought to bring with him several hundred dollars worth of local currency to be used for the purchase of information from the local citizenry. With his new information in hand, he identified a number of Vietnamese naval officers as the sources of the loot now on display in the local markets. This included bolts of uniform cloth, watches, imported perishables, and fruit originally destined for Phnom Penh.

The watches, stereo equipment, and cameras had been packed into barrels with false baffles, over which apples and other produce were packed for their concealment. Spradley bought several watches as evidence, and then he and Sergeant Trieu engaged the services of two young local men with motorcycles to take them back downriver to the Navy logistic support base.

"We hired these two cowboys with Vespas to take us down the trail which skirted along the bank of the Mekong. In many places, the

[289]

jungle grew right up to the edge and the trail was never very wide. I remember the local people, undoubtedly surprised to see a large American on a motor scooter, coming out to wave and saying, 'OK, GI' as I passed. As soon as we had gone by, they all vanished into the foliage. I found it disquieting and couldn't help but wonder if the enemy had been told I was out there."

Spradley and Trieu arrived safely at the base, caught a helicopter ride back to Saigon, and were briefing Al Kersenbrock soon afterward. In the meantime the Dutch captain was embroiled with South Vietnamese officials in a nightmare of bureaucratic red tape.

Even worse, the Hong Kong merchants sponsoring his voyage abandoned their support of him because he had left his ship. None of them had permission to enter the Republic of Vietnam, so permission could not be granted for their departure.

Aware of the captain's travails, Al Kersenbrock befriended him and offered the hospitality of the villa at 98 Phan Dinh Phuong. The Dutchman accepted with gratitude. In the days that immediately followed, the captain visited the Dutch and British diplomatic missions in Saigon and ultimately arranged for the crew to fly out to Hong Kong. Before leaving, he granted Special Agent Kersenbrock access to his Chinese communist crew. Valuable intelligence was soon gathered and forwarded to eager analysts at N-2.

Kersenbrock and the master had a number of evenings together at the villa, characterized by animated conversation about the relative merits of Chinese communism versus Western capitalism. The Dutchman considered communism an unstoppable social force that would ultimately overwhelm all opposition to it.

But his political orientation was influenced much more by opportunism and circumstance than by his personal conviction. He preferred a mainland Chinese crew because they came complete with Mao's Little Red Book and exhibited discipline most other nationalities lacked. He had first learned his trade through navigating the waters of the Dutch East Indies. Commercial circumstance and Indonesian independence had naturally moved him northward.

That a friendship had developed between the two men was made evident at a restaurant shortly before the captain's departure. A reporter chasing a vague rumor of piracy on the Mekong, approached their table and asked the captain if he was the Dutchman whose ship had been attacked. The captain not only denied his identity, but also his knowledge of any incident. Al Kersenbrock was understandably relieved. Any stories in the international press about the Vietnamese Navy's participation in acts of piracy would have had wide-ranging negative political consequences.

His final gesture of goodwill came as he prepared for his flight from South Vietnam...the captain left the ship's log and correspondence in Kersenbrock's care. His instructions were that they be mailed to him in Hong Kong, in the certain knowledge that every binding would be carefully disassembled and each word pored over by U.S. intelligence analysts. It was his way of expressing his thanks. N-2 had a Chinese expert on their staff, and he knew that the trading consortium underwriting the voyage of *Yellow Dragon* was a notorious communist Chinese front, which had been involved in all sorts of nefarious intelligence acquisition activity.

Yellow Dragon's papers and crew interviews helped add important new information to the Naval Intelligence files. A week later as promised, the log and the correspondence were mailed to the captain in Hong Kong. There was nothing to indicate that they had been examined in any way.

*****

13 THE DELTA EXPERIENCE, 1968 TO 1971

By far the greatest number of U.S. Navy men were concentrated in the area south of Saigon in the region known as the Mekong Delta. This made perfect sense since the rich alluvial plains that produced most of the nation's rice was the home to South Vietnam's densest population concentration.

The mighty Mekong splits in Cambodia, and the branches split again in the delta becoming four substantial rivers that eventually spill into the South China Sea. These rivers, their tributaries, and the innumerable canals have provided the region with maritime communication links for centuries. The Communist National Liberation Movement maintained strong links to riverside communities in the south, especially a place called My Tho.

A strong U.S. naval presence in the waters of the delta was an absolute necessity to maintain a military advantage for the allies. The U.S. Navy would create key command structures at Binh Thuy, immediately adjacent to the important delta city of Can Tho.

A construction program for improving roads and bridges was soon begun, and temporary buildings were erected in a self-contained base just inland from the Mekong's southernmost tributary known as the Ba Sac River.

Before long as increased concentrations of naval personnel created more work for NISOV, a full-time agent presence became necessary...NISSU Binh Thuy was born. It was a one-man post manned by a special agent on a six-month rotation.

Special Agent Bob Tugwell established the office in early 1968 and was relieved later that year by John Triplett. Triplett had begun his tour in Vietnam with his first assignment to NISRA Da Nang. Triplett was a well-liked and respected agent with considerable field experience, and was a logical choice for the post.

NISSU Binh Thuy was a demanding assignment. The "open" boundaries of the posting covered the entire southern area of Vietnam. In contrast the Saigon agents normally covered commands only as far south as My Tho and Dong Tam, and they were typically accessible by road...tactical considerations permitting.

The Binh Thuy agent had to master the geography of his area quickly, along with the locations of all key command elements. He also had to establish a working knowledge of the labyrinthine transportation systems so that he could respond to requests for investigative assistance in good time.

[292]

Helicopters provided the majority of the rides around IV Corps Tactical Zone…the Delta, to those who worked it.

Special Agent Don Masden would replace Triplett as NISOV's delta agent, and Masden had the advantage of an excellent grounding in criminal investigation. Formerly a Kentucky State Police trooper, he was appointed special agent ONI in December 1956 at Norfolk, Virginia.

"Our financial situation meant that I had to leave my wife, our two sons, and a daughter behind in Frankfort to take up the appointment."

Masden would remain at Norfolk until 1958, when he was posted to the U.S. Naval Ordnance Plant in Louisville, Kentucky. Responsible for sixty Kentucky counties, he travelled extensively for ONI until 1966 when a position opened up at the Camp Lejeune North Carolina offices. During most of the Vietnam conflict, Camp Lejeune was a crucible of racial tension and crime. The office was easily the busiest "shop" for criminal investigation on the East Coast. Masden first went to work for SRA Matt Hudgeons who would later be replaced by Al Kersenbrock. In January of 1969 Don Masden requested a transfer to Vietnam.

"Like others in the organization, I thought this was an appropriate move for a career special agent". The Masden family moved back to Louisville and on June 19, Masden boarded his plane at Travis Air Force Base for the flight to Saigon.

"I was met at Tan Son Nhut by Special Agent Jeff Baker and taken to the office in Cholon for processing. Saigon was a pretty big shock to the system."

Masden was quickly phased into the NISRA Saigon team under SRA Royce Logan. He soon learned the unique aspects of working in Vietnam, most notably the challenges to one's personal safety. Assigned to investigate narcotics violations at the Navy's riverine base at Dong Tam, Masden accompanied Special Agent Ben Johnson on the forty-mile drive to the location southwest of Saigon.

Aircraft were not available and this was one of those times when driving would be necessary to accomplish the mission. The two agents left Saigon in a Navy Bronco and were in Dong Tam by late morning.

The investigation was complete that afternoon but by then it was far too late to return to Saigon, and the two agents were assigned quarters in a SEA hut for the night. At 3:00 AM, awakened by insects and the other sounds of a strange environment, Masden decided to get up and take a walk. Stepping outside as quietly as possible to avoid awakening Johnson, he had taken only a few steps when he heard the sound of an explosion. It seemed to have come from one of the anchored crane barges nearby. They were under attack, and a VC mortar round had scored a direct hit. Others were in the air. Wasting no time, the startled Don Masden made for the nearest bunker only to find Ben Johnson there before him.

The next day while Ben Johnson ran down other leads, Masden elected to fly back to Saigon. Two young Army warrant officers flying a LOACH helicopter offered him a seat in their small craft, and the three were soon winging at treetop level across the thick jungle canopy. Several minutes out of Dong Tam he learned that they were on their way to put a strike in on a suspected Viet Cong base camp. Soon he was hanging on for his life as the pilots made repeated strafing runs over the camp. Don Masden learned to ask detailed questions in advance of any flight plans in Vietnam after that one!

In August 1969 as the new Binh Thuy agent, Masden packed up his gear at the Five Oceans BOQ, drove to Tan Son Nhut, and found a ride south aboard an Army Huey. It was his first trip to the delta, and he soon discovered that he had responsibility for a very large patch of unfamiliar terrain. Landing at Can Tho, he was greeted by the mixture of pungent odors typical of a delta town: "There was raw sewage running down the street in Can Tho, and I said to myself how glad I was to have all those inoculations up to date."

A passing Navy truck on its way to Binh Thuy stopped to give him a lift, and after a short drive Masden was deposited safely inside the Navy base. He found there a bustling complex in the grips of rapid changes and expansion. The parent command, Naval Support Activity Binh Thuy, maintained a substantial fleet of U.S. Navy patrol craft throughout the delta. They were now training the South Vietnamese sailors to assume these duties and were building facilities for the Vietnamese Navy at key strategic locations throughout the region.

Earlier that year the U.S. Navy had established a combat aviation capability at Binh Thuy to support its delta forces. These were comprised of the squadrons HAL-4 and VAL-4. The aviators and their Fleet Air Support Unit crews quickly increased the base population by about twelve hundred men.

Binh Thuy had a twenty one hundred foot runway to accommodate its various aircraft. The two squadrons added a formidable air attack/support capability to the Navy's delta arsenal.

The main force of the Binh Thuy base had always been River Patrol Boat Flotilla Five, the Navy's PBR force comprised of about 180 vessels. Charged with interdiction on the myriad waterways of the delta, the Brown Water Navy sailors found the jet boats to be well suited for their mission. The fiberglass-hulled boats could travel at speeds of twenty-five knots, and they were armed with three .50 caliber machine guns, assorted small arms, and many had radar.

River Flotilla Five officers quickly found office space for Don Masden in their administration building, and he was assigned a room at the base BOQ. He didn't have long to wait for his first investigation. It was the shooting death of an enlisted man who had been a passenger on a U.S. Navy truck.

The victim had been seated in the center of the cab; the round had been fired through the rear of the cab and had struck him in the back. He died instantly. Masden's investigation established that the fatal shot came from a .45-caliber pistol carried by one of the Navy men riding in the rear of the truck. It had been an accident, but nevertheless to formally conclude the investigation; a postmortem examination was necessary. Don Masden flew to Saigon and the Army mortuary to observe.

"I had attended autopsies at Camp Lejeune, and these were never pleasant. But my recollections are most vivid of other bodies at the mortuary in Viet Nam...the maimed victims of modern warfare."

[295]

Shortly after the conclusion of the accidental discharge case and while on a routine visit to headquarters in Saigon, Don Masden received a call for help from the Navy detachment at An Long. Upriver from Binh Thuy a PBR had been sabotaged, and there had been injuries.

"I was in Cholon at the time, so I caught the first available aircraft down to Can Tho, where the injured coxswain had been hospitalized. When I interviewed him he told me that there had been an explosion aboard his PBR, apparently originating in a one-gallon salad-oil container. He said he had been on a routine mission."

Pressed for details about the moments before the explosion the man told Masden that he thought he had seen an object drop from overhead just seconds before. A Vietnamese sailor had been seated above him and was acting as lookout at the time. The coxswain mentioned too that he was not on the best of terms with this sailor having refused him permission to take leave.

Doctors said the coxswain's injuries to his legs and feet were consistent with those caused by fragmentation. Needing to inspect the scene of the explosion, Masden turned to the aviators for his transportation. But it was one of the rare occasions when they couldn't help him. However the explosive ordnance disposal officer in charge, CWO3 John Lomburg, offered his Boston Whaler to take him upriver. Masden and Lomburg made the trip to An Long, where they inspected the vessel in question. While there, Masden interviewed the suspect Vietnamese sailor. "The Vietnamese sailor was cooperative, but not surprisingly he denied any responsibility for the explosion."

Masden turned to the other crewmembers for their recollections about the PBR mission. He learned that two vessels had been assigned, an older Mark 1 PBR and a much newer Mark II. The newer boat was much more powerful and had a better top speed than the Mark 1.

"One of the crewmen told me that the victim, the coxswain of the Mark II, had been driving in circles around the slower boat. This had caused the wash to splash the Mark 1, especially on the twin .50

machine guns in the forward mount. The gunner's mate whose guns were getting wet became angry with the coxswain when he refused to stop circling, and he threw a grenade at the offender. This was clearly not sabotage after all, it was a serious assault."

In February 1970 Don Masden took R-and-R leave in Honolulu. While in Hawaii, he saw his former SRA from Camp Lejeune, Al Kersenbrock, who was on his way to relieve Don Schunk as supervising agent in Vietnam.

"I was amused to find Al on his way to Vietnam because he had told me at Camp Lejeune that he couldn't understand why I was taking an assignment at NISOV in preference."

Kersenbrock asked Masden where he was assigned and how long he had been there.

"I told him how long I'd been in the delta, and he promised me a transfer back to Saigon as soon as it was feasible." He was a man of his word and Don Masden was returned to NISRA Saigon in April 1970.

*****

Adding to the challenges posed by a one-man posting to a busy delta area, fate often dictated that the agents assigned there were newly arrived. Special Agent Clayton Spradley took over Binh Thuy fresh from the United States. Spradley recalled that his takeover of the new post had required some adjustment.

The delta was a new and very foreign environment that was overtly hostile. The agent's workload could quickly reach unmanageable status without careful prioritization of what was worthy of investigation. An early lesson for Clay Spradley came just days after moving into an office space he shared with the officer in charge of the SEAL Team. The base commander came to him with a complaint that his personal jeep had been stolen.

In a normal environment a complaint of this type would have been investigated as a felony larceny. Spradley dutifully accepted the case and filed paperwork that formally initiated the investigation.

This meant that all levels of the NIS chain of command knew the case was pending and would be monitoring its progress.

Spradley quickly found out that he had entered an environment where stealing jeeps was endemic. Record checks determined that the Navy had no jeeps entered on their inventory even though a number of the vehicles painted Navy colors and with Navy numbers stenciled on them were present on the base. When the commander's jeep was finally located, the paint scheme had been changed to Air Force colors. As the Air Force paint was removed, it was not surprising that Navy colored paint came up beneath it.

But by the time the investigations were complete, it was clear that the jeep had at one time been the property of all three services. Spradley speculated privately that the base commander had recognized him as the gullible newcomer that he was and offered him the bait. Spradley accepted no cases involving jeep stealing after that one.

Prime Navy contractors RMK-BRJ were very active in the delta, building roads and bridges. In the unique environment that was the war zone, the construction conglomerate had arrangements in place that allowed claims to be made against the government for losses of both material and equipment. NISOV had never had sufficient resources to fully investigate RMK's claims against the Navy, but when paperwork was processed claiming the loss of ten six-by-six five-ton trucks, Kersenbrock assigned Spradley the investigation.

Spradley quickly uncovered a pattern of criminal behavior where persons assuming responsibility for inventoried equipment assigned to RMK would report it stolen or destroyed. The trucks in question had not been stolen and were found at a new, but distant, construction site in full working order and still wearing the RMK-BRJ livery.

Soon after this the same contractors reported the theft of an asphalt mixing plant worth several hundred thousand dollars from the barge being used to transport it. It too had never been stolen but had been secreted away. "I often wondered how much gear the Navy paid for twice," Spradley mused.

[298]

Death was never very far away in the delta, and agents were often astonished at the futility and stupidity surrounding much of the killing that they became involved in. An illustration of this involved two longtime buddies assigned to the NAD at the Gulf of Cambodia seaport of Rach Gia. Both were NCOs, and had located an off-base room to share for their liberty time in the town. Coincidentally, the building was also home to a number of prostitutes and to local business people. It was not in the best part of Rach Gia, but it had a refrigerator and phonograph, and it served its purpose well enough.

One afternoon the two friends were drinking beer, playing cards, and listening to records in their room. They had had a long day and had already consumed a lot of alcohol. The smaller of the two men, by now unsteady on his feet, lurched into the record player tumbling it over.

Enraged by this his friend staggered to his feet, announcing his intention to "Kick your ass." "Like hell you will" was the reply as the smaller man grabbed his issue sidearm and shot his buddy four times. The last shot was fired into the victim's head at close range.

The investigation would be pretty straightforward, and Spradley flew to Rach Gia to conduct it. The witnesses were located and cooperated fully, and the suspect was formally interviewed and readily confessed to the crime.

"What I remember most vividly was my visit to the small Navy compound in Rach Gia where the deceased's remains were. A group of sailors were enjoying some rare time off with a barbecue and a few beers. Perhaps ten feet from the group was the body bag with the victim in it. I was anxious to see if a bullet could be recovered because previous experiences with the Army mortuary and physical evidence had not been good."

"I opened up the bag, swatted away the flies, and probed two wounds with my government-issue ballpoint pen until I found a projectile lodged immediately under the skin and was able to remove it for evidence. Through it all, the sailors were unconcerned

[299]

about what I was doing. It was as if that sort of thing was pretty routine. It was another example of the crazy ways we had to operate in Vietnam."

*****

The most distant and remote Navy detachment was located down at the tip of the Ca Mau Peninsula, the southernmost tip of South Vietnam.

This was flat mangrove swamp, intersected by an occasional river. The U Minh Forest to the northwest had been under enemy control for many years. It was truly Indian country.

To establish a logistic support bridgehead, the Navy moored several flat barges in the river. Upon these were erected sandbag protected SEA huts. Dubbed Sea Float, this was a favored jumping-off place for SEAL operations. It was also a place wise men avoided if at all possible.

Stories circulated in Navy rear echelon circles about ambitious officers who arranged a visit to Sea Float for a trip up around the first bend of the river. Enemy fire was guaranteed, as was the career-enhancing Combat Action Ribbon.

Clay Spradley's last exposure to Sea Float was memorable not because of the investigation that took him there but because of the journey he took once his business was completed. After wrapping up his investigation, Spradley began asking about transportation out; being in almost any other venue was preferable to where he was. An LST was anchored off the coast, and helicopters readily landed on its long deck…this seemed a good bet for a ride back to Binh Thuy. The Sea Float sailors were happy to take him out to the ship in a motor launch. Once there, he settled back to wait.

[300]

Sea Float

Before long, a small group of SEALS came alongside in one of the flat-bottom boats they used for raiding. Dirty and covered in green camouflage face cream, they had two VC prisoners whom they had snatched during an overnight operation. SEALS were extremely adept at abducting enemy prisoners, who were usually a rich source of intelligence about movements and intentions. Because he shared an office with their OIC back in Binh Thuy, Spradley knew all the men and they happily greeted one another.

They told him a helicopter mission was scheduled to take the prisoners to the rear for interrogation, but the pickup would be made from the detachments small outpost upstream. Not wanting to find himself stuck on the LST, Spradley joined the men.

With their business at the ship complete the SEALs and their bound and blindfolded prisoners, (and now Spradley as passenger), sped over to the coastline then worked their way up the river to their base camp.

On the river, the fresh air was replaced by the fetid and closed atmosphere of a mangrove swamp. The tide was going out, exposing the tree roots in the dense black mud that supported the forest. The lowering water levels required that the boat be taken upstream slowly, and several times it was necessary for it to be

[301]

dragged over obstacles. Firefights could be heard in the distance, adding to Spradley's unease. Eventually they arrived at the team's camp in the forest. It was an unpretentious rest area that did nothing to make the agent feel any more secure.

Upon hearing the comforting whump-whump of a Huey approaching in the distance, Spradley felt a good deal of relief. He was in the company of the world's toughest Special Forces operatives, but he knew that there were far better places to be than sitting under a tree in the U Minh Forest.

He thanked the SEALs, boarded the helicopter along with the two VC prisoners, and was soon winging away over the swamp. The flight took him as far as Ca Mau, and the following morning an Army helicopter dropped him off back at Binh Thuy.

Like every agent who consistently worked "in the field", Clayton Spradley wondered what his fellow agents outside of the war zone would think of what he had to go through to complete this lead request.

Investigative leads had to be completed and it was as simple as that, but there were always strange twists in the environment of Vietnam.

"The tour in Vietnam was just absolutely amazing. The investigations were so intense; the friendships we made there are just everlasting-'til the day we die".

*****

As his six-month assignment at Binh Thuy was ending in midyear of 1971, Spradley looked forward to getting back to the relative comforts of Saigon. He would have been glad to fly out on the same day Rudy Dees arrived to take over from him, but Dees insisted that he needed to learn more about the job and its area of coverage from him. Knowing it was the right thing to do, Spradley stayed on.

There was a lingering case involving a stolen portable swimming pool that they could pursue together. There were rumors that it had been seen at a small detachment situated up on the Cambodian border…they might go up and have a look together.

[302]

The two agents retired to the Binh Thuy Officers' Club for drinks...it was the most likely place to find helicopter pilots who could tell them about missions being flown that next day. As they enjoyed their drinks, an Army medevac pilot named Pretcher approached them. He told Spradley he was rostered to fly a Dustoff mission early the next morning, and could take both men to Chau Doc if they were on the flight line by 7:00 AM.

Plenty of good company kept the agents in the club until it closed, and not yet ready to call it a night, Spradley suggested it might be a good time to introduce Rudy Dees to the bright lights of nearby Can Tho. Three hours after the 8:00 curfew, they left in their jeep and headed for the city.

They were disappointed to find that Can Tho was closed. Apparently nobody was interested in having a party. There was nothing else to do but head back to the base. The occasional kerosene lamp lighted the Vietnamese houses set back from the road, but being past curfew, they encountered no road traffic except for the occasional Army patrol. A dog ran across the road and Dees swerved to miss him. Losing control, they skidded into a nearby canal. With the jeep half immersed, they considered their predicament as the now awakened Vietnamese began to gather to see what had caused the commotion. Before long an Army MP patrol came by with a motor pool wrecker. The jeep was pulled from the water and somehow restarted, and the two agents were sent on their way none the worse for wear. The dog was fine too.

Dees and Spradley were not on the flight line in time for the early morning mission.

They were ragged and hung over, but still determined to track down the stolen swimming pool. Sheltering behind the revetments that protected the aircraft adjacent the flight line, they were approached by an Army warrant officer pilot. "Hey," he said, "Did you hear that Pretcher crashed? They're bringing the bird in now."

In the distance the outline of an Army CH47 Chinook could be seen on the horizon, carrying a load slung on cable beneath it. Soon it became apparent that this mass was a crumpled Huey, the same helicopter they would have been aboard that morning. Clayton

[303]

Spradley was convinced he would have died in Pretcher's helicopter. That would have been bad enough, but the thought that he might have been killed chasing a lead about a stolen swimming pool really bothered him.

Years after the war Spradley boarded a commercial flight in Washington, D.C. bound for Jacksonville, Florida. Aboard with him was Tom Truxell, the SEAL OIC with whom he had shared his office space at Binh Thuy. They enjoyed the flight together, sharing animated recollections of shared experiences in the delta.

"Clayton," Truxell said at one point, "do you remember that missing swimming pool?" "Yeah," Spradley replied. "Y'all took it didn't you?"

Truxell acknowledged that his SEALS were the ones who had "liberated" the swimming pool, taking it to their forward base at Ca Mau. They thought they had a greater need for it than the rear echelon troops at Binh Thuy.

*****

14   DA NANG, 1970 TO 1971: MURDER, RAPE, AND THE BLACK MARKET

When Edward J. Fitzpatrick arrived in early March 1970 to take over NISRA Da Nang, he inherited from Don McCoy a smoothly running team of agents who were experienced and self-directed. Fitz stepped into an office beset with cases of fraggings, narcotics, and the effects of growing racial tensions. He was well liked from the outset, and enjoyed the loyalty of those who worked for him.

I was in Da Nang for only a matter of weeks before I flew south to take over the satellite unit at Cam Ranh Bay. After several months there, I was asked to return to Da Nang to help them with a caseload that was out of control.

There had been big changes by the time 1970 rolled around. Naval

Support Activity Da Nang was responding to Vietnamization cutbacks and redeployments and had moved to reduce its presence in the city. Both NISRA Da Nang's office and billet were axed, and were moved inside NSA's compound at Camp Tien Sa. The move was unsatisfactory but necessary…the Navy was going, and eventually NIS would be going along with it.

The Naval Security Group detachment that had been housed at Tien Sa had already left the country, and we inherited their windowless Quonset hut with its high-gated fence. The agents would find rooms in the BOQ.

Our office maids were transferred to Tien Sa with us, and our interpreter Mr. Nam came along with them. The NSG had lived a cloistered existence, (their duties required them to), and they left a small barbecue area and a place to have a few beers after work. The Quonset, despite being windowless, was spacious. Yeomen and clerks occupied the forward portion and Fitz occupied an office built for the NSG detachment commander. A large room at the rear was set up with agent desks, filing cabinets, and other paraphernalia. In a corner a bunk had been set up alongside a battery of command radios and the telephone. This was where the rotating duty agent slept …available to answer after-hours emergency calls.

By the time I reported back to Da Nang, the move to Tien Sa had been completed. One of the first things I noticed about the new space was its enforced insularity.

We were no longer among Vietnamese. We now had little contact with them and virtually no opportunity to get a feel for what was happening outside the "Navy world". NISOV was so utterly focused on trying to cope with a huge load of serious criminal investigations that its other mission was going by the board. I had a gut feeling that NIS was just trying to ride out the wave it was on without crashing along with it. It made me feel very uncomfortable.

The transition back to the Da Nang agent team was effortless, and working for Fitz was a pleasure. He had built his reputation by being a man who led from the front and I admired him for this, but it worried me too. He had a wife and large family back in the States, and was a long way from being a trained infantryman. He would not send an agent out to do a job that he would not do himself, and he often became personally involved in major investigations. I was always glad for his help, but it made me feel anxious.

Two incidents illustrate Fitz's determination to provide best quality investigative support. The first was the murder of a Vietnamese peasant woman by a Marine officer and the second was a gang rape involving Marine Combined Action Group Team personnel.

The murder investigation began curiously enough, with loose talk by a group of reconnaissance Marine team members in a rear area enlisted club. An NCO, back from operations in the hills south of An Hoa, talked about the mission over several hours and too many beers. Recon marines were normally careful about talking shop outside their own circle of team members and were not known to share their experiences with other marines.

What the NCO said was therefore noteworthy, and when he mentioned that the young officer commanding the unit had shot a Vietnamese peasant woman, everyone listened carefully. The story found its way to the First Marine Division staff judge advocate, who contacted Ed Fitzpatrick with his request for assistance.

Witnesses were soon located and interviewed. The information divulged implicated a young Marine first lieutenant as the killer of an unknown woman near an observation post manned by the recon marines. In their role as the forward eyes and ears for the division these marines typically manned the high ground. From here they could observe the comings and goings of NVA and Viet Cong units within the fertile plain of the An Hoa Basin and similar hotly contested areas.

The lieutenant had led a team to a ridgeline that overlooked the rice paddies and trails from the west that were used by enemy units marching in from Laotian sanctuaries and the Ho Chi Minh Trail. They had with them a bolt action sniper rifle. Apparently the officer had used it to shoot a peasant woman who was working in the paddy field far below them, possibly as a demonstration of his skill with the weapon.

There was understandable angst among senior Marine officers at the allegations. If true, a member of their elite corps was a murderer. A thorough and professionally conducted investigation was imperative. Only one organization was equipped to do it and that was NIS.

A few major difficulties had to be overcome in this investigation, and more than a week had passed since the alleged shooting had occurred. Most problematic was the location of the crime scene. It was in an area that had never been pacified and where major clashes with North Vietnamese troops occurred regularly. Witnesses would need to be located and interviewed, the victim's body would have to be exhumed and examined, and the search for physical evidence would need to be carried out. And none of us were recon marines!

For the NIS agents, the location of the crime scene illustrated perfectly a long time confused dichotomy between where we were supposed to go and where we were not. Guidance from headquarters policy makers had never been specific. Agents were simply told they should avoid travel to forward locations and uncontrolled areas. If an agent were injured, (or worse), in a forward area, headquarters would require justification and a damned good explanation.

On the other hand, NISOV had sent a clear message to the commands it serviced, and the word was that we would investigate major incidents. Imperiling successful prosecution of major cases by relying on military police investigators was unacceptable. Ed Fitzpatrick and his agents never doubted whether they should visit the crime scene out in the Indian country. Headquarters in Washington could read about it in their report.

Division headquarters left security arrangements for the mission in the hands of the commanding officer of the reconnaissance battalion. The colonel was taking no unnecessary chances with either the NIS team or with his marines. Marine CH46 helicopters would transport the agents and their Marine security team to the area and Cobra gunships would be escorting them. Each agent would have a recon marine assigned to him in the event enemy forces were encountered.

[307]

The operation began as planned, and the agents boarded their transport helicopters where they joined the heavily armed marines. A back up CH46 joined them. The gunships flew ahead to begin prepping the landing zone, where the victim was believed to be buried. Fusillades of rockets and mini-gun fire searched out potential enemy hiding places, and then the landings began. A Marine security element pushed out to secure the landing zone. Landings prompted enemy attacks, and the agents had little time for a detailed crime scene search.

Despite the difficult nature of the unsecured area, Vietnamese witnesses were located and convinced to return back to Da Nang for in-depth interviews. The victim's shallow grave was also found. Agents had come armed with the necessary documentation issued by Vietnamese authorities in Da Nang authorizing disinterment for the purposes of formal medical examination. The grave was opened, and the victim's shroud wrapped remains were placed in a body bag.

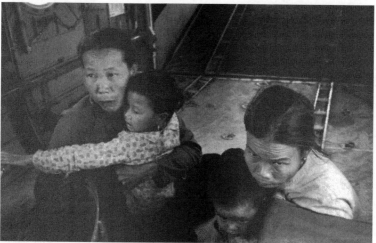

Vietnamese villagers who were witnesses to the crime return with agents to Da Nang

Vietnamese witnesses told agents that the victim had been working in a nearby rice paddy when a shot was heard from the ridge above them. She had dropped, mortally wounded. They could offer no explanation for the event. There had not been recent enemy incursions or actions between marines and VC or NVA.

[308]

Interviews conducted later in the Da Nang rear area produced no new information beyond what was originally reported at the scene. The recon marine observation post (OP) was checked for evidence relating to the crime, but none was found there. The medical examination confirmed only that a single high-velocity round had struck the victim, causing near-instantaneous death.
The suspect exercised his right to decline interview by agents.

The investigation was classified secret, which was unusual for a criminal inquiry. Recon marines, with their operations often classified in any event, kept the lid firmly on any potential leaks about what one of their officers had done. The matter was never referred for trial. NISRA Da Nang agents heard that some reparation had been made to the victim's family. There was a good deal of after-the-fact reflection about how difficult life could be for Vietnamese peasants living in actively contested areas, even without irresponsible young junior officers.

*****

The first information received about the alleged rape of a Vietnamese peasant woman was vague and unspecific and failed to confirm the identity of the victim. She had been prompted by family members to make a complaint at a refugee facility in the coastal community of Tam Ky, some distance from where the crime was said to have occurred.

After further refining the complaint information with interviews conducted in the rear areas of Da Nang, Fitz decided to start the investigation by visiting the Marine Combined Action Group units.

I had not been involved in the early stages of the investigation. But by this time I had worked with marines in the I Corps bush for nearly two years. Although I was not dismissive of the allegations, I was surprised to hear that CAG marines might commit a gang rape. CAG members were volunteers, many of whom extended their tours to participate in the program. CAG teams lived in Vietnamese communities, training and assisting the people in the defense of their lives and property.

Combined teams were the product of a doctrine that Marine leaders

[309]

began developing in the Central American Banana Wars, during which the value of marines living on the ground with local allies had repeatedly been proved. The concept was further expanded in Vietnam and it worked - Viet Cong influence diminished where CAG operated. NIS had little contact with CAG because it received very few complaints about its team members.

In the latter stages of the war, the First Marine Division was heavily deployed in the Que Son Valley that formed the southern border of the AO. The Army's America I Division AO began at the valley and extended south to well below Chu Lai. The alleged rape had occurred in the Que Son Valley, and CAG units were dispersed in small teams at strong points in various parts of the valley where security was problematic.

At that time, Que Son was definitely in Indian country. Several large and bitter clashes between the NVA and Marine battalions had occurred there since 1966. Viet Cong forces remained very active as we were soon to learn. For reasons of security we decided to take two vehicles, one of which was equipped with a variable frequency military radio. With Fitz at the wheel of one jeep and me at the other, and volunteers riding shotgun with us, we headed south down Route 1. We passed Dodge City, then drove onward to LZ Baldy and the turn-off for Que Son. Special Agent John Dill IV, a former marine himself, rode shotgun for me. I was glad to have him.

Baldy, initially developed by the U.S. Army, had become an important Marine strongpoint and artillery support base. Located near to Route 1 the national highway, and Route 535 the road to the Que Son Valley, its strategic value was obvious to all including the enemy. Baldy had formidable defenses with aprons of concertina wire, trip flares, tangle foot, claymore mines, and barrels of fu gas, a napalm-like substance stored in fifty-five gallon drums. These could be command detonated by the defenders.

There was a Marine checkpoint on Route 535 at a distance west of Baldy on the muddy, rutted dirt road. We stopped there to speak to the sentries, verified radio frequencies, and listened while they radioed ahead to another security element farther inland to advise them that we were using the road. As we were about to leave this position a U.S. Army jeep pulled up with MACV advisory staff

[310]

aboard. Marines noted their details, sent them through, and radioed the post ahead: "One doggy victor headed yours." We smiled; marines never missed a chance to address soldiers as doggies.

It was the rainy season, and the road had never been much more than a cart track even when French administrators had first carved it out decades before. We drove carefully but wasted little time on the way to the village that was the headquarters for the rice growing district.

Mountains surrounded the paddy plains and *ville*…these were the mountains that harbored the enemy forces. We first saw evidence of enemy activity at the compound that was home to district advisers. A cleanup was under way to repair damage from an overnight attack. Marines were repairing sandbagged bunkers, stringing fresh wire, and mending gate barriers.

We continued westward several more miles to a tiny outpost just off the road. On nothing more than a small elevation in a flat plane of rice fields, the CAG team and their Vietnamese allies had built a small fortress to defend surrounding villages and the valuable rice crop. There was wire around the outer defenses festooned with empty ration cans which clattered in the wind, and mortar aiming stakes had been driven into parapets. Several fire points had been built from sandbags and empty wooden ammunition crates. A central bunker, most noticeable because of the array of antennae it supported, doubled as a CP and sleeping spot for the OIC.

CAG teams did not normally receive many visitors from the outside. A young clean-cut marine dressed in cutoff utility trousers and boots strode down to us as we drove in. This was the lieutenant officer in charge. Fitz first greeted him, identified himself, and then explained why we were there. I looked around, taking in the verdant rice fields beyond us and the sweating marines filling sandbags.

They too had been hit the night before. "We kicked their ass" the lieutenant said when I asked what sort of a night they'd had. "Just a routine VC probe," he said matter-of-factly.

[311]

DaNang Senior Resident Agent Ed Fitzpatrick interviews the CAG Team officer in charge only hours after the detachment had repelled an enemy attack

Unfortunately the suspects in the case were not available. Knowing that time was against us, ("the night belonging to Charles" being especially true in Que Son), we arranged for them to be sent to Da Nang. But we did identify a witness.

We could do little else while in the Que Son Valley, but our interpreter Mr. Nam believed our victim could still be in Tam Ky, south of us on Route 1. We decided to drive on. Fortunately the return to Route 1 was uneventful for us, and an hour later we arrived in Tam Ky and were surprised when Nam found the victim.

Though scarcely more than twenty-five, she was a typical peasant woman who had many children and an obviously difficult life. She was hesitant to talk about the incident, and did so only after Nam's repeated assurances that authorities genuinely wanted to find and punish those responsible for the attack.

Finally she gave in explaining how four marines had accosted and raped her in a bomb crater near her village. She did not think that she could identify the perpetrators if she saw them again. "The large-noses all look the same to me," she told Nam.

In his beautiful flowing handwriting, Nam took her statement and we started back up the road into the afternoon sun. There was no useable physical evidence since it had been weeks since the rape. The outcome of the investigation would depend entirely on witness interviews and interrogations. Fitz arranged that these be conducted in the NISRA office at Camp Tien Sa. Suspects and potential witnesses were carefully quarantined, traveling in from the bush on different dates and from different points of origin.

Carried out over several days, the interrogations corroborated and supported each other. The rape had occurred, it was not just a rumor created by a Vietnamese peasant with a desire for a compensation payment. The Judge Advocate General staff ultimately decided the case was not strong enough to expect a reasonable chance of success, but it was not for a lack of effort on the part of Edward J. Fitzpatrick and his team of investigators.

*****

In March of 1971, the small cadre of Fitz's remaining agents gathered to congratulate him on the occasion of his transfer from Vietnam. He had beaten the odds, and had done his very best to make a difference.

Replacing Fitzpatrick as senior resident agent was Charles M. Bickley. Before joining NIS Bickley, a quiet and thoroughly competent criminal investigator, had managed inquiries for a Southern California district attorney. He settled into the SRA office at Camp Tien Sa and quickly won the admiration and respect of the last of the remaining Da Nang agent corps. By now signs of the troop drawdown were everywhere, and the agents rotating at the end of their year tour in I Corps were not being replaced.

Although violent crimes in the Da Nang region were characteristic of most cases at the NISRA, there was also the undercurrent of black-market and currency related violations. NIS special agents worked these cases whenever resources allowed for it.

Special Agent Carl Skiff, between his trips to remote firebases in the Que Son Mountains, quietly gathered evidence about a currency manipulation operation. It appeared that the scheme was under the

control of a Marine staff sergeant at the facility operated by the
First Marine Division for R and R near Freedom Hill.

This was adjacent to the notorious Vietnamese *ville* of Dogpatch.
The suspect had access to U.S. currency, (known to all simply as
"green"). But the possession of "green" was illegal in Vietnam
unless one was being processed to leave the country on an
authorized leave or at the end of a tour. Personnel assigned to
Vietnam were paid in MPCs, a legal tender in military stores, post
offices, and the clubs in the country, but nowhere else.

The idea was to prevent personnel from trading in currency with the
Vietnamese and engaging in barter and trade with them. Vietnam's
national currency was extremely fragile and was not exported from
the country legally.

The piaster had been overvalued on the official government
exchange rate. Because of this, the Vietnamese had a strong
incentive to move cash to external banks where they could purchase
hard foreign currency. Service personnel were incentified to
exchange MPC's for piasters at the favorable black market rates.
The Vietnamese always preferred U.S. dollars, although there was a
healthy market in MPC's too. An added element in the black-
market equation was a Viet Cong initiative to acquire U.S. dollars
to fund their war effort.

They needed hard currency to buy any items that were not readily
available in the Vietnamese economy. Skiff's suspect had access to
"green" because marines processing to fly from Vietnam for
external leave were allowed to exchange MPC for U.S. dollars.
There were indications that the NCO was banking tidy sums from
currency manipulation and perhaps from selling sought-after items
offered at the nearby Freedom Hill post-exchange.

Dogpatch was always hungry for tape recorders, refrigerators,
televisions, and other PX goods. The Vietnamese purchasers could
pay in MPC, which had been lavished illegally by Americans for
prostitutes and narcotics. The suspect was in a perfect position since
he had the means to convert MPC to U.S. dollars, a legal tender that
could be exported virtually anywhere. Skiff decided to insert a
trusted informant into the R-and-R facility in hopes that more

[314]

details about the suspect's operation could be learned. A fellow Marine NCO was issued legitimate orders that would place him in areas frequented by the suspect, and the process of accumulating evidence was begun. Skiff soon realized that the suspect was a creature of habit, moving around the R-and-R facility in predictable ways.

He was known to carry U.S. dollars with him at certain times. The unauthorized possession of U.S. dollars was an offence in its own right, and Skiff believed the suspect could be apprehended for possession of contraband. He began preparing his surveillance and arrest plan.

Like most transit facilities, the R-and-R center at Freedom Hill was awash with new faces, and special agents in Marine battle dress could go unnoticed. The agents took up positions inside the compound and waited for the suspect and Skiff's informant. He would give a prearranged signal to them if the offender was carrying contraband.

Takedown

The operation went down like clockwork. The suspect walked from his comfortable barracks quarters across to the adjoining parking area, and when the informant signaled, both men were taken into custody and handcuffed. A wad of "green" was taken from the suspect's pocket and he, a career marine, was transferred to the United States where he would face court-martial proceedings.

*****

15   THE MEN

At its peak, NISOV had fewer than twenty five agents assigned. They were a diverse group of former military officers, police officers, grunts who'd gone back to school, and even a school teacher. All were volunteers. Without making gross generalizations, it is fair to say that most were conservatives and few were shy about their patriotism.

In the best of times, assignment to Vietnam might have offered exoticism and interesting work. In wartime, it offered danger and the unexpected. As they prepared to leave for Vietnam, newly assigned agents faced many unknowns.

This form letter to Special Agent Peter Hopkinson from NISRA Saigon Assistant Senior Resident Agent Don Webb illustrated what the new volunteer might expect. In this case, Webb was kind enough to add a personal note to the standard message.

U.S. NAVAL INVESTIGATIVE SERVICE OFFICE VIETNAM
APO San Francisco 96243

From: Commanding Officer, U.S. Naval Investigative Service Office, Vietnam To:

Subj: Information for Special Agent reporting to Vietnam

1. *General.* As a Special Agent selected for assignment to Vietnam, you are entering a unique and valuable phase of

your career. Your tour in Vietnam will expose you to more criminal and counterintelligence investigations and activities in one short year than your contemporaries will gain in many years of stateside duty.

It will present you with more opportunities to exercise your judgement and make independent decisions than are available to any but supervisory personnel in the States. Thus, with these opportunities to gain unique experience and exercise your initiative, this should be a rewarding tour.

2. *Assignment.* Presently, USNAVINVSERVO Vietnam [NISOV] maintains two NAVINVSERVRAs (NISRAs): Saigon and Danang. USNAVINVSERVRA Saigon has satellite offices in Cam Ranh Bay and Binh Thuy, and USNAVINVSERVRA Danang has satellite offices at Chu Lai and Quang Tri. Every month one agent makes a trip to Bangkok to conduct investigations in Thailand. The preponderance of these cases are PSIs. The nature of combat operations encompassing sudden and dramatic shifts of personnel, make it difficult to give you any assurance as to your initial duty assignment. Notwithstanding that factor, after arriving in Saigon and getting a short orientation, your initial assignment will be in either Saigon or Danang.

3. *Areas.* There is wide disparity in the living conditions between those in Saigon and those elsewhere in the country.

Saigon is a big city which has grown larger and is overpopulated with both Vietnamese citizens and U.S. military and civilian personnel. Saigon has all the problems associated with overpopulation. Living conditions are crowded, garbage is piled high, traffic is unbelievably chaotic and prices are high. Danang is a small city which has been surrounded by the U.S. military. Danang has been declared Off Limits to US. military and civilian personnel. In other areas of the country, your life will be generally confined to living and working aboard a military base or cantonment.

4. *Saigon Billeting.* In Saigon you will be billeted in a BOQ occupied by U.S. and Free World Military Forces personnel. This BOQ was a former Vietnamese hotel which has had air conditioning, showers, and other "conveniences" added by the U.S. Military. These "conveniences" sometimes overtax the electrical and water systems and thus are not always operational, but they exist. Rooms are usually occupied by three permanent residents and the cost of the room is $5.00 per person per month.Laundry, room cleaning, water bottle filling (since tap water is not potable) and other miscellaneous services are provided by a Vietnamese maid costing you about $10.00 per month. Officers' open messes are available in several BOQs. Breakfast runs about 50-60 cents, lunch 65 cents-$1.00, and dinner $1.00 or more if you eat heartily. Beer is 20 cents, mixed drinks are 25 cents-50 cents. Entertainment is BOQ movies or floor shows or whatever you can find on the economy at exorbitant prices. If you like good French or Chinese food, floor shows and night clubs, you will find yourself spending plenty of cash. The curfew for Saigon, however, is currently 2200-0600.

5. *Danang Billeting.* All of the USNAVINVSERVRA Danang personnel moved into their new home on July 1967. It is a three story villa type structure which has all modern conveniences plus a few luxuries (from a Vietnamese standpoint). Maid service is available at low cost. There is an excellent Navy Officers' Club in Danang which boasts of the best facilities in-country. Breakfast is about 50 cents, lunch 65 cents, and dinner $1.00. Drinks are 25 cents-50 cents.

Danang also has an older Army Club as well as an Air Force Club at the Air Base. A curfew of 2000-0600 is still in effect, and outside entertainment is minimal.

6. *Saigon Working Conditions.* The office space can only be described as adequate. It is air-conditioned and is conveniently located to the post exchange. Agents work six and a half days a week. You will find yourself fully occupied during these hours and on occasion will even put in some "overtime." There is a duty agent each day, currently a 1 in 5 rotation. Cases in Saigon are to a large extent criminal in

nature and are in support of Saigon based commands or those units in the Mekong Delta or in coastal port areas. Counterintelligence collection is based largely on liaison with other government agencies, personal observation, and contact with Vietnamese sources or foreigners who are in some manner associated with the U.S. Navy/Marine Corps. There are four compact automobiles, two International Scouts, and one truck available for in city travel while out of area travel is by any aircraft available. This will provide you with any thrills you might otherwise miss.

7. *Danang Working Conditions.* The office in Danang was formerly a combination office and billet. It has now has been renovated and equipped exclusively as an office. It is a large, well cared for structure and makes a comfortable office. It is partially air-conditioned, and rooms not so equipped have ceiling fans and open-air ventilation. The office hours are basically the same as in Saigon. The work is almost exclusively criminal in support of U.S. Naval Support Activity, Danang or U.S. Marine Corps commands. Any of the latter cases are in remote areas far from Danang and thus agents will occasionally find themselves uncomfortably close to combat area. There are eight vehicles available for local transportation and, as in Saigon, distant travel is by any available aircraft.

8. *Finances.* Most officers and agents find they can live on an average of $150.00 a month while in Vietnam if they do not partake of much outside entertainment or buy elaborate gifts. In addition to the regular salary, each agent while in Vietnam, receives a 25% differential which is subject to Federal income tax. Agents in Vietnam also get Separate Maintenance Allowance (SMA) which is tax exempt, in the following amounts: $2,500 for wife; $2,900 for wife and one child; $3,300 for wife and two children; and $3,700 for a wife and more than three children. Additionally, agent personnel in Vietnam receive premium pay at the maximum rate which is 25% of the employee's rate of basic pay which does not exceed the minimum rate of basic pay for a GS-1O. Agents assigned to Vietnam are paid by the Naval Regional Finance Center (NRFC), Pearl Harbor, Hawaii. The NRFC will not mail

an agent's pay check to Vietnam; therefore, it is recommended that each agent maintain a stateside bank account to which his check can be mailed by the NRFC. You must designate a commercial banking institution, as your paycheck cannot be mailed to your wife, mother, or anyone else. Personal check cashing facilities are readily available in all locations to which you might be assigned. It is recommended that the agent arrive in-country with at least $100 available in cash or by check to tide him over until the first pay period. All "green" dollars and travelers checks are forbidden in Vietnam and must be turned in at the airport for Military Payment Certificates (MPC) used in Vietnam.

9. *Clothing.* Vietnam has two seasons-hot and wet and hot and dry. In the former, mildew is the great enemy; in the latter, dust. It is recommended that the agent not bring any good or expensive clothing White and solid colored short-sleeved shirts and slacks are the normal attire and sturdy washable varieties are recommended. Dry cleaning facilities are less than satisfactory. Only one summer suit should be brought for such use as out of country travel, leave, etc. Most agents prefer Hush Puppy type footwear because of the comfort and easy up-keep. Experience has shown that if you bring four or five pair of slacks, two-three pairs of shoes, half a dozen shirts, half a dozen sets of underwear, three or four towel and wash cloths, and an inexpensive vinyl raincoat, you will be adequately supplied. Presently, the only items that have been scarce are slacks and shirts. Electric razors will work on the Vietnamese current.

10. *Weapons.* Personal weapons are prohibited in Vietnam. You are to bring your ONI-issued weapon with you. This Office maintains a good variety of official weapons which may be drawn as needed.

11. *Mail.* Air mail to and from Saigon to the U.S. West Coast takes three days and five days to the East Coast, on the average. To and from Danang may take one or two days longer. The addresses: Saigon: U.S. Naval Investigative Service Office, Vietnam APO San Francisco 96253 Danang: U.S. Naval Investigative Service Resident Agency, Danang

FPO San Francisco 96695. We strongly suggest that you prepare for, and prepare your family for, initial and intermittent mail delays. By doing this you can preclude needless misunderstandings.

12. *Hazards:* It goes without saying that you will be operating in a combat area. There are no defined battle lines, and there is little question that the enemy controls more territory than do friendly forces, especially at night. The war can emerge almost any place, and you must face the fact that you are likely to observe it first hand during the course of your tour. This is not intended to magnify such hazards but merely to point out that they must not be minimized. Terrorism is almost an accepted occurrence in Saigon, and vigilance is mandatory. Mortar and rocket attacks are not uncommon, and it is essential that agent personnel know what to do when and if they are caught in them. Be aware of the fact that almost all Special Agents who have served in Vietnam have come under hostile fire at one time or another. If you are prepared for the possibility and exercise calm judgement, you are likely to emerge unscathed. Other hazards are of a health nature. Your required inoculations will protect you from theworst of these and weekly malaria pills will tend to offset that disease. There is little anyone can do to protect you from the "Ho Chi Minh Revenge," aka diarrhea, and you are likely to suffer from it on a few occasions.

13. *PX.* Exchanges are available in all areas and carry a good supply of the necessities of life such as razor blades, shaving cream, tooth paste, books and magazines, film, etc.

Luxury items such as cameras, radios, stereo equipment, etc., come and go, but may be special ordered at a considerable savings over stateside prices.

14. *Leave and R and R.* A five day trip to Japan, Hong Kong, Manila, Australia, Bangkok, Hawaii, Singapore, Taiwan, etc., is part of the benefits of a year tour. You are eligible for such a tour after being in-country a minimum of three months; however, due to the demand for Rand R trips the time required in-country can vary from four to nine months, depending on the place you desire to visit. At present, Hawaii

requires a minimum of six and one half months in-country. R and R trips are a package deal offering free round-trip transportation, low cost accommodations and does not count as leave. Workload permitting, other leave trips to the same areas may be taken on your own if you can arrange the required flights or can pay the fare in order to assure your return as scheduled.

15. *Passports.* Apply for an "Official U.S. Passport" well in advance of departure date to avoid delay. Obtain a passport with multiple entrance and exit visas to Vietnam. Visas are not required to visit Thailand and Malaysia as long as one has a valid U.S. passport. Visas to Hong Kong, Australia, Taiwan and Japan may be obtained locally without delay.

16. *Miscellaneous.* Bring your U.S. Government drivers license and have it effective through your entire tour in Vietnam. Licensing procedures here vary and are bound to be a nuisance when getting established. It is also suggested that you bring a supply of any pills, vitamins, or other medication you may need until you can obtain a local source of supply. Again, the Exchange has a good supply of aspirin, cough drops, and the more popular patent medicines.

17. *Arrival.* All incoming personnel check-in at the USNAVINVSERVO Vietnam regardless of their ultimate duty assignment.

For your benefit, it is suggested that you notify this Office, by letter or message, of the date, time and flight number of your arrival, in order that someone can be on hand to meet you and assist you in checking through customs, changing money, etc. Remember, you will be in a foreign country where the use of English is uncommon. In the event no one is at the Tan Son Nhut Air Base to meet you, call this office for transportation. From a Tan Son Nhut telephone, dial 98 and then our number which is 60845/ 60846 or 922-3967 during duty hours, and 922-3045 after duty hours.

[322]

18. If you have any further questions or need any further assistance to write this Office or the agent designated as your sponsor.

Commanding Officer
Naval Investigative Service Office, Vietnam

*****

Most newly assigned agents received a letter similar to this, with or without a personal note. Armed with this information, they packed and headed off to a NIS assignment none would ever forget.

24 February 1970

Dear Pete,

I will address you thusly, having derived same from the name that was given me. You, as you most likely know, have been designated as my replacement in the wonderful world of Vietnam come sometime in July 1970. I will not be here to meet you since I will be going to my next duty station in May 1970; however, I thought I would drop you a line to let you know that your presence in Vietnam, or RVN as we refer to it, will be greatly appreciated.

I am enclosing a little blurb that is mostly propaganda but it will help you in some ways. I will also endeavor to add to it or explain certain parts of it so that you will know what to expect once your reverse freedom bird touches down at Tan Son Nhut Air Base (where you will enter RVN). I have been here for 16 months having extended for six months, so it can't be all bad. Seriously, it is a very challenging but rewarding job. It requires unlimited enthusiasm, boundless energy, the hide of a water buffalo, and the eyes of an eagle. As an ONI agent, I'm sure you have these attributes and you will be in good stead over here.

Now down to the nitty gritty. Bring only wash and wear clothing. You will have a maid but her main job is to beat your clothes to rags on a wet rock. I brought six pairs of trousers and six shirts and I am still wearing them. I augmented my wardrobe with a few shirts and slacks from the PX at a very reasonable cost and I have stayed in pretty good shape. You will probably wear a suit over and you should have at least one suit and tie for out-country trips such as a Bangkok, Thailand, work trip, R&R, etc. Most of the guys wear Hush Puppies but I find Corfam leather holds up OK. That's all I wear. Either type will be fine.

You will be given two field uniforms and a pair of boots after you get here for your in-country trips so no sweat there. Bring at least six sets of skivvies. This should last you through and you can always buy more at the PX if needed. Enough for clothing.

I don't know how you want to handle your finances but you should be made aware of the fact that your paycheck can only go to your bank of designation. A joint checking account with your wife at that bank might be the most satisfactory arrangement. You'll have to work that out. Green is no good here. We use Military Payment Script, affectionately known as funny money. You can cash checks on a stateside bank here for $100.00 at the Bank and $50.00 at the px. This is how you get your funny money.

We live and eat at the Five Oceans BOQ located one block from the office. The rooms are adequate although nothing to write home about. The food is filling. You will have to pay your maid 1,000 piasters a month (local currency equal to about $8.20 US). You pay the BOQ 450 piasters a month (I have never figured out what that's for). The meals run about $2.00 a day depending on how much you eat or can stand.

Case-wise we handle the full gamut. We have worked, are working, or will work every category in the book. You will also probably travel the entire country to get the work done but it is not too bad. You get used to it. Upon arrival in country you may be assigned to either of the two NISRAs and subsequently may be assigned to one of four NISSUs. You will find that out upon arrival. Everybody coming here has different questions so if I can be of further assistance or if you have any specific questions please let me know and I will attempt to answer them.

On that note I will close and wish you best of luck on your upcoming Vietnam tour. It will be a good one, I can assure you.

Sincerely,

DONALD L. WEBB

[325]

NISO VIETNAM. DECEMBER 1967

The rather uncertain status of civilian Special Agents serving in an active war zone was the topic of Special Agent Mike Nagle's ironic 1967 cartoon.

*****

During my three years with NIS in Vietnam, I cannot recall ever hearing an in-depth political discussion between agents, but my colleagues were very aware of the changes both peaceful and otherwise, that were warping the American political scene throughout their tenure.

[326]

Agents were privy to classified reports about organizations in the United States and elsewhere that openly advocated the violent overthrow of American government and its institutions.

The Weathermen were building bombs (and occasionally killing themselves with them) in Greenwich Village; the University of California was rife with insurrection; and militant racial groups on both ends of the color spectrum used bombs, guns, and intimidation to achieve their aims.

America's enemies were quick to exploit U.S. divisiveness. None more than the North Vietnamese, who took succor from every newspaper article and television clip that added credence to the argument that a waiting game could win the war for them.

The Vietnamese politburo preached that patient Confucian values and internal discipline would ultimately triumph over despotic Western values. Some viewed demonstrations at home as an affront to the many dedicated people in Vietnam who genuinely believed a possible communist takeover would be an unthinkable tragedy.

When Jane Fonda traveled to North Vietnam, when NVA hospitals in South Vietnam were found to be operating with instruments and medication donated by zealots at home, and when captured American pilots were being tortured at the Hanoi Hilton, there was often little respect or appreciation for "rabble in the streets."

Far away in Vietnam, dependent on Armed Forces Radio and Television and *Stars and Stripes* newspaper for news from the home front, agents were frequently troubled by what they heard, particularly if they had not been home in nearly a year.

Mike Nagle on April 9, 1968, wrote to his mother, *"Received word of Dr. Martin Luther King's assassination and the subsequent wide-spread rioting. Was Los Angeles spared from this? Sometimes I'm kind of glad I'm not coming back to the States for a while."*

Later, in June, Nagle again wrote. *"Received word of Robert Kennedy being shot yesterday. I understand he is presently in critical condition in Los Angeles.*

[327]

It really makes me wonder, with the dissention, riots, and assassination what our country is coming to."

The Soviets and their sympathizers exploited American divisiveness whenever they could. Service personnel on leave from Vietnam in Japan, Korea, and even Australia were contacted by soviet agents and their sympathizers. On the assumption that they would speak out against the war and be good for propaganda, they were offered assistance to desert. Some were even courted for information about their duties in Vietnam, the initial contact in a potential espionage arrangement.

In Australia, where there was strong antiwar sentiment and a well-delineated left wing, service personnel with access to sensitive information were the target of groups with established links to the extreme left.

Because these events clearly fell within the NIS counterintelligence mandate, agents could be more than a little sensitive to the latest news from U.S. campuses.

In boozier moments, if such things were discussed, a quick-fix solution designed to add levity to the conversation might be put forward.

I recall one "Room 4" discussion in which it was suggested that a World War II B29 Superfortress fleet be reactivated and configured to drop huge quantities of fecal matter on street demonstrators, a slightly less bellicose purpose than the air raids on Japan for which they are famous.

And when American astronauts walked on the moon in 1969, somebody quipped, "Tell those clever people at NASA to send us something to help us kill more Viet Cong -- to hell with the moon."

Throughout it all, the Paris peace talks between North Vietnamese negotiators and U.S. diplomats ground on, punctuated by occasional ceasefires and bombing halts that seemed to change little for those on the ground in "the Nam."

[328]

The "Room 4 Gang" gathers on the occasion of Al Kersenbrock's relief as Supervising Agent, NISO Vietnam. He was replaced by Dick McKenna.

Seated, from left: Special Agent Andy Lambert, Mc Kenna, Kersenbrock, and Special Agent Bob Westberry. Standing, from left: Special Agent Rudy Dees, LTJG Chuck Palmer, Senior Resident Agent Fred Givens, and Special Agent Art Newman

Mike Nagle's April 9, 1968, letter to his mother in California mirrored the thoughts of many:

"Sure hope these new peace proposals are productive. Many here feel the bombing pause was a grave mistake-as we can see the tangible results when the NVA supply lines are not bombed. Personally, I feel it's a good move if it in any way will help bring an end to this miserable war. Also very surprised Johnson declined to run for re-election.

I think history will show that our involvement in Vietnam was a wise move-although I think the point has been made and we should do everything in our power to end it, save forfeiture of South Vietnam and/or surrendering what we have gained."

[329]

Mike Nagle's youthful observations make interesting reading in hind-sight, written a full seven years before South Vietnam finally collapsed under the communist onslaught.

*****

Those who lived through the late '60s and '70s will recall it as the time of the Afro haircut, long hair, and lamb chop sideburns. Dedicated military men have long believed that part of pride in the uniform they wear is a carefully shorn, regulation haircut.

But short hair was definitely uncool for young servicemen on leave trying to impress the women of that day. Beyond the desire to be fashionably attractive to the opposite sex, "pushing the regulations" also became a means for some to express individualism and for the true malcontents to go further by blatantly flaunting military regulation.

Some did their best to turn the debate into one of ethnicity. African American servicemen in less disciplined outfits strode the streets with haircuts that would have done a Fijian policeman proud. There were sensitivities on both sides of this debate, and I recall a senior Navy captain ordering a fellow officer out of the officers' club because he had sideburns which extended unacceptably. The captain told the man his appearance was disgraceful.

The haircut debate never made it to the agent corps while I was in Vietnam, though I recall my good friend John Morgan being branded a subversive because he had hair long enough to touch his collar. John was an exception to the rule. In the Marine Corps field units during one of my last visits in 1971 to the Fifth Marines I watched with quiet amusement as the battalion sergeant major approached a young first lieutenant, addressed him with great courtesy as Sir, and suggested he get a haircut before anything else. At chow half an hour later, the lieutenant was shorn.

The corps had its problems, but discipline in the officer ranks never seemed to be a part of it.

Through the twists and turns of the '60s and '70s and confusing, sometimes distressing events both at home and in Vietnam, the agent corps served with integrity. Although not impervious to forces of the day, agents assigned to Vietnam maintained their commitment to the best traditions of the U.S. Naval Service.

*****

16 NEARING THE END

Ever since evolving from underwater demolition teams (UDT)…the Frog Men of World War II fame…Navy SEAL teams have carried out important secret missions using small, highly trained squads. The SEALS are the functionaries of the Naval Special Warfare Group.

In Vietnam, important senior commanders did not always favor unconventional warfare, as the shady world of the Special Forces soldier became known. Their elite image with special uniform accoutrements and unusual equipment, did not sit well with the more conventional commanders.

The U.S. Army's Special Forces program came under heavy attack after several officers in Vietnam were accused of complicity in the assassination of a double agent. It was well known that the commander of MACV, army Gen. Creighton Abrams, was no fan of the Special Forces. Pundits saw the court-martials connected with the assassination as a swan song for the Special Forces, and many would concede that it very nearly was.

When in 1971 NISOV agents briefed the CO of Naval Special Warfare at his Saigon office about serious criminal allegations against his SEAL team members, there was immediate and genuine concern that a couple of bad apples might spell the end of the entire program. Reductions and extreme budget austerity were the norm in the Navy at the time. Nobody profited from the wrong type of publicity in that kind of environment.

The U.S. Drug Enforcement Administration (DEA) had come to the

San Diego NISRA with information gleaned from their local informant network. SEALS stationed at Coronado were alleged to have smuggled into the United States, kilo packages of opium concealed in their scuba tanks. As was the norm, their gear had traveled with them on special Navy C130 flights used to rotate the teams and their equipment in and out of Vietnam.

These special flights moved SEALS outside the normal personnel logistic systems, allowing them to keep classified special equipment under wraps. An example in 1971 was the night-vision devices called Starlight Scopes.

These carried a secret classification at the time, and required special handling. Though Customs had cleared the aircraft and its occupants on arrival, none of the contraband had been discovered at that time.

SEALS always seem to have favorite watering holes, whether abroad or at home. And so it was in San Diego where the bar of choice was also a favorite of accomplices in the opium-smuggling scheme. DEA agents quickly identified key players and set up an informant within the group. They soon learned that two SEAL team members, assigned at the time to Logistic Support Base Ben Luc, were planning to import another load. But before the two suspects could make their next move, the U.S. attorney in San Diego decided that the case DEA had built was adequate to support the immediate apprehension and return of the SEAL conspirators.

One of the accused SEALs was an officer, and the son of an active duty senior career naval officer. His involvement stung colleagues in Naval Special Warfare, even though his assignment had been one of logistic support rather than the command of any SEAL operations. There seemed to be little doubt that the man had taken part in the plan with greed and self-aggrandizement as his motives, neither of which reflected well on his proud organization. His co-conspirator had been a petty officer second class with a history of numerous successful combat operations in Vietnam.

Navy JAG staff at NAVFORV was consulted, and the decision was made to apprehend and incarcerate both men on the basis of documents furnished by the U.S. attorney in San Diego. Naval

[332]

Special Warfare advised that the officer was on R and R leave in Sydney, Australia, but he was expected back on a night flight into Tan Son Nhut. The petty officer was currently at Ben Luc on stand-by status.

Special Agent Marshall Whidden and I, accompanied by a SEAL officer, drove from Saigon to Ben Luc for the petty officer. We used the hour of driving time to devise our plan for the upcoming arrest in order to minimize the danger inherent in taking down a highly trained operative who we were sure would be armed. The SEAL officer told us we could expect the man to be carrying a short-barreled revolver in the breast pocket of his camouflage utilities. We all agreed it would be best if the takedown occurred in an open area away from the SEAL hooches. With this in mind, we hatched a plan to have the Ben Luc communication station summon our man to receive an operationally urgent message.

We reasoned that he would drop whatever he was doing and walk the short distance from the SEAL area to the sandbagged bunker that contained the message center. That would provide us with our opportunity.

At Ben Luc we briefed the command staff. A sailor in the message center was detailed to deliver a note for our man that summoned him to the bunker for a message. With this done, Marsh Whidden and I began our slow walk down the road we knew he would be using. We were dressed in our civvies and thought it likely that we would be seen as visiting civilian engineers.

The SEAL officer assisting us was in uniform; and he hung well back from us. Within a few moments our quarry approached us, walking hurriedly toward the communication bunker. Ignoring him, we continued an animated conversation about improving a drainage design until he was just past us. Then we drew our weapons and identified ourselves, ordering him to remain stationary. The SEAL officer accompanying us had drawn his .45 and covered the man from his right quarter…the accused was visibly rattled. I wasted no time removing a .38-caliber Colt Detective Special from his left breast pocket and handcuffing him.

Whidden remembers, "I recall my most vivid thought at the time of

[333]

the arrest was whether or not our SEAL companion was going to shoot him on the spot. As I recall emotions were high and solutions to problems in Vietnam were a little different than they would have been Stateside. I certainly didn't want to be in his line of fire, that's for sure."

We marched him directly back to his quarters, where he had a small private cubicle in the main sleeping hooch. There I began a careful search of his personal effects, looking especially for correspondence and other evidence of the conspiracy. Whidden moved into an adjoining area to search the gear belonging to the co-accused.

The man's cubicle contained a formidable arsenal. There were captured Chinese AK47 assault rifles, an SKS, and even an Australian self-loading rifle whose barrel had been shortened. This was a favorite weapon of the Australian Special Air Service, with whom the SEALS operated.

There were concussion and fragmentation grenades, flares, and other pyrotechnics that would have rendered the hooch a very unpleasant environment in the event of fire, rocket attack, or any accidents.

In a wooden ammunition box, I found a number of letters. These contained information that would support charges against both of the accused. Marshall Whidden's search produced evidence, but of a much more circumstantial nature.

With our search complete, we loaded up and drove back to Saigon and the brig where the accused was incarcerated. One was down, but we still had one to go.

Given the nature of SEAL team camaraderie and the communication equipment at their disposal, we considered it fortunate that the accused officer was out of Vietnam. We reasoned that even if they wanted to, finding and alerting the man in Sydney would be very difficult. So when the chartered Boeing 707 landed at Saigon's Tan Son Nhut Airport that night, a team led by Senior Resident Agent Fred Givens was waiting for it.

Givens who was renowned in the organization as a man who could

[334]

look after himself, had been a Texas Ranger. Quiet in nature and always calm, Givens never seemed to have problems with ne'er-do-wells once his blue eyes had fastened on them.

With Givens in charge, we had a strong measure of confidence that our man wouldn't be tempted to do anything silly. And so it was. The NIS agent team was first aboard the plane when the door was opened. Givens asked cabin crew to page the accused and we watched him make his way forward past rows of bleary-eyed service personnel just back from a week in the fleshpots of Sydney's Kings Cross. Once identified, he was handcuffed and then ushered off the aircraft. In the security spaces, a full search was conducted of his person and luggage. We did not elect to interrogate him at the airport.

As an officer, he was entitled to incarceration in facilities for officers only. The Army maintained a stockade with a section reserved for officers at their massive Long Binh facility. This also accommodated the U.S. Army Vietnam headquarters elements. Known in Vietnam as the Long Binh Jail (LBJ), it was in these spartan confines that our accused spent his first night while awaiting transport to the United States to stand trial. We reflected that a hard bunk at the LBJ must have been a harsh change from the soft living and gentle company he had found in Sydney. Both men were returned to the United States and tried in federal court. We later heard that convictions had been upheld for both.

Marshall Whidden remembered fondly the camaraderie between NIS agents and SEALs: "The one thing that stood out most in the SEAL drug smuggling case was the camaraderie that developed between the SEAL team guys and us."

"We always had good relationships, probably because our organizations were both kind of bastard outfits, and they did do some jobs for us through the years. That was a terribly embarrassing event for those guys, especially the teams in Vietnam. It would have been convenient for them to turn against the messenger. But to their credit they didn't and in fact it made the relationship stronger. I remember some mock knife fighting in room 4, them against our man…and the usual winner was Uncle Fred Givens."

[335]

National presidential elections were scheduled in August 1971. President Nguyen Van Thieu was running for a second four-year term and was opposed by both former President Nguyen Cao Ky and Gen. Duong Van "Big" Minh. Unexpectedly both men suddenly withdrew, claiming that the incumbent had rigged the election. Students at Saigon University demonstrated, as did Buddhist activists who also contended that the entire election process was faulty. Students spilled into the streets not far from NISOV headquarters. Because of concerns about festering anti-American feelings, all hands were ordered to limit their travel and exposure in the cities.

Thieu won the election by an even larger majority than in the previous one, and was sworn into office on October 3. The communists expressed their displeasure by firing rockets into Saigon, killing several Vietnamese civilians. Viet Cong and NVA regulars mounted similar attacks elsewhere around South Vietnam. By the last quarter of 1971, the U.S. force withdrawal and Vietnamization ramp up was apparent in every quarter. When the Cholon PX closed, it marked an end to the compound area that first housed the Navy headquarters in the early '60s, Headquarters, Support Activity Saigon.

The building that first housed the Provost Marshal and then later NISOV, was no longer available to Naval Intelligence. The Five Oceans BOQ, home to agents and officers since 1962, was also closed.

It was clear that the U.S. Army was getting out of Saigon in a hurry, and as it had at the outset, the Navy found a home in Cholon with U.S. Army MPs. Only a short distance from the offices that were now being vacated was a former Vietnamese hotel, which at that time housed an Army CID unit.

The Army unit was also downsizing, which would leave two of the floors available for NISOV billeting and office space.

No office move is ever easy, especially after an organization has been in one place for nearly a decade. For a unit with security

[336]

responsibilities and the paraphernalia required for safe custody of classified material, moves are complicated even further. Naval Investigative Service Office, Vietnam, had numerous four-drawer document security containers. In affect armored filing cabinets. The containers were protected against forced entry with combination locks and steel plating. There were desks, typewriters, personal effects, unclassified reference documents, the entire contents of the NISRA evidence locker, photographic equipment…a seemingly endless list.

The entire office staff, from the CO to our one assigned seaman, turned out to help. Drawers were removed from their security containers and transported in trucks closely guarded by armed agents. The moved items were carried individually from the trucks past the armed sentries at the MP building, the heavier items stockpiled in the breezeway between the two wings of the building. The teams raised the heaviest items upward with block and tackle.

This was not the work that federal agents normally did, but it was unavoidable. Our various "customers" had to wait until we were re-established, and with our radios and telephones operating once again. All but the commanding officer, Cdr. Gene Moore, and Supervising Agent Dick McKenna moved their gear into rooms in the building adjacent to the offices.

The CO and McKenna remained billeted at the 98 Phan Dinh Phung villa under the watchful eye of the housekeeper, Hai. Whidden said of the move, "The only time I can remember security being tighter is when we were transporting a truckload of liquor to the NIS company bar from Tan Son hut."

In retrospect, I think the move probably exacerbated the already prevalent feeling in our command that we were all on borrowed time. The United States was going to leave Vietnam in any event and the reassuring rhetoric that was being proffered to our South Vietnamese allies was hollow.

I had been in country at this point for more than two years, and I found it very disquieting when Vietnamese asked me if things would be all right after we all left.

[337]

Moving

But I had neither the foresight nor the cynicism to realize what was really happening. I could never believe after the monumental sacrifices that had been made that the United States would just walk away, and I told them so. I remained reassuring to my Vietnamese friends and associates regarding their future. *Mea culpa.*

By the latter part of 1971, the U.S. presence in Cholon had dwindled further and we and our MP hosts were largely on our own. We no longer had messing facilities, as the Five Oceans was closed. I found myself purchasing food from the street vendors who came out in the evenings to sell their bread, warm beer, and a few specialty items such as boiled mussels. Bunkie John Morgan had an electric frying pan (which frequently blew the electrical circuits) and he would occasionally create meals for us with frozen food purchased by the CO on his periodic shopping runs to the commissary.

None of us had authority to shop at the commissary though, and more often I could be found at dinnertime on the sidewalk in front of the old hotel sitting on a stool with a bowl of cooked mussels, French bread, and a quart of warm Tiger beer.

Marshall Whidden: "The food was certainly one of the up points for the tour. Probably one the greatest treats was simply eating a butter-smeared loaf of French bread freshly purchased off a local street corner and washed down with a bottle of beer. There were some great restaurants and soup kitchens. Those that stand out most were the great Cholon Chinese restaurants. Many times it got exciting as we had to sit with a handgun in our lap, under the dinner napkin, to have ready to discourage disabled veterans, cowboys, and just common Asian criminal folks."

None of this was genuine hardship, merely a reflection of the state of things at the time. Our caseload remained largely unchanged and agents drove to Nha Be and downtown to COMNAVFORV every day to cover the latest incidents. Few high-profile investigations were under way at the time, but we dealt with an increasing number of incidents involving Vietnamese Navy personnel.

Most U.S. Navy facilities were being handed over to the VNN in one form or another, meaning that the Vietnamese command area now encompassed areas from which non U.S. personnel had previously been excluded.

The incidence of burglary and theft rose appreciably after this happened.

Providing needed services to the scattered U.S. Navy commands, which in many instances were becoming isolated in much the way we were, became more of a challenge for NISOV. Cutbacks and Vietnamization affected our transport and communications too.

In Da Nang at this time, Special Agent Ed Giblin, later to become SRA in Saigon, operated a one-man office in the vastly reduced area of Camp Tien Sa, in use at the time by U.S. naval advisers. This was the third office space NIS in Da Nang had used since the original office in the city had been given up the year before. Giblin, and a petty officer yeoman to manage the phone and clerical duties, was doing his best to stage an orderly withdrawal from I Corps. He operated there in a climate of pandemonium until the decision was finally made to pull him back to Saigon permanently.

[339]

The area south of Saigon that encompasses the Mekong Delta remained important in the allied naval effort, but increasingly Vietnamese Navy units were taking over combat operations and patrolling. The U.S. Navy role was steadily moving back toward advisory status as the Americans turned over equipment and withdrew men. For Naval Investigative Service special agents, this had several important ramifications. Getting to commands and people was getting more difficult since it was no longer possible to rely on U.S. military aircraft and vessels for a ride. In addition, advisory staff was more difficult to locate.

*****

I had established useful ties with the CIA proprietary airline Air America. As the once dependable Navy and Army medevac chopper service grew increasingly undependable, I would occasionally rely on the Air America pilots to get me where I needed to go. This usually happened aboard fixed-wing Pilatus Porter turboprop aircraft. Catching these rides was a matter of getting out to the Tan Son Nhut Terminal and waiting to see what developed on the flight manifest.

Porter flights were not always rostered, but pilots always seemed willing to help if they could. One memorable mission was my very first ride in a Porter during the 1971 monsoon season. I needed to get to Moc Hoa, which was located on the Plain of Reeds near the Cambodian border. We didn't leave Saigon until late morning with a heavy and dark cloud cover building up. I was seated next to the pilot, a former Marine aviator who seemed to have an air of adventure about him. I learned that this unique aircraft was designed by the Swiss to land in difficult and inhospitable places like glaciers.

The pilot guided the aircraft with a stick as would a fighter pilots, and he adjusted flap settings by reaching overhead to a handle and sprocket, which looked as though it had come off a bicycle. Rotating the sprocket drove a chain that operated the flap gear. It was basic, but it worked very well.

Once in the air, we leveled out at about three thousand feet and adjusted to a northwesterly course. As was typical at this time of

[340]

year, water stood everywhere below us in the paddies rivers and canals. There seemed to be more water-covered terrain than there was dry land. Closer to Cambodia, there was even more flooding. I began to wonder what the airstrip at Moc Hoa would look like.

My anxiety increased as we began our descent after the short flight.

I could see a strip ahead, and the pilot nodded above the roar of the big turboprop to signal that this was our destination. Most of the strip was covered in water. The pilot turned and yelled in my ear, "Do you really need to get in there?" I nodded affirmatively, still wondering how he planned to pull the landing off. I soon found out.

The pilot made the sort of approach one would expect when landing on an aircraft carrier. With flaps down and emulating a landing pelican, we swooped over the end markers of the tarmac where the pilot reversed the propeller pitch... we simply stopped in the air and dropped the foot or two to the ground.

I was amazed, and just sat there with a silly grin on my face. My ex-Marine jet jockey grinned back and helped me open the door. I grabbed my rifle and gear and closed the door, walking quickly to the edge of the strip. The pilot had revved his engine with brakes full on and then released them to roll a few yards and stagger into the air...a minute later he was out of sight.

I was alone there except for a couple of Vietnamese in uniform who were sleeping in the shade some distance away. I sat on some nearby sandbags, cradling my rifle and waiting for another aircraft to arrive.

An aircraft eventually did stop. It was an Army Dustoff Huey assigned to the medevac squadron in Binh Thuy. Alighting next to a fuel hose that was connected to nearby storage bladders, the crew chief jumped out and began fueling while the pilots remained at their controls. Crouching down, I ran up to him while waving to the pilots, and asked if they could drop me at a forward base nearby. The crew had a short discussion via the intercom and then the chief gave me a thumbs-up and I crawled aboard and strapped in.

[341]

The Dustoff was empty now, but the state of the floor suggested it had not been quite recently. Streaks of congealing blood revealed where a body had been pulled out the door.

Moments later we were in the air and gathering altitude over the inundated plain below us; the afternoon sun reflecting off the glistening stalks of flooded fields of reeds. I was somewhat comforted by the knowledge that my briefcase and I would be in a reasonably secure position for the night. In the countryside I noticed familiar American faces much more than in the cities.

There were good reasons for that. Troop levels at the beginning of 1971 were pegged at 280,000. By the end of the year the number had declined to 159,000. The South Vietnamese were assuming more responsibility for the actual prosecution of the ground war, and their casualty rates reflected it.

In theory, Vietnamization seemed to be working on the ground, although the United States was still committed to an aggressive air campaign in support of them. Large B52 strikes continued to hammer NVA troop concentrations in Cambodia, Laos, and Vietnam. One had to wonder how long they would last against the communists if the airpower were no longer on call to support them. We heard news almost daily about the seemingly unending peace talks in Paris, which optimists hoped might not only provide a tolerable political solution but also get American prisoners of war released. The only certainty at the time was that we all seemed to be leaving Vietnam.

Being the most "ground experienced" agent in the office had its disadvantages. I could be sent just about anywhere. More than two years of in-country experience had taught me where the units we serviced were and how best to locate the people assigned there. Agents always had the option of asking the command to send a person of interest rearward to Saigon, but inevitably the person concerned would want to know why he was traveling. The valuable commodity of surprise, along with access to the individual's personal effects and compatriots, would be forfeited if agents took the easier option. An agent finding his way out to a field unit and doing his job there always achieved best results. So we went to our customers.

In late 1971 South Vietnam was a long way from being at peace, but it had become possible with very careful planning, to drive places where helicopter flights had once been the only option.

I drove from Saigon to Can Tho twice. The second time I was halted at a new bridge that had just been completed with American foreign aid. VC sappers using ammonium-nitrate fertilizer mixed with diesel fuel had demolished some of the support structure. The irony of seeing empty fertilizer bags nearby bearing the familiar "hand-clasp" U.S. Agency for International Development logo was not lost to me that day. They lay there on the banks of the small and picturesque river, the bridge approaches shaded by palm trees and bamboo.

The cars jeeps and trucks were backed up there for miles, and the Vietnamese drivers and passengers became increasingly uneasy as the sun reached its zenith and began to fall. ARVN military police (QC) were having problems keeping the jeeps off the damaged bridge, so they resorted to halting traffic by firing their M16s overhead.

The only other U.S. vehicle I could see anywhere was a grey Navy International Scout, which I quickly learned had Navy SEALs on board who were growing as uncomfortable as I was with the situation. After a brief conference we decided to bluff our way past the QC using my Military Security Service identification.

Taking the initiative, the SEALs pulled off on the steeply sloping road shoulder and drove toward the increasingly agitated QCs. Following closely behind them, I held the MSS card out for inspection and was approached. The SEALs, after stopping only briefly, pulled away once again. Seeing this I shouted "MSS" to the Vietnamese and followed the speeding Scout as a burst of fire erupted from the ARVN. We drove as fast as possible, made the ferry crossings across the Mekong and Ba Sac Rivers, and were safely at Binh Thuy that evening.

Nursing a beer that night, it occurred to me this had been an unnecessarily risky trip, the sort of situation that had killed complacent travelers in Vietnam for years.

[343]

Sea Float heliport

I resolved to be more alert to potential dangers in the remaining months of my tour.

I continued to run my leads in the delta, working there with the Binh Thuy agent. Special Agent Rudy Dees had an unenviable caseload, and I assisted from time to time. Being billeted with both Army and Navy aviation units at Binh Thuy made helicopter transport fairly dependable and hassle-free. We ranged over Cape Ca Mau to the Navy Sea Float outpost at Nam Can, where industrious sailors had constructed the first base aboard flat barges anchored there in the river. Never far from the fight, "Sea Float sailors" drew fire just by venturing upstream and around the river bend.

They were surrounded by hundreds of square miles of mangrove swamp, and to the northwest, by the infamous U Minh Forest that had been home to NVA battalions for many years. SEAL teams operated with great success in the region, taking the guerrilla war to the enemy. The area had earned its reputation as Indian country. In the opposite direction, the riverside border towns of Chau Doc and Tan Chau had advisory outposts, a legacy of Special Forces unit ventures across into Cambodia.

The Naval Air Facility in Cam Ranh Bay, operated helicopters that flew regular milk runs from the depot in Saigon. When I first arrived, the aircraft were old green US34Ds, which had obviously come from the Marine Corps inventory. The "34" looked like a flying tadpole largely due to the monstrous radial aircraft engine housed in the nose under the pilots. It was an aircraft with a lot of character, and I usually enjoyed my 34 flights high above the rivers and canals of the delta. I would sit looking past the door gunner as we overflew the remote, triangular forts that the French had left behind.

The 34s were scheduled for replacement by the much larger twin--rotor CH46 helicopters. Summoned to an LST that was anchored in the Gulf of Cambodia, I joined one of the last flights of the venerable old bird. It was a long flight by helicopter standards, and on this occasion there would be no views. Clouds and fog covered the coast as we beat our way over the final vestiges of terra firma somewhere down the coast from Ha Tien.

The flight over water seemed to be lasting a very long time. I was not wearing a headset, so I could not hear the pilots, but we had reduced our elevation considerably and were no longer flying in a straight line. I eventually caught the eye of the crew chief/door gunner and said slowly so he could read my lips, "Lost?" He nodded his head in the affirmative, then slid across and said, "The fucking ship won't give us directions to their position." I nodded my understanding. Ships' positions were classified, especially when they were anchored in hostile territory.

More minutes would pass before the long, grey shape of the LST loomed out of the fog. We gratefully set down across her open tank deck...there was not a great deal of fuel left in the old bird. I jumped off with the mail and was quickly replaced by men due for rotation home. The crew chief busied himself with getting just enough fuel into the tanks to deliver them to the next airfield that had high-octane aviation fuel available. Soon they were flight-ready.

[345]

The pilot cranked over the big motor which caught immediately and belched smoke out of cavernous exhaust stacks. Moments later they were circling the ship and climbing above the fog.

It had been a long time since I had been aboard a ship that was at anchor in open waters. The atmosphere was eerily quiet without the thump of screws and the other sounds of the machinery that go to drive a ship through the water.

Rainwater Shower

With the helicopter gone and the rain now falling, sailors came out on the tank deck, stripped their clothes off and began lathering up with soap. The freshwater falling from the skies was most welcome. Freshwater shortages are endemic to LSTs, and this was a not-to-be missed opportunity for men who had endured water rationing for a long time. My business aboard the ship did not take long, and by mid-afternoon I was beginning to consider my next move.

[346]

Being marooned aboard a stationary LST in the Gulf of Cambodia until the next resupply mission flew in was not an attractive option, so I asked the CO if another underway vessel might be in the area. He agreed to check for me. This was not as simple a matter as it had once been. The Vietnamization effort was well advanced at this point.

Friendly small vessels in the area would most likely be those of the Vietnamese Navy. The weather was not improving, and I watched the waves sweeping across the open water. I began to wonder which was the better option, the pitch and roll of the notorious flat-bottomed LST, or a smaller vessel under way in foul weather.

A young sailor approached me and said, "Sir, a swift boat will be coming alongside for you directly." The question was settled.

Swift

He beckoned me to the railing where a Jacob's ladder was being readied. As I neared, I heard the swift's engines as it throttled back to approach us from astern. As I looked down, crewmembers dropped fenders over the side to prevent any damage from collision...a real possibility considering the existing conditions. As lines were thrown to the boat, I had a close look at her. Fifty feet long, the "patrol craft, fast", was a sleek shallow-draft vessel designed to work coastal waters and rivers.

[347]

With its alloy hull, it cut a rakish appearance except for the pilothouse that was perched only a few feet back from the bow peak. It was a practical design, but lacked the romantic silhouette of a patrol torpedo (PT) boat.

On top of the wheelhouse was a gun tub, mounting a pair of .50-caliber machine guns. Now looking down into the gun mount, I could see where it would command an excellent field of vision above the waves. On the aft deck and behind the wheelhouse, the boats crew scurried around the centrally positioned 81mm mortar-machine gun combination mount.

Unlike conventional ground based mortars, this one could actually be aimed in the manner of a typical deck gun.

Only one Westerner, a young U.S. Navy petty officer who towered over his shipmates, was on board. As soon as the vessel had been made secure alongside and the engines had been shut down, he had the covers off the two massive Detroit diesels and began to check them.

My gear was secured to a line and lowered over the side of the LST to the waiting hands below. A good deal of slop splashed up between the two hulls, and my pack swung in an arc with the vessel movement. I gritted my teeth and swung over the side, grimly clutching the Jacobs ladder which by then was swinging in much the way my gear had.

Once at the end of the ladder, there was nothing to do but jump to the rapidly rising deck of the Swift. My landing was neither soft nor gentle, and it caused some good-natured grinning from the Vietnamese. How, they must have wondered, was this tall Yankee going to fare in the seas ahead?

I was offered a comfortable spot below but prudently elected to find a standing position in the wheelhouse where I reasoned, there was likely to be more fresh air. It proved to be a wise decision, and we were soon under way with crewmembers preparing a meal in the spaces below.

First they slaughtered a chicken, began heating water, and broke out the *nuoc mam* fish condiment. Nuoc mam has many wonderful flavors but also an overpoweringly pungent fish odor, which some have compared to unwashed athletic socks. The aromas wafting around the vessel as we plunged into waves that threw water clear over the pilothouse were not conducive to pleasant travel. It took a great deal of concentration to convince my churning stomach that I was not now nor would I become, seasick. A grizzled Vietnamese coxswain hung onto the wheel skillfully, occasionally checking my color with a cheerful grin. Shirtless, he had a collection of tattoos and illustrations on his chest, the most prominent of which was the statement, "Sat Cong," which translated meant "kill Viet Cong."

Thankfully the "swift" made landfall at An Thoi on the island of Phu Quoc without my disgracing myself.

I thanked my hosts for the ride and made my way to the Navy outpost, established there in the early '60s to support the Vietnamese Navy's force of junks. Successive groups of American advisers had transformed the outpost into a reasonably comfortable spot, replete with spectacular ocean views. With a clean beach and fresh breezes, it certainly offered conditions vastly superior to those that the inland Brown Water Navy had to endure. The only drawback I detected was its close proximity to several thousand hardcore enemy prisoners of war that were interned on the island.

At the Navy base I soon would learn that the next aircraft back to mainland South Vietnam would not be departing until the following morning, when a USAF C123 Provider was due in to their airstrip. Asking about the space availability, I was told, "Don't worry about it, just show up…you'll be okay."

Just to be sure, the next morning I was at the airstrip an hour before flight time. With more than two years of experience dealing with U.S. Air Force air movement personnel, this seemed to be a wise precaution. I need not have worried.

The morning was beautiful, with a gentle breeze blowing in off the Gulf of Cambodia and seemingly unlimited visibility. No U.S. Air Force personnel were present, only Army aviation maintenance men and armorers servicing the Cobra gunships and loading rockets into their pods in preparation for the next mission.

I watched the sweating armorers work until my reverie was broken by the arrival of an aging military fire truck festooned with fully outfitted firefighters. They were Vietnamese civilian employees, but their helmets, jackets, and boots were of U.S. manufacture.

All was correctly buttoned and buckled up, but many times larger than the small-framed firemen...I was quietly amused. I reasoned, correctly, that the fire truck's arrival was an indicator that my aircraft was inbound. I was soon rewarded for my patience as the twin-engine cargo plane touched down, reversed props, and taxied quickly off to a seaward parking area.

By this time, a crowd of Vietnamese Navy personnel and dependents had clustered on the verge of the hardstand area. I did not see any live pigs in their woven baskets, but they were clearly moving...everything else seemed to be with them.

In the meantime the aircraft was refueled, and the pilots carried out their preflight checks. I caught the eye of the crew chief who beckoned me over with a casual turn of his head. Just then the Vietnamese dependents broke ranks from the grass verge and headed en masse for the aircraft loading ramp. I was fortunate in the ensuing skirmish to win for myself a sling seat far forward, next to an open window.

The aircraft quickly filled with chattering Vietnamese, their gear piled unceremoniously onto the cargo ramp. I heard the sound of breaking glass in the back amidst the chaos. With the ramp up a harried crew chief pushed forward to the cabin area, shaking his head as he reached me and warning-"nouc mam." He was followed soon by the pungent odor of the renowned Phu Quoc fish sauce leaking onto the cargo deck.

The pilots made haste to get us under way, and minutes later I was watching An Thoi's beach fade away behind us as we climbed into the cooling atmosphere. I wondered if this would be my last trip to Phu Quoc; as luck would have it, it was.

*****

[350]

About this same time, NISRA Saigon received a request for assistance from one of the Navy barrack ships (APLs) anchored in the Mekong near the Cambodian border. Irregularities in the ship post office had been discovered, and it was feared that the postal clerk was stealing from the mail.

I inherited the case which from the outset seemed fairly straightforward, as did locating and getting to the ship. The APL was basically a floating barracks configured to function as an assault support vessel. She was home not only to a resident helicopter gunship from the Navy Sea Wolf squadron but also to a variety of river patrol craft.

By this time, the old CH34s had been stood down, and the Naval Air Facility Cam Ranh Bay Detachment Tan Son Nhut now had a CH46 Sea Knight. It had already been christened *Ha Tien Hattie.*

The seaport of Ha Tien, adjacent to the Cambodian border, was the farthest point this aircraft flew to. Somebody had thought the name a good one and stenciled it in black over the Marine green fuselage.

The big Boeing Vertol twin-rotor helicopter could carry much bigger loads, and much faster than previously. The aircraft were new to the Navy detachments, but they were not new by any means. "Checking the bulkheads and seats in the old CH46s to make sure you didn't get lined up with a known active hydraulic leak…that was normal," Whidden recalls.

On this occasion, an agent who had a case to work near Tan Son Nhut Air Base dropped me off at the Navy depot. There, seated around a Navy grey SEA hut were twelve sailors dressed in green utilities. Each was trying to kill time in his own way until the flight was called.

Some read tattered paperbacks or recent copies of the Stars and Stripes newspaper. Others who had found a post or wall to lean against were trying to doze. One or two smoked while staring off into the distance.

I reported in and signed the manifest in the office…stood on the scale, and then wandered out to check on progress with our bird.

[351]

Ha Tien Hattie's crew chief was closing the inspection ports on the rear rotor. As he did so, the pilots walked out past me and began their preflight check.

Roughly ten minutes later, we were called over to board the helicopter. Passengers perched in the sling seats anchored along the fuselage, with most of the men cradling their issue rifles between their knees. Turbines whined, and the big overhead rotors picked up speed. We began taxiing, finally lifting off and rapidly gaining altitude over the perimeter fence of the air base. Below us, scores of Vietnamese cyclists and pedestrians scurried like ants. Saigon quickly fell away, and we soared over the rice paddies on a southbound course.

The APL, which was my destination, was our first stop. Our pilots approached the small landing pad on the vessel with caution even though they were accustomed to landing on underway ships. Standing prepared behind the man guiding us in on the tiny ship platform was a fireman dressed in a reflective fire suit that covered him completely.

As we hovered and began our landing, I could see the image reflected in his face protection panel. We exited from the rear ramp and moved quickly off the landing zone and down the ladder way. As I surveyed the barges boats and men who were all a part of this combat platform, the helo pulled pitch and clattered back off over the broad muddy expanse of the Mekong to its next destination.

Permanently moored alongside us were large flat barges. These served as mooring points for PBR vessels and as a location for the recreation area, a plywood SEA hut christened the Last Chance Saloon. Air-conditioned and inviting, it dispensed cold beer to the men who walked "ashore" down the ship gangway.

The Navy had found the means to allow the men a few beers in off-duty time without violating its longtime policy of dry ships. As I watched, two sailors walked out the door to the barge edge to relieve themselves. The ship's master at arms had joined me at the elevated railing. "Biggest urinal in the entire United States Navy," he commented. And who could argue with that?

[352]

Navy CH-46 *Ha Tien Hattie* makes her approach over the Last Chance Saloon

The investigation was routine. After briefing the executive officer and obtaining the command-authorized permission to search, I examined the suspect postal clerk's locker and his personal effects. Jewelry and watches were recovered, together with documentation

[353]

that indicated that these items were the property of others.

The clerk chose not to speak to me about the allegations against him. I took photographs, and bundled up the evidence. With most of the preliminary paperwork completed, I went topside. It was late afternoon, and the sun was beginning to dip low over the flat delta countryside. From upriver, two Cambodian patrol boats were approaching us.

I had not seen the Chinese-built boats this close before, so I watched with curiosity as they throttled back and approached berthing positions alongside. From my vantage point, I could see the Cambodian flag with its distinctive stencil of the temples of Angkor fluttering from the mast.

How quickly things had changed I reflected. Not that long ago, this same boat might well have fired on us. But all that had changed when the allies crossed into Cambodia and cleaned out the North Vietnamese that were there.

Testing the 50's

A nearby pair of gunner's mates test firing .50-caliber machine guns into the river below them shattered my reverie. Satisfied that their repairs had rendered the weapons combat ready, each shouldered

[354]

one of the fifty-pound guns and walked back toward the armory. Soon the guns would be back in place, fastened into their mounts on PBRs.

At the evening meal in the wardroom, I noticed with interest the conduct of the Vietnamese and the visiting Cambodian naval officers. They obviously did not like each other, though each group was quite capable of communicating with the other had they wished to do so.

I was aware of their cultural animosity, which had origins that stretched back to ancient times, but had never been this close to it. How long could an alliance of convenience with this sort of history be expected to last, I wondered? It did in fact prove to be only temporary.

The following day I faced the routine challenge of how best to get back to Saigon...this ship was not expecting any aircraft visits. With Vietnamization in place, air traffic movements were far fewer than in previous times. I elected to take my chances at an airstrip that was likely to be busier...Chau Doc. A Vietnamese PBR took me south and down the canal that crossed the tributaries of the Mekong. Chau Doc, a longtime border post, was situated at the confluence of the canal and the southern main Mekong tributary, the Ba Sac.

We cast off after our breakfast, joined up with another PBR, and made our way down the canal. The VNN crew was friendly enough, but our language barriers made real communication difficult. They were not in any hurry, and I relished the opportunity to watch the river-dwellers whose stilted structures and picturesque boats lined the banks and tributaries.

There were friendly calls and waves for the young sailors. Had the crew not been manning machine guns, I might easily have imagined myself in an idyllic setting. I tried to imagine how it must have been when the French who had plied the waters back at the turn of the century. Chau Doc, with its crumbling French architecture and towering banyan trees, seemed to have avoided the war. I admired the minarets of the mosque as we passed.

[355]

There were no Americans anywhere to be seen. This place too was a step back in time. The spell was broken suddenly by the distinctive thump of a Huey landing in the distance.

Bidding the boatmen good-bye, I found my way to the helo pad and was in Binh Thuy that afternoon. I was just in time to bum a ride from there back to Saigon. The life of a traveling field agent was certainly never boring!

Marshall Whidden's recollections of agent air travel in Vietnam are memorable. "I flew to Da Nang on an Air America C46 to pick up a frozen turkey, parlayed from the Army, for Hai to prepare for Christmas dinner at the CO's villa. I then manifested the bird on the return flight as T. Turkey so as to have a seat on which to stow the old bird coming home."

Whidden recalls that Vietnam special agents were often challenged to improvise their travel arrangements. "Being dropped off in a clearing in the jungle to hopefully be retrieved later by another helo, or having a T39 stop on a darkened runway in NKP [Thailand] at 0400 because you could not get manifested on a flight the normal way [and after all having good friends in OSI does pay dividends]...that was 'normal'. Of course explaining the situation to the Air Force general who happened to be aboard the aircraft was even more challenging. I don't know why the pilot ever stopped for me."

When the Vietnam agents ushered in the 1972 New Year, all were housed together in the Army CID building in Cholon. The Army had drawn down the number of staff too, and there was talk that another move was not that far away.

In the meantime, Special Agent Ken Seal came aboard as supervising agent. He would remain in that capacity until Ed Giblin finished his tour. NISOV was downgraded in March to a resident agency under the control of the NISO Philippines...exactly as it had begun seven years previously.

In January of 1972, I inherited an informant at the Newport Dock facility. He was a young SeaBee who reported seeing increasing signs of the large-scale theft of goods from waterside by

[356]

Vietnamese Navy personnel. This was apparently with the complicity of U.S. Navy men that were assigned there. I was in contact with the informant regularly while awaiting an opportunity to catch the offenders with the goods.

In mid-March I unceremoniously finished my third year in the Republic of Vietnam and my NIS career. I flew out of Saigon on a commercial flight to the Philippines away from Vietnam and the war. Marshall Whidden would take over running the informant at Newport Docks.

I left behind me a lot of memories and people that I felt I was betraying with my departure that day. But I turned my back on it all. Certainly I was relieved when the Pan Am flight cleared the coast...I had survived. But a part of me would remain there in Vietnam. So too did some very close friends and colleagues.

*****

By the end of March 1972 Whidden's informant was confident that a large-scale theft of material was being planned at the Newport docks by Vietnamese naval officers. A Vietnamese officer had approached the informant, asking him to prepare fictitious documentation to authorize the transfer of a vast quantity of building materials from U.S. control.

These supplies would be readily salable on Saigon's black market, and the informant was promised that he would be well paid once the material had successfully cleared the heavily guarded gates of Newport.

Whidden told the SeaBee to play along with the would-be thieves, and to establish a day for the operation with them in advance that would allow for preparation of the sting. With a firm date now set, Whidden approached his counterparts at VNNSB to participate in the operation with the arrest of the Vietnamese suspects. In his seventh year of working for NIS, interpreter Lo Han Thang assisted with the day-to-day planning as the operation matured.

[357]

Whidden recalls, "On the day of the arrest we set the trap at Newport. Even though we went to a great deal of trouble to disguise our presence we must have been obvious. But I guess the bad guys were pretty slow and had no inside people because they never picked up on it."

Preparing for the arrest: Special Agent Marshall Whidden briefs the Vietnamese

Two armored cars were positioned in concealed positions outside the entrance to Newport prepared to block the convoy of trucks and their stolen material. NIS special agents dressed as guards and workers had positioned themselves at various vantage points to monitor progress as trucks were loaded. "The hardest part was hiding the Security Bloc troopers who were there in mass, mainly in jeeps and some with vehicle-mounted machine guns."

It would be a long day. Though the sting had been set up for that morning, the suspects remained inactive until well into the afternoon. Whidden had no way to contact the informant and grew increasingly concerned at his inability to control events.

He bought the VNNSB troopers drinks and candy to discourage their wandering around and potentially compromising the operation.

When the Vietnamese Navy officer conspirators did arrive, things moved quickly. Ten two-and-a-half-ton trucks were soon loaded with everything from cement to toilets. They formed up and drove to the gate as a convoy, expecting to be waved through as one. When they arrived at the gate however, Whidden gave the signal.

The bills

The gate was blocked and the trucks were surrounded by edgy and heavily armed Vietnamese. Whidden: "Thank God no one fired a shot because had they opened up they would have killed all the drivers and loaders who most likely were innocent of knowingly doing wrong."

A large wad of notes was seized from the suspects, and the several hundred thousand dollars worth of U.S. property was returned. The U.S. naval command was pleased not only because a theft was thwarted and a strong message sent, but also because NISOV had run another successful operation with the help of their Vietnamese Navy counterparts.

Whidden recalls the aftermath: "We put the source up in a hotel in Saigon for the next couple of nights for his own safety, paid for meals and entertainment as a reward, and then he was shipped out to preclude any retribution." The Commander of the U.S. Naval Forces in Vietnam, Rear Admiral Robert S. Salzer, would commend the informant in a letter for his official personnel file.

[359]

John Morgan left soon after this incident to take a post in the Philippines. Marshall Whidden and Ted Hicks stayed on longer, enduring yet another office move. This time it was to spaces in the central Saigon compound of the commander of U.S. Naval Forces, Vietnam.

Their workload shrank as more and more naval personnel departed. Those who remained were most often career sailors who were disinclined to stray from the established rules. Counterintelligence matters remained a low priority for the agents. Two new agents, Bob Bagshaw and Ham Maedor, were later assigned to work the Saigon office but were short-toured after a matter of months.

Whidden and Hicks were transferred to Subic Bay in the Philippines. Certainly now one of the busiest offices in the NIS network, their area of responsibility included a nearly dormant Vietnam, where only the offices of the Military Sealift Command continued to operate. Thailand was also included, and was where Marine aviation units had deployed from Vietnam. In Subic they worked for Special Agent Don Webb (of Saigon fame). They would find themselves returning to Saigon periodically to run their investigative leads.

Marshal Whidden: "After we totally withdrew from Vietnam, we probably made trips back in country, from the Philippines, every two months or so. I don't think anyone other than Ted Hicks, John Odom, and I made those trips, except for the final one. Sometimes the agent would stay two weeks in Vietnam, sometimes a month or longer. No one else wanted to go. In conjunction, we would normally make a swing through Bangkok and run to ground those leads that had built up in the interim. It usually required a good bit of travel throughout the country."

"We also started covering, on a monthly basis, the Marine Base at 'the Rose Garden,' Nam Phong, Thailand. For about a year we would fly in by C130 and one, sometimes two agents would stay for a thirty-day period. That was another experience unto itself. Live in a SEA hut, shit in a ditch, and roam the countryside. What an idyllic life. That's when John Odom and I started somewhat seriously considering the option of leaving government service to become chicken ranchers in the Northern High Country of Thailand."

In February of 1973, the U.S. Army assumed responsibility for military message communication from Vietnam. This created some challenges for agents used to the naval communication station, from which even sensitive reports could be quickly dispatched with no questions. The Army wanted to know what was in the reports, and this could lead to awkward questions about from where some of the reported information had originated.

That same month Marshall Whidden was dispatched from NISRA Subic Bay to become "agent afloat" aboard the USS *Oriskany*. "I was aboard in the gulf when Peace with Honor, (president Nixon's much vaunted peace plan with North Vietnam) was announced. Two battle groups steamed all night to form up together to parade in celebration. It may have been a sad-even dishonorable-time in American history, but it was a glorious spectacle on that morning.

I don't recall how many ships were present but there were four carriers. Much to my wife's chagrin I left her pregnant and alone living on the banks of the shit river in Olongapo City…her first excursion out of the US of A, to accomplish this mission. Many more would follow."

Of course, North Vietnam never intended to honor the peace agreement and aggressively continued its prosecution of the war against the South. With no longer any direct U.S. military assistance, it was just a matter of time before the final capitulation of Saigon in 1975.

In March of 1973 Special Agent John Odom, a counterintelligence specialist assigned to Subic Bay, made his first trip into Vietnam accompanied by Marshal Whidden. Odom was ordered to determine what potential threats of terrorism existed in the Saigon and Mekong Delta areas. There was particular interest in initiatives that might be directed against the ongoing "Supply Cambodia out of Thailand" program.

This supply initiative was designed to prop up the fragile pro-Western government of Lon Nol, who was at the time, engaged in a bitter fight for Cambodia against the communist Khmer Rouge. The plan itself was relatively simple. Supplies were first shipped from the United States to Thailand. Here they were restaged onto barges and taken by tugboat across the Gulf of Thailand to the port of Vung Tau. A tributary of the Mekong was accessed from there.

Odom reactivated Lo Han Thang, who was working for the Army in Saigon, to help him source information about threats to shipping. True to form, Thang unearthed reports that the enemy had advanced a plan to attack the large fuel depot on the Saigon River at Nha Be.

A longtime target of the communists, the port was now only lightly defended after the U.S. Navy withdrawal and was apparently quite vulnerable. The plan had the Viet Cong attacking the depot and either scuttling or sinking a ship across the waterway…isolating the Port of Saigon.

Though the attack did not come when predicted, it did occur successfully at a later date and caused considerable disruption to South Vietnam's military fuel supply.

Odom continued his long-standing relationship with the Vietnamese Navy Security Service (VNNSS), which was still under the command of Captain Thanh.

Often working alone, Odom sensed that the security situation in Saigon had changed. Initially he used the Embassy Hotel as a base, but nighttime activity in the hallways and on the street outside soon convinced him that little stood between him and a determined attacker. He moved to the Grey House, an Air America establishment near Tan Son Nhut Airport. The house was located within a secure compound guarded by Nung mercenaries, and it had a fine bar and restaurant and a safe place to park a vehicle. The Navy's Military Sealift Command (MSC) offices in central Saigon provided him an office.

The sense of uncertainty about the future of South Vietnam was becoming more pervasive. During this time, an unattended warehouse opposite the MSC offices in Saigon was found to contain boxes of unsecured classified messages. An investigation into the origins of the boxes was launched immediately. It seemed

[362]

quite possible that at best, unauthorized persons had access to sensitive classified material. The worst case scenario was that the enemy had been reading the Navy's mail for a considerable period of time.

Odom began his inquiries and determined that a U.S. civilian office employee had neglected to destroy the classified documents. They had been accumulating in the safes over a prolonged period of time. The documents had been put into boxes and stored in the rented warehouse space, where they remained for many months. Fortunately, when the boxes were opened, they were found to contain almost nothing but ship movement reports. These were classified as "confidential" and were really of no value at all once the vessel had moved on.

What first brought John Odom to Vietnam later became a reality when one of the tugs used to push transport barges to Cambodia was sunk by what was reported to be Viet Cong swimmer-sappers. At the scene, Odom learned that the ARVN colonel in charge of port security regarded the sinking with some suspicion. Looking into the matter further, his investigation pointed toward a conspiracy by the Korean tug owners to collect compensation from the U.S. government.

Perhaps realizing the lucrative barge transport program would not last much longer, the Koreans sank the boat at its moorings. As the investigation proceeded, the owner of the vessel, a Madam Wu, contacted Odom unexpectedly at the Embassy Hotel. The agent had seen her at the Vung Tau Wharf without knowing who she was. Madam Wu wasted no time informing the agent that she needed his cooperation, and asked what kind of compensation would be required for him to leave the case alone...Odom declined her bribe.

The Koreans turned up the heat, calling a meeting of officials at the Korean embassy. Odom attended the meeting after advising U.S. embassy staff, and was subjected to a range of questions aimed at undermining his investigative conclusions. In the end, the agent returned to Vung Tau where he borrowed diving equipment, and inspected the sunken hull personally.

His inspection clearly indicated that the blast that damaged the tug

[363]

had originated within, not from the outside as had been reported. After Odom reported his findings, the Korean claim for compensation was dismissed. More intriguing in Odom's counterintelligence assignment was a chance contact in Vung Tau with a Vietnamese woman who was consorting with a colonel in the Czech Army. In the 1970s, Czechoslovakia was firmly cemented into the Soviet-dominated Eastern Bloc. Any opportunity to gain information about a military officer was always keenly sought after.

Odom learned that the man had been assigned to the International Control Commission, the body originally charged with overseeing provisions of the 1954 treaty between North and South Vietnam. The colonel had traveled extensively, presumably also into North Vietnam.

His Vietnamese lover was more than happy to share her secrets about his family, career, and personal habits. Conversations that they had inevitably returned to the theme of the love they had for each other and the colonel's unhappiness in his Czechoslovakian home.

There seemed to be an opportunity here that was now outside the purview of NIS. The CIA became the grateful recipients of Odom's reports.

*****

17   THE FALL

In April of 1975, the fall of Saigon appeared imminent and a final decision had to be made about the last remaining NIS office in Vietnam.

Subic Bay Senior Resident Agent Don Webb decided to close the small office that was maintained for visiting agents at the Defense Attaché Office (DAO) compound at Tan Son Nhut Air Base. Electing not to send either of the somewhat uncontrollable former Vietnam agents, he decided to dispatch Special Agent Gary West, a young man who he knew would carry out instructions without question.

West was directed to make his own judgment call as to what would be brought back out and what would be left there for destruction. West decided to leave everything where it was. Counterintelligence manuals, crime scene kits, all of the assorted detritus of years of agent activity in Saigon would be destroyed. He came back out and left the office in the hands of Army demolition experts. They began wiring their charges of thermal and white phosphorous grenades, preparing the safes and their documents for destruction.

Whidden and Hicks, back in Subic, were increasingly restive as events began to overtake their vaguely laid plans to travel to Saigon to rescue former NISOV employees... in particular Lo Han Thang. Whidden broached the subject with SRA Webb, who refused permission on the grounds that the situation in Saigon was unstable and far too dangerous. Their plan had been left for too long and groups of angry ARVN soldiers were reported to be interfering with ongoing evacuation plans.

Whidden was able to get through to U.S. Army personnel in Saigon and asked them to look after Thang and his family; it was the best he could do. Two trusted allies, Maj. Andy Gambara, U.S. Army Military Intelligence, and SAC Josh Billings, US. Army CID, agreed to help in whatever way they could.

Thang was working at the time in the DAO compound at Tan Son Nhut. In the days before Whidden's call for help, some Vietnamese had been evacuated from the nearby Bien Hoa Air Base. But with the NVA armor drawing nearer, Bien Hoa was no longer a safe option. The enemy was in Saigon within days.

Back in the Philippines, with unreliable communication to Saigon, Whidden worried about whether Lo Han Thang and his family had been safely evacuated. He drove to the massive U.S. Air Force facility at Clark Air Base and enlisted the assistance of OSI agents to help him locate the family among the many refugees being sheltered there after their harrowing flights from South Vietnam. Thang's name did not appear on any flight manifests; nor could he be found among the evacuees.

[365]

Whidden noted with considerable disgust that many of the early evacuees were not direct-hire Vietnamese employees of the U.S. government. Many seemed to be politicians and streetwise "cowboys" off the boulevards of Saigon. Crestfallen, the agent returned to Subic Bay and passed the word to the other concerned agents that Lo Han Thang, his wife, and his daughter were likely casualties.

Several days passed before Whidden returned once again to Clark. He was disappointed to find no trace of the family. SRA Don Webb was becoming unhappy about the amount of time the agent was devoting to the search.

On his third trip to Clark, Whidden strode once again into the OSI offices…sitting in the waiting area was Thang. "Where the hell have you been?" were Thang's first words to him. Always the professional, Thang and his family had traveled under an assumed alias, never knowing for certain whether his past "in the shadows" might be known to the Viet Cong.

Everyone knew that the Subic Bay naval facilities would bear the brunt from seaborne evacuations after the fall of the South. Thang's first job would be to assist in the screening of the hundreds of Vietnamese evacuees, many of whom would not have even the most basic identification.

But instead after researching the Vietnamese repatriation process, the agents decided that it would not be in Thang's best interest to remove him and his family from the bureaucratic pipeline that would provide them with a new life in the United States. A cash collection was taken up for them in anticipation of their next leg on the way to America: Guam. Ted Hicks's sister and her husband agreed to sponsor the Lo family in Southern California.

Whidden: "We individually, and as an organization, owe a great deal of gratitude to Maj. Andy Gambara , U.S. Army MI, and to SAC Josh Billings, U.S. Army CID."

"These two men were both American patriots in the truest sense. We would have been unable to do as well as we did in-country after the pull out, without their assistance. After it was all said and done,

[366]

a lot of folks owed them a debt of gratitude."

Harrowing stories were surfacing from the final hours of Saigon. Defenders of the Defense Attaché Office compound spoke of having to shoot their way through the streets of Saigon, while defending the busloads of evacuees on the way to their aircraft. So too came the account from a witness to the final moments of the NIS office at the compound. He said the building had literally melted from the heat of the thermal grenades set to destroy the classified material and property.

When it came, the fall of Saigon precipitated a massive evacuation of Vietnamese aboard anything that would float. The U.S. fleet at their station off the coast rescued many of these brave souls. Others elected to strike out directly for the Philippines and the U.S. Navy base at Subic Bay. The CIA had evacuated its important Can Tho facility earlier by vessel, dispatching their personnel down a tributary of the Mekong, into open waters and on to Subic.

As the deluge of refugees began to reach Philippine waters, their vessels were each boarded by junior officers of the U.S. Navy. The Stars and Stripes was then raised to facilitate their entry into the U.S. base, as required under Philippine law. All weapons were ordered surrendered and were either cast over the side or impounded for later destruction.

The NIS agents were charged with screening all evacuees upon entry, to ensure their status as legitimate refugees. Grande Island, which was a recreation area for the naval base, had a facility quickly erected that was then manned by a Marine security force. NIS agents used PBRs to intercept the incoming vessels before they reached port, and what they found was often distressing. The people had been without food or water while in their leaky, overloaded, and decidedly unseaworthy boats.

Marshall Whidden would recount, "The welcome we got when we boarded those boats was just unbelievable. The bravery and dignity the Vietnamese people presented was incredible. They were scared...they were terrified really, but they weren't rabble."

One of Whidden's fondest recollections of the flotilla arrival at

Subic was passing a heavily laden South Vietnamese Navy water carrier in a PBR. Hearing a plaintive cry of "Marsho!" he quickly turned to see the waving figure of VNN Commander Khoa, a longtime NIS ally of the VNNSS.

Their happy reunion was marred by the news that Khoa's commanding officer, Captain Nguyen Van Tan, had stayed behind to gather his family and had not made it out in time. Tan was reported to have been heard the evening Saigon fell on a South Vietnamese radio, calling for Navy men to return to port with their vessels. The broadcast had obviously been made under duress.

Included in the seaborne mass of humanity were general officers of the South Vietnamese military forces, the mayor of Saigon and well-known movie stars. Many carried what remained of their wealth as small gold bars or gold leaf. All assets were receipted and locked in a CONEX shipping box that was under the control of armed Marine guards.

Accompanying the CIA contingent came scores of large bags, packed with U.S. currency...the agency's black money for their operations in the Mekong Delta. This too was put under guard.

The agency sent in their own teams of case officers to assist with the screening. Agents that were proficient in the languages of Vietnamese and Khmer arrived from stations around the globe. CIA interrogator/translator teams came from Okinawa and set about identifying their own people and those of the Vietnamese Military Security Service. Agents were very careful to scrutinize all of the internees. Clothing and their manner of dress, as well as reactions amongst fellow evacuees were all carefully observed and noted. All were interrogated at least once and some were also polygraphed.

Throughout it all, a frustrated press corps tried unsuccessfully to get to Grande Island and to its temporary inhabitants. The Navy and Marine Corps successfully kept them all at bay, going so far as to seize and destroy film taken in the restricted area. Many in the military felt very strongly that the press had done the armed forces and our country a great disservice in Vietnam...the restrictions put on the media were enforced enthusiastically.

The screening lasted for weeks, and this should have been the swan song for the former Vietnam agents.

But for John Odom, there would be one final episode when Khmer Rouge soldiers seized the USS *Mayaguez* and took it to an island near the Cambodian mainland. After refusing to return the vessel, the communist forces were attacked by both U.S. Marine infantry and airpower.

Marine counterintelligence teams on the island later seized everything of intelligence value that they could find. The carefully searched the Khmer Rouge casualties and scoured their camp, and facilities. There they found diaries, photographs, official papers, and even some French brandy. Odom and a team of specialists would carefully scrutinize it all before forwarding the parcels on for formal evaluation.

With that, the war was truly over.

*****

From the perspective of personal experience, Supervising Agent Dick McKenna's letter to his agents at the end of his tour says what most of us felt...

"Good-byes are sometimes hard to express, and my attempts on my final parting proved to be a complete failure as far as you so and so's are concerned. But I must say to you all what is in my heart. Working with you for the past year was an honor and a finer group of men exists nowhere. You are individually and collectively that factor that adds up to a unique, once in a lifetime experience. It is rare that one has the opportunity in life to share the frustrations, the tensions, the joys, the laughter of a group so molded by common goals and interests-and I feel privileged to have been part of that group. You made my tour, and I shall remember each one of you."

Vietnam veteran agents present the NISO Vietnam flag to NIS Director Captain Barney Martin, USN, at Subic Bay From left, Special Agent Ted Hicks, Captain Martin, Special Agent Marshall Whidden, Special Agent Don Web and Special Agent Michael B. Jones

*****

Through the entire story of Naval Intelligence involvement in Vietnam, from 1965 to 1975, only one man played a continuous role throughout and that was Lo Han Thang. Officers, agents, and enlisted men rotated through Vietnam every twelve months. Thang remained, always providing continuity, a man who consistently could be counted on. A man that was tried, trusted, and true.

Thang was a man tempered in the crucible of contemporary Vietnamese politics. Born in the North, he had begun his education when France was defeated at Dien Bien Phu. When the Geneva Treaty of 1954 was signed dividing the country into communist-North and pro-Western South, the Lo family knew there would be no future for them under Ho Chi Minh's pro-Moscow regime.

They made ready to take what few belongings they could carry with them and found their way to the port of Haiphong. The U.S. Navy was ferrying those who wished to leave from here, down the coast to Saigon in the Republic of Vietnam.

How strange that Lt. Bob Kain, introduced already as Naval Intelligence's first agent in Vietnam, was then an officer aboard one of the LSTs assigned to this duty. Perhaps Kain's own ship removed the Lo family to their new home in the South; we'll never know for certain. Many years have now passed since the young Vietnamese boy passed through the cavernous jaws of the ship that carried his family to a new home, and that ship's name has faded with time.

A bright student, Thang mastered English and found employment with the interpreter pool of the American embassy in Saigon. The Office of Naval Intelligence discovered him and then recruited him to become a full-time interpreter and functionary for them.

He was bright, diplomatic, and well connected with various Vietnamese government agencies. Agents liked and trusted him, and soon Thang was actively involved in counterintelligence operations with ONI special agents.

As the office grew along with its' mission and a NISO was established, Thang was assisted by other Vietnamese who exhibited language skills. But his primacy was never in doubt, nor was his loyalty to the agency and its personnel. A skilled interviewer,

[371]

Thang had the ability to talk with Vietnamese and learn facts without suggesting any particular outcome. This was a strength few other interpreters had.

His Navy employment ended in 1973 when NIS ceased a full-time presence in Vietnam. The Army was glad to share his services, but he continued to assist the Naval Intelligence agents until the very end, in 1975.

That Thang was successfully evacuated with his wife and young daughter only hours before Saigon fell reflects very little on the people who employed him for all those years. His escape was much more a function of his own toughness, determination, and professionalism.

I believe, as I know most of my fellow agents who shared the dangers of the Vietnam War with Lo Han Thang do, that we could have done a far better job of looking after our trusted friend and ally. His story certainly is not a unique one in this regard.

*****

Epilogue 18

The last of the NIS special agents with Vietnam experience had reached mandatory retirement age by the new millennium. Several rose to senior rank in the organization, leaving lasting marks of a leadership style that was forged in the crucible of war. Most, now in their sixties, enjoy retirement, though several have gone on to excel in private enterprise.

Lo Han Thang

Lo Han Thang is settled in Southern California. The infant daughter he and wife Phuong carried out of Saigon in the final hours of freedom is an honors graduate of the University of Southern California.The family has not returned to Saigon, even for a short vacation.

[373]

They are another truly American success story, as are many Vietnamese who were forced to flee their country.

Of the Vietnamese officers and families of VNNSS who successfully escaped Saigon when it fell in April 1975, several families were sponsored and accommodated by the U.S. Navy officers with whom they had previously served. The Brooks and Schneider families-among others-assimilated and patiently restarted the lives of their traumatized former allies. In the time since the end of the war, the sponsors have witnessed a remarkable litany of educational and professional successes among the children of those families, now all proud Americans.

In 1999 retired YNC Jon Springer, still believing his Vietnamese wife Cang and their two children had been lost in the war, was stunned to learn that they had made good their escape from Saigon immediately before the fall in 1975. Cang's sister had married an American civilian who arranged for the trio to leave Vietnam as a part of his family. After stints in various refugee facilities, they settled temporarily in California before establishing themselves permanently in Las Vegas, Nevada. One of the daughters, who had never believed her mother's story that her father had been killed during the Tet Offensive, had determinedly used the Internet to find her natural father. Not only was Jon Springer reunited with his family, but he also found that he was a grandfather four times over. This may be the only happy ending to come out of the Tet Offensive of 1968.

As he rushed to gather together his large family of eight children for evacuation, VNNSS commanding officer Capt. Nguyen Van Tan ran out of time. He was captured soon after North Vietnamese troops overran Saigon and was hurried off to North Vietnam for interrogation. Incarcerated in a series of brutally primitive jungle camps in the mountainous provinces of Vinh Phu, Thanh Phong, and Nam Ninh, he was subjected to isolation and torture, and years of hard-labor. A small man already, Tan lost sixty pounds while in captivity. For more than sixteen years the North Vietnamese worked to extract secrets from their captive.

Throughout his prolonged captivity, Tan's ailing wife worked for his release with the assistance of concerned former U.S. Navy colleagues. V.Adm. Rex Rectanus rallied to assist Tan, and in June 1991 he was finally released and repatriated with his wife and their four children in the United States. Sadly, his wife died just shortly after their reunion.

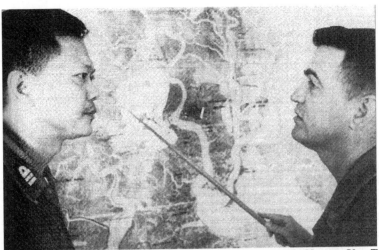

In better days: long-time captive of the communists Captain Nguyen Van Tan, VN. Here he receives a briefing from an American advisor about conditions in the Rung Sat Special Zone

Now remarried, Tan has settled happily in southern California as has his brother, who survived more than fourteen years in various North Vietnamese prisons himself. The four children repatriated with Tan are grown and settled. Three others remain in Saigon, and one now lives in Australia. A grandson is a serving U.S. Navy officer.

My return trip to Vietnam in the late 1990s was in many ways a step back in time for me. There are changes of course; zealous revolutionaries have renamed streets, and new high-rise buildings line the horizons in both Saigon and Hanoi. In many respects though, the trip to Saigon was an experience in *déjà vui.*

The old French colonial architecture has survived the years, though in most cases it is now showing its age.

But modern Vietnam is still a very young country. At the time of my trip, more than half of the population of 65 million was less than twenty-five years old. Most do not remember the war. They operate "in the moment" and are looking determinedly at the future.

I have no doubt that they will continue to accelerate toward a true market economy and away from state control.

As their war-era revolutionaries retire and die, many more positive changes can be expected from them. The Vietnamese remain as resourceful and courageous as ever, and are committed to catching up with Asian neighbors. There is little doubt in my mind that they will succeed in doing so!

In Cholon, the NISOV office has been demolished to make way for a service station. The HSAS compound that once housed the PX is sealed shut and appears to have been for some time. On the opposite corner, Fuji's Restaurant has been totally razed with no traces remaining. Even the bamboo grove and gardens, which once were a pleasant escape from the bustling streets outside the walls are now gone.

In the late 1990's much of the city center remained as it was in the sixties. The Continental Palace, Caravelle, Rex, and Majestic hotels had all seen facelifts. The town hall had also been restored, but interestingly, all of the park statuary had been changed. The hordes of motorcycles still remain, and in the evening hundreds of young people and children turn out to walk amongst the parks and fountains.

Thieu's monument of ostentation, the Presidential Palace, has been preserved as a national museum, as has the tank that symbolically breached its gates on the evening that Saigon fell in 1975. Young female guides suitably indoctrinated into Vietnam's modern socialist ideal, escort the visitors. The grand halls, lovely art work, and rooftop helicopter pad complete with a parked Huey, have been carefully maintained as examples of capitalist excess. A basement war room, resplendent with wall maps showing the progress of the war, is also a popular attraction.

The American embassy, once the hub of Saigon, simply looked old and tired. Its concrete starkness streaked with dark mold. The new government does not encourage visits to it.

[376]

Da Nang, reflecting its perennial status as a commercial seaport, has been largely rebuilt. The White Elephant is gone, as is the 20 Duy Tan Street residence where Naval Intelligence was first established. The billet at 23 Doc Lap has curiously survived change, with its rooms now converted into tiny apartments.

I found a widow and her young daughter living in the first floor room Carl Sundstrom and I shared in 1969. She received me graciously into her tiny home, which had changed very little over the years. Nearby, General Lam's villa housed a bank. Its well-manicured neocolonial facade had seldom looked better. Opposite 23 Doc Lap, the old French villa that took the fatal rocket strike that night in 1969 served as the offices of an oil company.

With assistance from sympathetic communist nations, the national highway over Hai Van Pass north of Da Nang had been widened and improved. Were it not for the presence of French, pre-French Vietnamese, and former South Vietnamese bunkers clustered around the crest of the pass, visualizing just what a hostile environment these mountains had been would not be easy. Whether the victim of allied defoliants (as the communists claim) or desperate starving peasant woodcutters, the forests that graced the mountains are mostly gone. What remained were magnificent and unforgettable views: Looking to the south, the village of Nam O, Red Beach, and Da Nang's grand harbor, and to the north, the idyllic lagoon and sand isthmus upon which was built one of the Orient's most picturesque villages…Lang Co.

During the war southbound convoys would assemble and join the gun trucks and armor at Lang Co for the perilous trip over the pass. The assembly point today is a roadside market at which the occasional European backpacker can be seen bargaining for marble trinkets or cold drinks.

Hue is less than an hour farther north. The airport at Phu Bai and the French military buildings which once sheltered the most important Marine enclave north of Da Nang, are now largely abandoned. The airport receives daily flights from the domestic airline; otherwise it is as quiet as the sand dunes around it. Another ten minutes further north through the rice paddies, the outskirts of Hue appears. Little seems to have changed…perhaps

[377]

with the exception of the absence of concertina wire, sandbags, and sentries. The Catholic cathedral, a glorious monument to the best of Gothic-French Oriental architecture, arises in the west with its spires reaching up above the groves of palms and bamboo.

Soon, I found myself on the banks of the Perfume River...precisely where I had stood in awe on my first visit to the Imperial City in mid 1969. On the river were sampans, Vietnam's own unique brand of bustling pedicabs-cyclos, and of course pedestrians. Beyond was the towering flagstaff, but this time resplendent in the colors of the communist Democratic Republic of Vietnam. There could be no surer reminder of the war's outcome.

The south bank of the Perfume River where I was standing was the epicenter of some of the most savage house-to-house combat of the war. To my delight, few indicators remained of those desperate times when U.S. Marines blasted their way through the university buildings, provincial headquarters, a prison, and even the hospital as they removed very determined VC and North Vietnamese regulars. The tamarind trees had fully recovered, spreading a leafy canopy over the waterfront boulevard. Villas constructed in the art deco style of French Indochina were worn and moldy, but lacking nothing for character. I felt a little like I'd come home, after my many years away.

An old French hotel near the railway station served as my home for the more than a week of exploration. This time it was possible to visit the outlying legacy of the Nguyen dynasty...the imperial tombs. During the war, visiting the rural surrounds of Hue was a very dangerous enterprise, and I had left Vietnam disappointed that I'd never made it. The Perfume River's many sampans provided a peaceful and placid journey upstream to the burial sites. Each location had been carefully chosen by its intended occupant, and all were an individual expression in symmetry, carefully considered landscaping, and artistic taste.

The more than two decades of war left their mark, but the pockmarks of small-arms fire hardly detract from the simple beauty and aura of peace found at the imperial tombs. This was a side of Vietnam I'd never seen, and I found myself reflecting with envy on what the life of a Hue-based French colonial must have been like.

[378]

Venturing into the cloud-shrouded mountain ranges only a short distance to the west of the Imperial City, is like journeying into a different world. The narrow track first built by the French and then improved by the Americans to ease the resupply of the important firebases protecting the city, is in disrepair. But it is passable, and the striking mountain country that the road winds through is stunning.

Firebase Bastogne, the home of the 101st Airborne, is now only a grass covered hill. The ville that developed during the war as a venue for trade with American service personnel still surrounds the site of the former base.

As the plains and paddy fields fade, Bru villages built on the steep hillsides begin to appear. The Montagnard people, the aboriginals of Indochina, performed sterling service as irregular soldiers under the leadership of the U.S. Special Forces.

They now pay the price for their well earned reputation as killers of Vietnamese. They have been forcibly moved by the government, and survive as subsistence farmers practicing slash-and-burn agriculture. A benefit of land clearing, albeit an extremely hazardous one, is the scrap metal and unexploded ordnance that is found. Bru households proudly display cluster bombshells, unexploded mortar rounds, and piles or artillery shrapnel.

The mention of the Ashau Valley, strikes a quiet chord of terror in those servicemen who operated against this harboring spot for the NVA. It is nestled in the Annamite Cordelera adjacent to the Laotian border. It was from here that the Northerners came via the tributaries of the Ho Chi Minh Trail.

Until 1966, a U.S. Special Forces camp supported on-going reconnaissance of the trail. Then the NVA decided upon a strategy of attrition against the vulnerable and difficult to supply border camps. Operating during the monsoons when clouds cover the ranges and limit air observation, the communists moved anti-aircraft batteries onto the low hills and mountains that encircle the camp and its airstrip. Once in place, they began systematic heavy artillery attacks soon followed by the infantry. The U.S. soldiers and their Montagnard irregulars were significantly outnumbered,

[379]

and they were eventually driven out. Withdrawing overland, they were ultimately plucked from the jungle by Marine aviators based at Phu Bai.

Ashau has become a small school and collection of grass huts for the Bru students. All are within a short distance of shattered bunkers and unexploded bombs. Because of the danger, visitors are not encouraged to visit Ashau, but determined ones still get through.

The Cubans helped their communist allies extend and pave a former branch of the Ho Chi Minh Trail northward from Ashau clear through to Route 9, connecting the coast with Khe Sanh. The new road snakes its way under mountaintops, which once bore names like "Firebase Bradley" and "Tun Tavern."

Khe Sanh has become coffee and pepper plantations. Plants now cover much of the former Marine base where the media tried to equate the siege to the 1954 French defeat at Dien Bien Phu. The once scarred hills are once again verdant. But Khe Sanh base -- though now gone -- still retains its aura.

Piles of unexploded ordnance are uncovered regularly, sometimes at considerable physical cost to the collectors. A thriving trade in excavated military memorabilia flourishes, with buttons, badges of rank, boot soles, and scraps of webbing.

In the midst of the DMZ stands a low hill known as Con Thien, or "Hill of the Angels" to the Vietnamese. Marines heavily fortified this geographic reference point after their first battles with the NVA intending to block enemy attack routes into the zone and to points beyond. As a firebase, it took hundreds of rounds of heavy artillery fire from North Vietnamese guns to the north. Its muddy trenches, interlocking water-filled shell holes, rats, and incessant stench compared in many respects to the conditions of trench warfare in World War I.

Driving through pine plantations, I finally found the bloody hill where so many lost their lives. It was covered by thriving banana plantations.

A visitor to Vietnam who was familiar with the country during the war will ponder what difference America's brave attempt to rescue South Vietnam made. As I stared out over the rice paddies in the former demilitarized zone, I had to admit that despite a preponderance of altruism, we had mattered very little.

My American compatriots are now dying at an alarming rate, as are their one-time Vietnamese enemies. The leaders and educators have reared the youth of Vietnam on a diet of one-sided war stories, and this too will fade into the realm of ancient history. Time marches on, and in this instance, that is not a bad thing.

Returning again to Hue, afternoon rains provided a backdrop that helped connect my memories of the war and more contemporary images of this visit. During the war, the rain often granted me a visual and aural escape from the cacophony.

Low clouds would sweep in with the atmosphere heavy in anticipation of the following deluge. Large raindrops would fall on palm leaves, creating a patter and then a steady drumming that blocked out all. At these times when the air was damp and once again fresh, the leaves and flowers took on a luminous sheen. They were reborn, and time stood still.

I was now very much at peace with myself and with Vietnam. It was somehow intended that I have the experience of the storm in that once troubled place, as a reminder of the greater scheme. And so it was all those years later that the rains brought me back to the temporary tranquility of an earlier time.

Very little had really changed with the Perfume River and her
people in the years that had passed. Vietnam's history has somehow
always been a story of stoic endurance. The part I played there was
just a grain in the sands of time.

*****

GLOSSARY OF TERMS

AO: Area of operations.

ao dai: Traditional Vietnamese lady's dress.

APL: A floating barracks ship.

ARVN: Army of the Republic of Vietnam, the South Vietnamese Army.

ASA: Army Security Agency, a highly classified command charged with signal security and electronic intelligence acquisition.

BEQ: Bachelor enlisted quarters.

BIs: Background investigations.

boonies: From *boondocks;* out in the wilds; the bush.

BOQ: Bachelor officer's quarters.

C47: Douglas DC3, a twin-engine transport. Most were built during World War II.

C117: Super DC3, an upgraded version of the C47. It had larger engines and a different tail assembly.

C130: Lockheed Hercules, a four-engine turbo-prop transport aircraft in service with all service branches except the Army.

CACO: Casualty assistance coordination officer.

CAG: U.S. Marine Corps Combined Action Group. Part of the Marine Corps strategy in Vietnam to assist friendly villagers to protect their crops and assets from the Viet Cong.

CBMU Construction battalion maintenance unit, a unit designator for naval engineers (SeaBees) often assigned to maintenance duties, as opposed to construction.

[383]

CH46: Twin-rotor Boeing Vertol medium helicopter widely used by U.S. Marines and to a lesser extent, by the Navy.

chow: Food

CHP: California Highway Patrol.

CIA: U.S. Central Intelligence Agency.

CIB: Combat infantry badge, a U.S. Army decoration. Also the Combat Information Bureau.

CIC: Army Counterintelligence Corps.

CID: Criminal Investigation Division. The criminal investigation component of the U.S. Marine Corps and U.S. Army Military Police commands.

CINCPACFLT: Commander in chief, Pacific Fleet.

CO: Commanding officer.

Cobra: AH1 Bell Huey Cobra, a purpose-built helicopter gunship.

COMNAVFORV: Commander, Naval Forces, Vietnam.

COMUSMACV: Commander, U.S. Military Assistance Command, Vietnam. Originally Gen. W.C. Westmoreland who was succeeded in 1968 by his assistant, Gen. Creighton Abrams, U.S. Army.

CP: Command post.

CS: A refined form of tear gas.

DAO: Defense Attache Office.

DEA: Drug Enforcement Administration.

dinky-dau: Corrupted Vietnamese term for crazy.

DMZ: Demilitarized zone. The area along the eighteenth parallel that separated North and South Vietnam.

DNI: Director of Naval Intelligence.

DRV: Democratic Republic of Vietnam (communist North Vietnam).

EOD: Explosive ordnance disposal.

flak jacket: Body armor.

FLC: Force Logistic Command.

frag: A fragmentation hand grenade.

fragging: The act of murder by use of a fragmentation hand grenade.

grunt: A field marine.

gunny: Gunnery sergeant, a Marine Corp senior NCO, E-7.

HAL-4: Helicopter Attack Squadron 4, the Sea Wolves; Navy helicopter squadron assigned to the Mekong Delta region.

Ho Chi Minh Trail: A network of improvised roads and trails extending from North Vietnam to the south, most of it in neutral Laos and Cambodia and thus out of reach of U.S. ground troops.

hooch: A hut, often of the SEA design, used as rear-area accommodation in Vietnam. Also describes an improvised field shelter.

HSAS: Headquarters Support Activity, Saigon.

Huey: Utility helicopter. The Bell UH1 series of utility helicopters were the workhorses of the Vietnam War.

I Corps: Pronounced "Eye" Corps, the first of four corps areas adopted by Vietnamese and consequently U.S. forces. I Corps was the northernmost corps, IV Corps being the Mekong Delta Region.

ICC: International Control Commission.

IIR : Intelligence information report.

investigative lead: A logical next step or task in the investigative process, often an interview or a simple inquiry. Leads were sent to NISOV for action by other NIS offices and similarly, it was often necessary to request another office or agency to complete leads.

JAG: Judge Advocate General, the legal arm of the U.S. military organization.

JPRC: Joint Personnel Recovery Center.

LAAM: Light antiaircraft missile.

ladderway: Stairs, in naval jargon.

LCM: Landing craft, medium. A ramped landing craft capable of carrying vehicles and personnel.

LCU: Landing craft, utility.

lifer: Derisive term for a career military man.

LSB: Logistic support base.

LST: Landing ship, tank.

Lt. Cdr.: Lieutenant commander. Naval officer rank 0-4, equivalent to a major.

Lt. j.g.: Lieutenant junior grade. Naval officer grade 0-2, equivalent to a first lieutenant in other services.

LZ : Landing zone.

M1 Garand: Semiautomatic, .30-caliber rifle first issued to U.S. troops in early World War II.

M16: Issue U.S. rifle which began service in Vietnam during 1966.

MACV: Military Assistance Command, Vietnam.

MAF: Marine amphibious force.

magazine: An ammunition storage facility, especially on a warship. On a modern military firearm, a magazine carries ammunition ready to fire.

MI5: British national counterintelligence agency.

MIA: Missing in action.

MP: Military Police. Applies to both Army and U.S. Marine Corps.

MPC: Military payment certificates.

MSC: Military Sealift Command.

MSD: Vietnamese Military Security Directorate.

MSS: Vietnamese Military Security Service.

MSTS: Military Sea Transportation Service.

N-22: Counterintelligence officer of COMNAVFORV.

NAD: Naval advisory detachment.

NAF: Naval air facility.

NAS: Naval air station.

NAVFORV: Naval Forces, Vietnam.

NCO: Noncommissioned officer. The enlisted ranks E-4 to E-9.

newbie: A recent arrival to Vietnam; a new guy.

NILO: Naval Intelligence liaison officer.

NIS: Naval Investigative Service.

NISOV: Naval Investigative Service Office, Vietnam. The command headquarters for NIS, located in Cholon, Saigon.

NISRA: Naval Investigative Service Resident Agency, a NIS field office. There were two in Vietnam: Saigon and DaNang.

NISSU: Naval Investigative Service Satellite Unit, typically one-man outposts assigned to area requiring the fulltime presence of a NIS special agent. There were NISSUs at Binh Thuy, Vung Tau, Cam Ranh Bay, Chu Lai, and Quang Tri.

NLF: National Liberation Front.

NSA: Naval Support Activity.

NSG: Naval Security Group, a highly classified command charged with electronic intelligence missions.

NVA: North Vietnamese Army, the regular standing army of the DRV.

OIC: Officer in charge.

OICC: Officer in charge of construction.

OP: Observation post.

OSI: U.S. Air Force Office of Special Investigations, the Air Force counterpart to NIS.

padre: A military chaplain.

PBR: Riverine patrol boat.

PCF: Patrol craft, fast; swift boat.

PCS: Permanent change of station; a permanent transfer.

[388]

PF: Vietnamese popular forces, South Vietnamese militia.

PFC: Private first class.

POW: Prisoner of war.

PX: Post exchange. A retail outlet designed to provide military personnel with quality goods at the best prices.

refueling pod: Device fitted on aircraft to allow fuel to be taken from aerial tankers while in flight.

revetment: Typically, blast walls erected to protect equipment from damage by rocket and mortar attack.

RFPF: Vietnamese regional forces militia; ruff-puffs.

RVN: Republic of Vietnam; South Vietnam.

SEA hut: Southeast Asia hut. A temporary building design utilizing basic timber framing, plywood decking, fly screen, and roofing iron.

SeaBees: Naval mobile construction battalions.

SEAL: Elite Navy commandos.

skivvies: Underclothing, in particular, underpants.

skivvy honcho: A man possessed of winning ways with the opposite sex.

skivvy house: A brothel.

SRA: Senior resident agent. Senior agents at the Saigon and Da Nang NISRAs.

SU: Satellite unit.

TDY: Temporary duty (as opposed to permanent station change) orders.

UCMJ: Uniform Code of Military Justice.

UDT: Underwater demolition team.

VAL-4: Navy fixed-wing squadron assigned to the Mekong Delta region.

VC: Viet Cong.

VCI: Viet Cong infrastructure.

Viet Cong: Enemy guerrillas, most often local people. The main fighting force of the communist National Liberation Front.

ville: Any Vietnamese settlement or village.

VNAF: South Vietnamese Air Force.

VNN: Vietnamese Navy. Naval forces of the Republic of Vietnam.

VNNSB: Vietnamese Navy Security Bloc. In 1970 it became VNNSS.

VNNSS: Vietnamese Navy Security Service.

YNC: Yeoman chief petty officer (E-7). Senior naval NCO with clerical specialties.

XO: Executive officer. Second in command, under a commanding officer.

The First Crew, Saigon Office late 1964

Agent Mord Tucker, Special Agent Maynard Anderson, Agent Sam
Houston, Special Agent Bob Kain, LT Lee Hayden

Second Saigon Crew 1965

Mr. Q.V. Ngau, Agent Mord Tucker,YN3 Smith, Special Agent
Maynard Anderson, LT Leroy Hayden, Agent Sam Houston, YNC
Schlief, Special Agent Bob Kain, Mr. Nguyen Van Van, YN1
David Walker, Mr.Lo Han Thang.

ONI Office SAIGON 1966

<u>First Row</u>: Mr Lo Han Thang, Special Agent Tom Brannon YN1 (unknown), Mr. Q.V. Ngau, Lt. Dothard.

<u>Second Row:</u> YN2 J. Springer, Special Agent John Nester, Special Agent Milt Steffen, Special Agent Maynard Anderson, LTJG Dixon, Special Agent Paul Carr, YN1 Don Weinel.

NISOV April 1966

Front Row: Q.V. Ngau, YN2 R.G. Krause, YN1 J.M. Springer, YN2 R.D. Lancing, YN1 A. Lingway

Second Row: Special Agent F.F. Givens, Supervisory Agent K.W. Nickel, Special Agent J.A. Renwick, Special Agent D.A. McBride, Lo Han Thang

Third Row: ENS D.L. Carr, LCDR W.H.J. Manthorpe Jr., W.H. Fry

<u>Front Row:</u> Special Agent David Roberts, LCDR Lou Costa, Special Agent Carl Merritt, Special Agent George Meglemere, Special Agent Jim Leavitt.

<u>Second Row:</u> YNC Gary Hall, Special Agent Milt Steffen, YN1 John Moore, Special Agent Bob Hall, Senior Resident Agent Charlie Baldwin.

<u>Front Row</u>: Special Agent R. Gallow, N. Vinh, YNC G. Hall, LT
G.P. Wheeler, Senior Resident Agent J.A. Meyer

<u>Second Row</u>: Special Agent H.V. Dilkes, Special Agent J. Seach,
YN2 T.V. Curry, Special Agent M. Nagle

<u>Third Row</u>: Special Agent P.G. Segersten, Special Agent R.J.
Powers, Special Agent R.R. Ryan, SN B.G. Dukes, YN1 R. D.
Martin

Front Row: YN1 J.M. Springer, Special Agent J.P. McMullen, Special Agent J.A. Renwick, YN1 J.K. Hendrickson

Second Row: Q.V. Ngau, Special Agent D.A. McBride, Lo Han Thang, Special Agent R.J. Tugwell

Third Row: Special Agent H.J. Hoem, Special Agent F.R. Seehorn, YNC A. Lingway, LCDR W.F. Brubaker, Supervising Agent B.G. Truxell, Special Agent W.J. Ward, W.H. Fry

Front Row: YN2 P.D. Haley, YN3 T.E. Fisher, T.T. Danh, Special Agent R.J. Tugwell, H.H. Hon, T.N. Nam, YNC R.L Rosengrant

Second Row: YN1 D.H. Page, Supervising Agent R.G. Morrice, Special Agent H.J. Hoem, Special Agent J.P. McMullen, Special Agent N.D. Nelms, SN G.V. Williams, Special Agent T.R Ferguson

Third Row: LCDR W.F. Brubaker, Special Agent J.P. Pender, Special Agent J.J. Caldwell, YN1 J.K. Hendrickson, Special Agent W.J. Ward, Special Agent F.R. Seehorn, YN3 D.S. Bodine

NISRA Da Nang May 1968

Front Row: YN2 J.M. Telencio, Special Agent R.D. Gallo, N.V. Vinh, Special Agent J.P. Seach, LT W.R. King, Senior Resident Agent Peter Reilly

Second Row: LTJG L.B. Coffey, Special Agent J.E. Rodriguez, Special Agent M.D. Nagle, Special Agent R.H. Cook

Third Row: YNC L. Taylor, SN S.L. Beshear, YN1 G.A Hulme

NISRA Da Nang 1968

Front Row: Mr. Duong Cong Nam, LTJG M.S. Quinn, Special
Agent John Tripplet, Senior Resident Agent Peter Reilly, Mr.
Nguyen Van Vinh

Second Row: Special Agent T. Y. Stallings, Special Agent Vernon
Oakum, Special Agent David Hall, Special Agent Frank Orrantia,
Special Agent Larry Coleman, Special Agent R. H. Cook

Third Row: LTJG Timothy Klee, LT Herman Hughes, YNC Leroy
Taylor, YN3 S. N. Beshear, YN2 Jim Pagels, YN2 J. M. Telencio

First Row: YNC D.H. Page, YN3 T.E. Fisher, YN1 P.D. Haley, YN2 R.L. Reed

Second Row: Senior Resident Agent R.E. Logan, Q.V. Ngau, T.T. Danh, Special Agent R.J. Tugwell, LoHan Thang, Special Agent T.E. Ferguson, Special Agent A.D. Newman, Special Agent K.R. Doktor, N.B. Duy

Third Row: LT J.W. Gainor, Special Agent G.B. Johnson, LCDR W.A. Armbruster, Supervising Agent R.J. Morrice, Special Agent N.D. Nelms, Special Agent J.P. Pender, Special Agent J.J. Baker, LT J.L. Law, LT L.B. Coffee

Fourth Row: YN1 C.E.Crisp, Special Agent J.J. Caldwell, Special Agent L.E. Ferrell, Special Agent D.L. Webb, YN2 D.S. Bodine, YN2 R.W. Piland, Special Agent C.V. Page, YN1 W.A. Schenker

NISOV, NISRA Saigon May 1969

First Row: Miss D.T. Tuyet, Mrs. T.T. Danh, SSgt L.H. Thang

Second Row: Senior Resident Agent R.E. Logan, Special Agent C.D. Liles, YN1 P. Haley, Special Agent E.K. Bonner, YN1 D.W. Lagerstrom, SSgt Trieu, LT N. Idleberg

Third Row: Supervising Agent D.C. Schunk, Special Agent M.B. Jones, LTJG S.J. Crowley, YN1 G.A. Borrelli, YN2 J. Pagels, CDR T.A. Brooks, YN2 D. Bodine, YNC C. Crisp, Special Agent D.P. Masden, Special Agent J.J. Baker

First Row: YN2 L. Dennis, Special Agent L.A. Gonzales,
"Peanuts", Special Agent J.F. Washko

Second Row: Special Agent C.W. Sundstrom, LT S.J. Zapatka, LT
E. Donaldson, Miss Dieu, Miss Lai, Senior Resident Agent D.L.
McCoy, Special Agent E.W. Hemphill

Third Row: Special Agent W.M Biscomb, YNSN R. Jacobs,
Special Agent Lance Arnold

Fourth Row: Special Agent D.H. Hubbard, YN1 R.D. Martin,
Special Agent Michael Bourke, Special Agent John Schlictman,
Special Agent Walter Focht

-

NISOV, NISRA Saigon May 1970

First Row: LCDR T.A Brooks, YNC W.C. Miller, YN1 D.W. Lagerstrom, "Sweet Thing", YN1 G.A. Borrelli, YNC G.C. Schenecker, LT S.J. Zapatka,

Second Row: LT N. Idleberg, Supervising Agent A.J. Kersenbrock, Senior Resident Agent B.C. Taylor, Mr. Duy, Mr. Ngau, Miss Thu, Sgt. Thang, Sgt. Trieu, Special Agent C.M. Spradley, LTJG S.J. Crowley

Third Row: Special Agent D.P. Masden, Special Agent M.B. Jones, Special Agent D.L. Webb, Special Agent E.K. Bonner, Special Agent C.D. Liles, Special Agent D.H. Hubbard

NISRA Da Nang 1970

First Row: Miss Vo Thi Dieu, Miss Lai, Special Agent C.W. Sundstrom

Second Row: LT Leonard Karp, Special Agent L.A Gonzales, YNSN R. Jacobs, Mr. Duong Cong Nam

Third Row: Special Agent John Dill, Special Agent William Biscomb, Special G.F. Grim, Special Agent Larry Upchurch, Senior Resident Agent E.J. Fitzpatrick,

Fourth Row: YNC Robert Martin, YN2 Neal Van Duyn, YN1 Carl Thatcher, Special Agent Walter Focht

NISOV, NISRA Saigon November 1970

First Row: YN2 J.J. Thomas, LT S.J. Zapatka, Miss Thu, Senior Resident Agent F.F. Givens, LTJG C.A. Palmer II, YN1 W.A. Schenker

Second Row: LT S.F. Argubright Jr., YNC W. Ludchak, YN2 D.M. Johnson, YN2 B.S. Robinson, YNSN D.E. Sedivy, CDR D.T. Burrows,Special Agent A.T. Lambert, Special Agent R.D. Dees

Third Row: LT J.D.Whitmire, Special Agent C.M. Spradley, Special Agent D.H. Hubbard Jr., Special Agent P.A. Hopkinson, Supervising Agent A.J. Kersenbrock Jr., Special Agent R.G. Westberry

Left to Right: Supervising Agent Richard E. McKenna, CDR Donn
T. Burrows, LT S.F. Argubright Jr., YN2 Bruce S. Robinson, LT
James D. Whitmire, YNC William Ludchak, YN1 James J.
Thomas, YN1 William H. Adams, YN1 William A. Schenker, Miss
Thu, YNSN Dale E. Sedivy, SSgt Trieu, SSgt Thang, Special Agent
Wallace M. Beasley, Mr. Duy, LTJG Charles A. Palmer II, Senior
Resident Agent F. F. Givens

NISRA Saigon March 1972

Front Row: Miss Thu, Special Agent William Worochok, Mr. Duy, Supervising Agent Kenneth Seal, Lo Han Thang

Second Row: Special Agent Ted Hicks, Mr. Ngau, Special Agent C.T. Cauble

Third Row: YN2 Ross, YN3 Dale Sedivy, LT Alan Sipe, LT Klampfer, CDR M.E. Moore, Special Agent D.H. Hubbard, LT Coughlin, YN1 Ottney, YNC Mopps, YN1 Watson, Senior Resident Agent Ed Giblin

NISRA DaNang, 1971

<u>Front row:</u> Mr Duong Cong Nam, YN1 William Adams, Miss Vo Thi Dieu, Senior Resident Agent Charles Bickley, Special Agent John Dill IV, LT Leonard Karp.

<u>Rear row:</u> Special Agent Douglass Hubbard, Unknown YN1, YN1 Lee Foster, Special Agent Carl Skiff

NISRA DaNang, 1970

Front row: Mrs. Sat, Miss Tiu, Miss Vo Thi Dieu.

Second row: Senior Resident Agent Edward Fitzpatrick, Mr.
Duong Cong Nam, Special Agent G.F. Grim, LT. Leonard Karp.

Third row: Special Agent Douglass Hubbard, YN1 Lee Foster,
Special Agent Lorne Hamilton, YN1 Carl Thatcher, YN2 Neal Van
Duyn, Special Agent John Dill IV.

Left to Right: Special Agent Robert Bagshaw, LCDR W.D.
Derryberry, Miss Thu, Special Agent H.W. Meador, Mr. Lo
HanThang, YN1 P.A. Jenson, Mr. Trieu

Made in the USA
Columbia, SC
03 January 2020